In Every Place

Settling Into the Unsettled:
A Missionary Story of God's Faithfulness in
West Africa and Beyond

Amy,

Keep on Keeping on
with Jesus!
I love you,
Kim Abernethy
Jn. 16:33

Kim Lennon Abernethy

IN MEMORY of My Brother

Robert Edison Lennon Jr.

"Eddie"

March 2, 1961 - July 23, 2001

The world was a much better place with you in it.
Looking forward to spending a couple of hundred
years visiting you when I get to heaven.
I'll bring the sunflower seeds and, oh yea, a jar of olives.
Won't be long...I don't think.

Dedicated to
"My Brothers From Other Mothers"

When my brother passed away, these guys, already special parts
of my life, stepped up and committed to love me like a sister,
tease me like a sister, and protect me like a sister.
They have.

I'm so blessed.

- *Tom Abernethy*
- *Glenn Benfield*
- *David Furman*
- *Paul Johnson*
- *Ed Propst*
- *Brent Roland*

ACKNOWLEDGEMENTS

To my four very keen editors: Lois Gillespie, Cynthia Long, Glenn and Debbie Benfield

Thank you so much for taking your time to read my story, and with your comments and corrections, making it even better...to the glory of our worthy Savior!

To Nancy Freund, a most creative book cover designer:

Love how you listened to the ramblings of my heart and were able to create something so *exact and beautiful.*

To all the Campus Bible Fellowship students who have blessed my life:

I don't know if you'll ever know how much I truly love you. So thankful that God, in His wisdom, placed Jeff and me in such a dynamic but fruitful ministry.

To Mark and Nancy Sheppard, our West African co-workers and forever friends.

We learned together. Laughed together. Cried together. Prayed together. Saw God do incredible things together in some of the darkest of times and brightest of days. So grateful for every day we served God together. Yes, I mean it. Every day.

Kim's first book, *In This Place,* prefaces the events of this book, covering her and her husband's earlier years as missionaries in Liberia, West Africa.

In This Place is sold online at:
Amazon
Barnes & Nobles
Books-a-Million

E-book versions for all reader formats can be purchased at ebookit.com

For more information about Kim's books and to view a gallery of photos from the time periods in these books, please visit her website:

www.kimlabernethy.com

~

All the way my Savior leads me;
What have I to ask beside?
Can I doubt His tender mercy,
Who through life has been my Guide?
Heav'nly peace, divinest comfort,
Here by faith in Him to dwell!
For I know, whate'er befall me,
Jesus doeth all things well;
For I know, whate'er befall me,
Jesus doeth all things well.

All the way my Savior leads me,
Cheers each winding path I tread;
Gives me grace for every trial,
Feeds me with the living Bread.
Though my weary steps may falter,
And my soul athirst may be,
Gushing from the Rock before me,
Lo! A spring of joy I see;
Gushing from the Rock before me,
Lo! A spring of joy I see.

All the way my Savior leads me
O the fullness of His love!
Perfect rest to me is promised
In my Father's house above.
When my spirit, clothed immortal,
Wings its flight to realms of day
This my song through endless ages—
Jesus led me all the way;
This my song through endless ages—
Jesus led me all the way.

~

Written by Fanny Crosby, 1875

PRELUDE

The great thing, if one can, is to stop regarding all the unpleasant things as interruptions of one's own or real life. The truth is that what one calls interruptions are precisely one's real life – the life God is sending us day by day. —C.S. Lewis

If I could have written the ending to our short, but illustrious ministry in the country of Liberia, it would have been a softer ending, a more complete ending, a smoother ending. But, we do not usually get to write our stories' endings. On that fateful day of the Liberian evacuation from our home in Tappeta in March, 1990, reality slapped me soundly, reverberating to the depths of my soul. Missionaries about thirty miles from our compound had been killed by rebels, so our American Embassy mandated all American missionary personnel to leave immediately. The Embassy had good reason to believe the rebels were heading our way, perhaps to takeover our compound since there was a radio station located there. Having only forty-five minutes to thrust my heart and mind into processing the words, *You are finished there. Pack your bags. Say goodbye. Get on the plane. Get out of there. The rebels are coming,* they fueled my overwhelming grief and disbelief. Two weeks after leaving Tappeta, though back in America with my family, I was still wrenched in the West African world through my memories. *The girls and I were safe.* My mind bounced from being thankful that we were out of harm's way to the consuming guilt for deserting our Liberians. Jeff was still there trying to encourage and help our Liberian Christians in Monrovia, the capital city. While I was glad he could be useful in such desperate times, any news of the war moving towards where he was changed my gladness into my begging him to come home to his family.

As helpful as anything during those first weeks in America, our pastor, Dr. Jack Hudson, interviewed me during a Sunday night service. I can see it in my mind's eye even now. Two leather wingback chairs on the platform. He sitting across from me. I was tired, overwhelmed, and seven months pregnant, but Dr. Hudson was a master at soothing frazzled nerves. He asked me questions, he listened, he helped direct my thoughts. He brought me back to God each time I faltered in my answers. Before *debriefing* was ever fashionable or deemed necessary, Dr. Hudson did it masterfully. For me, I remember the compassion in his eyes, the tears he wiped away as I told the evacuation story, and afterwards, the arms of church friends who held me tightly. It was a refreshing stream in my soul's dry, dry desert.

The mysteries of God are vast, limitless, intriguing. But God's work in the life of a Christian resolved to live out His purposes is astounding, masterful, breathtaking. I have seen Him etch out a providential design for my life, but even beyond that, I have seen Him keep His word in enabling me to fulfill what He has planned. He has never lied to me. He has never tricked me. He has never called me to go beyond what I could possibly do. He has never disappeared from my life - for even a second. And though I wish He would have, He never promised my life as a missionary would be easy, predictable, or tidy. And so it has not.

In This Place, the first of two missionary memoirs written from detailed and candid journals while we lived in Liberia, concentrated mainly on the uncharted perceptions I had of its culture. It entails the fruitfulness, foolishness, and both guided and misguided passions of a young, inexperienced missionary trying to find her place in the annals of missiology. This second book, however, projects beyond the borders of Liberia, painfully admitting in tiny increments that missionary life - for my family - was not to be settled. In my younger missionary updates, I undoubtedly proclaimed I had already seen my greatest challenges during our five years in Liberia as missionaries, mainly because of the dramatic evacuation from Liberia. True, it was measurable and life-changing, but there were to be other situations ahead just as significant. Some of those took me far out of my comfort zone, and at times, I feared that I would be annihilated by the fierce heartbreaks and challenges. But, I did not disappear in a puff of smoke. In all honesty, as I look back at those defining times, in actuality my spirit was being renewed more and more though my flesh continued (and still does) to scream its disfavor of where it is being led.

In the words of Fanny Crosby, there were days my weary steps faltered and my dehydrated soul lacked the energy to choose anything but fear itself. How grateful I am that the One consistently my Guide, my Rock, and my greatest Comforter never gave up on me. True, He usually did not allow the cup to *pass from me,* but He propelled me on with His strength, and so my faith grew even more. I did not always understand His purposes or even the places He directed us, but I did begin to perceive how truly perfect and sovereign His ways were. **Where else will we grow truly strong in the deep knowledge of Him unless we experience those vulnerable places where there is nothing else but Him?**

In Every Place will take you through the throes of volatile relief work with Liberians in the French-speaking country of Ivory Coast and then on to the tropical beauty of Jamaica where we ministered temporarily, but exactly on time. After Jamaica, we found ourselves back in Ivory Coast helping to establish a church which is still thriving in Liberia to this day. From a year of learning the French language in Quebec, Canada, the heart-wrenching loss of my brother, the rebellion of two of our daughters, and a final ministry in Bouake, Ivory Coast, it all culminates with another drastic evacuation. These stories and more are in this book. As you become caught up in the ride of my life, don't forget. It is the marvelous workings of our Giver of life, the Author of Wisdom, the Sustainer of our souls, I do not want you to miss. To Him, I give all the glory, the honor, the praise, the ultimate reason for the faith that lives in me today.

CHAPTER ONE

God moves in a mysterious way, His wonders to perform; He plants His footsteps in the sea and rides upon the storm. —William Cowper

The Realities of War

War is never pretty. Even more, if the conflict takes place on the other side of the world, out of our peripheral view, and does not involve anyone we love, we tend to shut out the horrors. I was determined not to do that with the Liberian Civil War even while we were living in the United States - waiting in the wings for God's green light to return as missionaries to the place where we left our hearts. Gleaning any news concerning the escalating Liberian conflict, I forced myself to imagine being in Monrovia as the fighting became an chaotic inferno. To see the blazing fear in the eyes of those caught in the middle, to gaze upon the traumatized, gaunt children too weak to run from danger; to hear the heart-wrenching laments and deafening blasts of rocket launchers; and to smell the sulfurous fumes of gunfire and the sickening whiff of carnage from any direction. It shook my soul.

During that first year of civil war, one of the biggest massacres in the country's history was committed. Over 600 Liberians from the Gio and Mano tribes, from the Tappeta region where we had ministered, were killed in an all-night shooting, stabbing, and beating spree. It was even *rumored* that President Doe was in attendance for some of the decimation. What prompted that particular massacre, we were told, was fulfillment of a Devil Bush society ritual. Two months after the massacre, a reporter visiting the Lutheran church where the atrocities had taken place, spoke of the butchery. She saw clusters of bodies still inside the church building, maggots crawling everywhere among the decomposing skin falling off bones. To bring matters closer to our hearts' doorsteps, within that first year, our Baptist Mid-Mission's compound in Monrovia was raided by a group of government

1

soldiers. Killed in that attack was a short term American missionary named Jake who had decided to stay and care for the many Liberians who sought protection. After killing most of those on our mission compound, the soldiers drove off with the vehicles parked there, including Jeff's Isuzu Trooper.

Where Do We Go From Here?

The war in Liberia seemed to be avalanching, making it impossible for us to even consider returning there for the unforeseen future. Though Baptist Mid-Missions (BMM) had worked amicably with us during the entire ordeal, they had no concrete answers for our plight. We felt strongly that we wanted to be close to our Liberian people, to encourage and minister to them. That desire, not just ours, but also on the hearts of other Liberian missionaries, precipitated a survey trip to the neighboring country of Ivory Coast where we had heard thousands of terrorized Liberians had fled.

After a meeting in Galipolis, Ohio, (fondly called the *Galipolis Conference*) with other displaced Liberian missionary families, it was decided that my husband Jeff and Chick Watkins would make a trip to Ivory Coast, traveling also to the Liberia-Ivory Coast border to see firsthand the needs and conditions of the Liberian refugees. They scouted out possible towns where we could live, as well as bringing back a comprehensive list of items needed by the Liberians. BMM helped us bring national awareness to the needs of the Liberians by setting up a *World Relief Fund*. Interested churches and individuals were able to donate money to help the Liberian relief operation when we were returned to the struggling region.

Chick and Jeff were gone for two weeks, and when they returned, it was with an encouraging report. The opportunities and needs were great. The time was now. They were able to meet with over a thousand Liberian Christians, passing out almost $6,000 worth of food (rice, canned fish, oil, etc...) to impoverished and traumatized Liberians in Ivory Coast. While on the survey trip, they had the opportunity to also enter Liberia. The Lord closed the door a couple of times, but then sent Charles Taylor's Inspector

General, Moses Blah (whom Chick had mentored as a teen), to give them a personal escort past all the checkpoints and other difficulties of traveling in a war-torn country. While in the vehicle with General Blah, Jeff was alarmed to realize the General had a *nine-year old* bodyguard decked out Rambo-style with bullet vest, gun, and sunglasses.

The one time the boy soldier took his sunglasses off, Jeff was saddened to see absolutely nothing behind those young eyes. Nothing. Blank and dull. Nothing that indicated a youthful, playful spirit as it should have been for a boy so young. Looking up, Jeff noticed multiple bullet holes in the top of the car, and upon inquiring, was nonchalantly told that snipers were always attempting to take out the rebel government leaders. Evidently, no big deal to those whom war had hypnotized slowly, but surely. On the other hand, to Jeff and Chick, fresh from the civility of America, it was a death knell, a feeling of vulnerability and apprehension attached itself quickly to the men following a divine call much more invincible than that evil war.

They arrived in Tappeta to a wonderful reunion with a few Christians still living there. Jeff was eager to see how our home had fared during the time we had been away, but when he tried to walk towards our house, a soldier quickly told him that he could not visit the Executive Mansion. *Excuse me? Did he say, Executive Mansion?* He learned that for nearly three months after our mandatory evacuation, the rebels had used our mission compound as a base of operations. Rebuilding and strengthening their growing army before advancing towards Monrvoia, Charles Taylor himself had taken up residence in our home. Why? We could only deduce it was because of the new American furnishings we were in the middle of unpacking when we were forced to leave. There was a new La-z Boy chair which I could envision Taylor himself sitting in and making decisions for his powerful revolution. Even his wife and children stayed with him there much of the time from what we understood. My children's toys being played with by the children of this rising star of war's - why did that bother me so much? It is not the fault of the children that their father had chosen to stir up civil unrest in the worst kind of way.

Almost a year and a half later, when we were able to visit our home in Tappita, the looming words **NPFL Executive Mansion** had been spray painted in large letters on the side of our storage building. NPFL stood for the rebels acronym, *National Patriotic Front of Liberia*. Notably, one of the only things left behind in our house after the rebel forces abandoned our mission compound were several of my cookbooks. On the inside flap of one of them was inscribed with the letters **NPFL.** I kept it as a memento though when I really thought about it, it bothered me greatly to think of those men roaming around and touching our things. Defacing my cookbook? Didn't they have a war to fight? What business did they have with **my** cookbooks?

The day after Chick and Jeff arrived in Tappita for a visit, they learned that their guide, General Blah, had left them unknowingly and returned to Ivory Coast. Because the missionary men had traveled into the country with a government representative, they had not brought the proper papers to travel anywhere on their own. The rebels in charge of Tappeta asked Jeff and Chick to remain in a house on the compound until someone could help them return to Ivory Coast. The reality of being under house arrest during that first visit back to our compound shoved reality into the faces of Chick and Jeff. Things were definitely different. Three days later, it was made possible for them to travel to Gbanga and meet with Charles Taylor's Vice-President, Enoch Degoliah, whom Chick had known since Degoliah had been a little boy.

A Snake is Still A Snake

Upon their return to Ivory Coast, Jeff and Chick continued to preach and encourage the refugees living in one of the larger towns near the Liberian border. Though it seemed a world away, it was only forty-five miles from our mission compound in Tappi. During their two week survey trip, the men had the opportunity to preach in five churches and saw twenty-four people accept Christ. Among the ones saved were a Muslim, an Ivorian, and a Liberian government soldier. It was heartening to realize that God was still on His throne and moving in the hearts of people despite the hellish situations around them.

On a lighter note, Jeff and Chick were visiting a police station on the border of Liberia-Ivory Coast, getting to know the officials and informing them of tentative plans to bring their families back to help with the relief efforts. While there, Jeff asked to use the bathroom inside the police station. As he was facing the toilet, his eye caught a movement where the water pipes came through the wall. Within seconds, a very long black snake had plopped into the 3x3 foot room with Jeff. Obviously there was not enough room for them both. Zipping up quicker than ever, my husband jumped over the snake and opened the bathroom door, screaming, *"snake! snake!"* Mind you, everyone in the building spoke French except Jeff and Chick, so the Ivorian men thought it amusing how the white man came barreling out of the bathroom, eyes bulging, screaming something incoherent to them. Within seconds, the snake slithered out of the confining bathroom behind the maniacal American and several of the African officials yelled appropriately, *"Le Serpent!! Le Serpent!!"* At those words, the building quickly emptied except for the two brave men who put an end to the tumult. The "serpent" was killed, putting to rest Jeff's dangled nerves!

Upon returning to the United States, Jeff and Chick presented a report to the BMM administration regarding the survey trip. After hearing the details, our mission board approved the transition from Liberian field to *On Loan to Ivory Coast* for an undetermined amount of time. The Mark Sheppard family, Ardith Maile, and the Abernethy family were able to team up and make preparations to leave within three months. The first team out of the gate, so to speak, we had not a clue what we were getting ourselves into. Missionaries are not the most patient creatures in the world and waiting seems worse than stagnation. Going into potentially dangerous and difficult circumstances was, to some of us, much better than not going at all. *Safety is of the Lord* and where He sends us, He is faithful to fulfill His perfect will.

Many Ivorian villages on the Liberian border were without a good gospel witness. Our goal was threefold: 1) Evangelism and encouragement, 2) Seminars and classes to help fill the time for the refugees since the Ivorian government would not allow refugees to work nor their children to attend schools, and 3) Relief efforts (physical and emotional) to continue as long as feasibly possible. The stratagem was created out of hearts full of fervor and desire to bring hope to those who had forgotten what it looked like. Though we knew it would take unprecedented efforts on our part, we really had no idea of what we were walking into. Sometimes that is best, isn't it? Our human hearts are not always able to handle events planned for our future. God knows everything and we do not. Some things are best left with Him. Well, **all things,** for that matter.

Trading in My Dreams For His

In light of our impending departure, our sweet eight month old baby girl, Lauren, had to take the typhoid, yellow fever, and tetanus immunizations along with the rest of us. Watching our girls go through the trauma of receiving extraneous immunizations along with the normal childhood vaccines was always difficult for me as a mother. **But for the sake of the call, we find grace to do the hard things**. Though I know there are varying opinions on whether to immunize children or not, we felt it was best for our girls.

Packing up what few belongings we could fit into large Rubbermaid Action Packers and backpacks, we felt somewhat prepared for our next missionary adventure. As far as material things were concerned, it was like we were starting all over. Everything left behind in Tappita was considered lost. However, between the arrival of our third baby daughter and the preparing of the new adventure in Ivory Coast, neither Jeff nor I had taken much time to ponder the tangible losses we experienced in our Liberian evacuation.

Not knowing where we would be living in Ivory Coast, we all felt it necessary to pack lightly and harbor no huge expectations. However, for a young missionary with three daughters ages 7, 4, and 11 months, that was an emotionally and spiritually taxing thing to do. I wish I could tell you that I put everything in God's hands and walked in full confidence of His provision and promises. Since I made a pact with myself at the inception of these books to always be candid and painfully honest in recounting our early missionary years, I must relate to you how extremely unsettled and unsure I was in spite of my desire to let God have it all. Tremendously afraid of what was ahead, especially for my children, I wanted so much to protect them from the unknowns.

In the Air Again!

In four short years, Michelle and Stefanie had been on seven international flights seven and Michelle wasn't even eight years old! In June of 1991, when we left for our Liberian refugee ministry in Ivory Coast, Lauren was eleven months old. While she was a fun-loving baby, she was also full of unconcealed energy. Just thinking of the two long flights from Atlanta to Europe, and then Europe to West Africa, I knew we needed to have a plan. Judge me if you will. My mom has always said, *"Don't judge another person unless you have walked in their shoes."* After buying a large bottle of children's Benadryl, we boarded the plane with five carry-ons and three excited children. Never mind what was on the other side of the flight, our girls were created to fly! Don't get me wrong: the goodbyes never got easy, though by this time, those closest to us had frequently heard our laments and desires to return to our African ministry. Saddened by the farewells, anxious about the uncertain days ahead of us, and excited for the opportunities we knew God was putting before us; we were a stockpile of emotions! *A missionary's life is a perpetual paradox.*

Despite all those feelings, I did my best to hold on to this truth: **the immense challenges and the shadowy unknowns were nothing compared to the overwhelming wisdom God would provide and the unlimited strength He promised to give.** You may understand when I say that I believed it *with my head*, but I needed for God to help me absorb it deep *into my heart*. Little by little, as the trip unfolded and we became more fatigued, circumstances were snatched out of our control, allowing me to see God at work. Sometimes He just needs to get our attention so that we will look UP - and only UP.

It was a long flight to Amsterdam. Lauren was too big for the small baby cradle which the flight attendant attached to the wall, so we made her a pallet on the floor at my feet. When she was finally asleep, Michelle started acting up because she didn't want to sleep on the floor while Stefanie was sleeping on the seats. Working out a fair solution, everyone finally fell asleep. Way too soon, the cabin lights of the plane were turned on and breakfast was served. To our bodies, it was only two in the morning. None of us really wanted to eat, but the girls woke up as if they were going to miss something important. Upon our arrival in Amsterdam, I quickly found the baby nursery at Schipol Airport. That airport, in my opinion, was one of the cleanest and best laid out airports we ever traveled through. In the nursery were cribs, bathtubs, and rockers; it was a traveling mother's paradise! Lauren slept soundly for almost three hours. The girls and Jeff stayed in the Missionary Lounge (Schipol was the only airport we had known to have one) to relax and wait on the Sheppard family who had taken a different flight from Minnesota. Somewhere in the midst of traveling, I turned 33 years old. That birthday was a blur, to say the least.

After reuniting with our missionary co-workers and their children, we made plans for our connecting flight to Sierre Leone, West Africa. Unfortunately, we did not arrive in that country until early evening, so we were forced to spend the night before hopping another plane to Ivory Coast. As we arrived in Sierre Leone, the heat and humidity hit us, bringing tears to my eyes as I realized how very close we were to Liberia. It had been fifteen months since we had abruptly evacuated from our Liberian home and my heart twisted to think we were not going back to that beloved country. Instead we were traveling to an unknown country, an undetermined ministry, to everything unfamiliar. Fears rose deeply within me and I prayed silently to God to take them away. In the midst of dealing with my personal apprehensions, we were told by Sierre Leone custom officials that if we wanted to carry our luggage off the plane, it would have to be throughly searched. I do not remember how many pieces of luggage both families had, but from experience, we always brought at least two or three per person. It would have taken **hours** to search through at least thirty bags or Action Packers. Nothing else to do, we chose to leave our luggage at the airport under "lock and key." That was to make us feel better. Right.

There was more to the story. Sierre Leone airport officials insisted we leave our passports with the luggage. That unusual demand made no sense to us, but we were not the ones in charge and we knew it. Arguing with foreign authorities is futile. Feeling extremely uncomfortable, we left the airport with only our carryons, no passports, and no luggage. We had no choice but to leave it in God's Hands. He delights in working when there is no human solution to our problem. Of course He would work even when we have a solution, but our propensity is always to try everything *humanly possible* first, then go to God. How much do we miss by living like that?

After paying $10 for a half mile taxi ride, we checked into the last two rooms available at a local hotel. Each room had two twin beds (considered a "double" room in European terms). After assessing the impossible sleeping arrangements, we decided to put both twin mattresses on the floor, pushing them together to make a king size bed. We hoped it would be large enough for the five of us to get some decent sleep. The next morning, after a fitful night of flailing arms, little kicking feet, two whiny children and a baby, we got up and meandered around, drugged from the lack of sleep and the time difference. Since our flight did not leave until 5:00 p.m., there was not a big hurry to do anything. Jeff went down to the hotel desk and asked for a small amount of milk powder, so I could make Lauren's bottle.

We passed the day by eating lunch in the hotel restaurant and exploring our immediate surroundings. Later that afternoon, Jeff and Mark took a taxi back to the airport to locate our luggage and have everything ready for our departure. Nancy and I sat in the hotel lobby and watched the kids play for a couple more hours before hailing another taxi for two adults and six children. When we arrived at the airport, we saw Jeff and Mark both looking a little frazzled around the edges, waiting on us with no luggage and no passports in hand. Our flight was scheduled to leave in less than an hour, so we all became unsettled about our predicament.

Michelle, my almost eight year old, took my hand as I was undoubtedly revving up for a good old pity party and asked me to go with her to a corner of the airport and pray. Honestly, it was the last thing I felt like doing. *Didn't she know that I was busy being worried?* All the same, I went with her. Her little prayer was short, to the point, and somehow calming to her mother's anxious heart. You know what happened, don't you? **No more than five minutes later, our luggage along with our passports appeared**. Humbled, I knew God had answered Michelle's simple prayer and was desiring to strengthen all of us to completely trust Him. What part about God wanting us to *trust Him like a little child* did I not understand?

STRESS: in all caps

Arriving in Abidjan, long pegged as the *economic* capital of Ivory Coast, we met up with the other member of our missionary team, Ardith Maile. Working out our plans for our team's move to the western part of the country took a couple of weeks in Abidjan. Though in the past, there had been BMM missionaries in western Ivory Coast, that had been many years ago. At the time of our arrival, there was no missionary to help with logistics. For that reason, Jeff and Mark felt it would be sensible to make a quick trip to the western region, leaving the women and children in Abidjan. During our two weeks in the bustling city, our missionary team stayed in various places. A guest house served us well for the first three nights, but as we realized we would need more supplies and additional government paperwork for moving upcountry, it became evident we needed to find provisional living arrangements in Abidjan. A missionary commissioned with a sister mission helped us find a temporary house in which to live. The house was owned by a missionary family who was in the States on furlough, so it seemed a good fit for the eleven of us wandering *pilgrims*. Unfortunately, what felt like a great solution quickly turned into a nightmare. My journal of Monday, June 24, 1991, reads:

> *If we were not committed to do God's will, we would
> have thrown up our hands a week ago. Our living
> conditions are beyond difficult. Though the house is
> very nice, the Baptist church which the missionary
> helped establish meets in the two front rooms of the*

house on Sunday, Wednesdays, and Fridays, and at other times for Bible study. At those scheduled times, we had to take the six kids (one who was an active baby) and go into the back of the house, trying to be quiet for at least two hours. Why didn't we join the services, you may ask? It was all in French. I had more French than anyone at this point, and it was still not enough to comprehend an entire message. But to ask our small children to do that?

In the part of the house we were given permission to use, there were two bedrooms, a bathroom, and a sitting room. The kitchen located in the front of the house was locked. So no kitchen for us. Improvisation seemed to be the buzz word at the beginning of that missionary adventure. Strangely, there was a stove in the bathroom located next to the sitting room. The refrigerator was in the small sitting room which was also what our single missionary lady was using as her bedroom.

Jeff and Mark spent much of their days traveling around the city: reporting to the American Embassy, tracking down the officer who was handling the paperwork for our container shipped from America, shopping for a refrigerator and stoves. At one point, there were three straight days where Nancy and I were stuck in the house's small confines with six active children. Maddening, I tell you. Outside those walls was a whole new world. While it was still in West Africa and bore some similarities to Liberia, the language barrier was enough to keep us holed up with our children instead of exploring the bustling area around us.

The Ivorian pastor who was in charge of the church was unmarried and living in a smaller house behind the main house. Suspiciously, he had four Ivorian girls working, cleaning, and cooking for him from sun up to sun down. He was never friendly to us and constantly complained about something we were doing or how disruptive our children were. It was hard not to believe we had interrupted his allegedly libertine lifestyle. Little did he know that we were as eager to leave that house as he was for us to leave. But the days crept by.

Lauren was eleven months old when we arrived in Abidjan and obviously still in diapers, so a washing machine would have been helpful. No such luck. It would be nearly six months before we would use one in the conventional way again. We washed our clothes by hand in the bathtub every morning in the bathroom while we cooked breakfast since the stove was also in there. Are you really following this preposterous situation? As for Lauren's diapers (yes, cloth ones), I remember vividly soaking the more soiled ones in a *bidet* (a French-influenced wash basin for a person's nether regions). When we finished doing our laundry - because it was rainy season - we draped our wet clothes over the benches in the front part of the house to dry. We had no idea what ramifications would come from that action.

If you read my first book, *In This Place*, chronicling our five years in Liberia, I wielded the phrase **cultural collisions** quite a bit. A situation arose while living in the missionary church-house which was definitely a collision of cultures. Being a missionary often requires you to be a diplomat and a mind reader. In our living situation, we desperately needed to do both of those well. One day, suddenly and harshly, we were accused of "defiling the house of God." This was told to us in French, of course, so every excruciating detail had to be translated in English. To this day, it is not clear if we sinned in God's eyes, but we did offend a couple of church members when they stopped by to visit. In their eyes, we had shown disrespect by hanging our laundry to dry in the church sanctuary (still part of our living quarters). In retrospect, after having gleaned carefully the truths in Romans 14, the concern of the church members should have been enough. We had offended those brothers and sisters in Christ. Though we saw those rooms as an extension of the house we were renting and desperately needed a place to hang our laundry, the offended ones saw those rooms as their church property. *Apostle Paul, what advice would you have given in this situation?*

Those were spiritually refining days, full of desperation brought on by physical inconveniences unlike any this American girl had ever known. More times than not, the ugliness of my soul acted spiritually delinquent. The whole living situation became tense;

and as Mark and Jeff returned from a survey trip to the western part of the country, Nancy and I pressed to be released from it. The men saw our distress and did their best to work out our departure expediently in a culture that moved to its own slow tempo. Completely embedded in a *grass is greener on the other side* mode, we felt sure the little town of Pehe in the western region of the country would be better than where we were. Surely.

Neither family had a tremendous surplus of funds with which to set up complete households, so we decided to pool our resources, buying one refrigerator to share between the two families and Ardith. The next logistical challenge was finding the means to haul two men, three women, six children, more than a dozen Action Packers, a refrigerator, and boxes of food on a seven-hour trip toward the Liberian border. Thankfully, Jeff and Mark secured a "money bus" for our Saturday morning departure. At 7:00 a.m, the driver showed up to inform us that it was a Muslim holiday, so the owner of the bus would not allow him to make the trip that day. The earliest he could take us would be Sunday afternoon at 3:00 p.m. Realizing we were at our wits' end with our living situation and having already packed up our belongings, we leaned on our husbands to find a way of escape. The truth be told, none of us wanted to stay in that house another night.

As an amazing reminder of God's perfect timing and abundant grace, our missionary friend Johnny brought his family to visit us that very morning. Being adept in French, he was able to go with our husbands to the parking station to find another bus which would transport us. Early that afternoon, a money bus drove up, and we loaded our belongings. After an hour of packing the inside of the vehicle, many of the Action Packers went on top of the bus along with a 50-pound bag of potatoes. There were bags, backpacks, and boxes of food stuffed under seats. Do not forget the large refrigerator looming over us all at the back of the bus. Most likely, there are pictures somewhere of this money bus loaded down with a refrigerator, missionaries, and all our belongings. Excitement masked the uncertainty of heading into unknown territory. There were no established missionary ministries waiting for us to join them in the western part of Ivory Coast. We were pioneers heading into a town where any missionary work done in the past was a faint memory.

The first couple of hours of traveling were a fresh new adventure for our children who were indeed ready to leave the dirty, busy city of Abidjan. Me? I was not so sure. Though it was a very loud city, as we left the progressive region behind, I became almost desperate for its frustrations. As we drove deeper into the quiet simplicity of the bush, I felt vulnerable as most likely did the others. Masking our reservations, we passed the time singing silly songs with the kids, reading books, and exploring the deepening countryside from our seats. We had packed sandwiches, chips, fruit, and plenty of water, making snack time a great diversion to the impending boredom. Our youngest daughter Lauren toddled around the money bus from seat to seat. Her need of constant entertainment was shared by the lot of us, which made her mother very thankful. When time for Lauren's nap, Jeff and I made a pallet with pillows across our laps for her sleeping pleasure which answered favorably our inward pleas for a little quietness from our busy baby girl. Hard to believe, but I do not remember having a car seat with us. Even if we had one, there were no seat belts on the money bus with which to attach it.

The driver seemed to be in a hurry to return to Abidjan, making it difficult to convince him to stop for necessary potty breaks with the children. In between those rare stops, when there was a need for a bathroom, we improvised with empty Pringle cans. Though none of us adults used them, the children had no qualms about "pottying" in the cans and then laughing hysterically as we attempted to "flush" the cans out a window. Is being a missionary glamorous? Boring? Predictable? I'll let you be the judge. After fifteen straight hours on the road, seven checkpoints, and a couple of Muslim prayer stops, we arrived in the small town of Pehe. It was around four o'clock in the morning and we were wiped out. For us, sleep was a distant memory. Unloading the bulging money bus, we were in total survival mode. Do the next thing. Then maybe sleep would be a blessed option.

CHAPTER TWO

You need not fight in this battle; station yourselves, stand and see the salvation of the Lord on your behalf. II Chronicles 20:17

Surrounded!

Pehe was situated in the heart of the cocoa-laden western rain forest of Ivory Coast. A very small town, notably no more than an advanced African village, it was a main hub for many smaller villages in that area. Because of two vacant missionary homes available and because it was only an hour's driving distance to the border of Liberia, we felt it was a good place to temporarily "put up tent." If we had only known more of the regional dynamics, we might have decided those conveniences were not worth it. Hindsight.....yeah, it's **gold**. Would it have helped to see the future? Probably not. Satan thrust his evil foot forward in the next three months and dared us to continue in our calling. Might I be candid and tell you that - in my case - he almost defeated me.

The two missionary houses in Pehe had been empty for nearly twenty years. That meant nothing warm and inviting welcomed us as we arrived in the inky black, pre-dawn morning. One of the houses had electricity, so we all bunked there, each desperate for some sleep. However, no matter how tired her parents was, baby Lauren woke up early, ready for the day and oblivious of the precarious living conditions. My first order of business was to find a broom to sweep the floors, so our busy baby girl could play freely. Since there was no running water in either of the houses, we borrowed buckets to bring water from a nearby well to wash off the travel dust. Tired or not, our first day in Pehe had begun. My journal after a week in Pehe reads better than I can retell it:

> *Someone washes our clothes everyday for about*
> *$1.50 per hour. We all (eleven of us) eat rice and*
> *soup together for lunch, but have our supper meal*

15

separately in our own houses. Kids and people
surround the house constantly from about 8 in the
morning until about 8 in the evening. Lauren loves
to play out on the porch and of course, she always
draws a crowd. Stefanie fits right in with the other
kids playing around the two houses and exploring the
small town. Cows, goats, and chickens have free reign
of the yard between our houses, so you can imagine
what our yard smells like. Our kids were reminded
constantly that there would be consequences if they
did not wear shoes outside for very good reason.
Dysentery was a very serious problem where animal
droppings and people co-existed.

The missionaries who had lived in the houses some years ago must have felt it best to promote an "open door" policy in their ministry. By that I mean, they chose not to put locks on the doors, amplifying their desire that the Ivorians would always feel free to visit them **at anytime**. While I personally cannot understand the benefits of that particular ministry style, I do not want to judge any missionary for doing what they felt was the right thing. Two fresh cultural collisions bombarded me during the first week we were in Pehe.

The first incident happened during one Sunday afternoon while we were taking glorious naps. Feeling refreshed after a bit of sleep, enjoying the rare quietness while reading a book, I was startled by a pronounced shuffle at our bedroom door. I gasped as an African man and woman stood staring at us. Some awkward moments ensued as I slid off the bed and grabbed a blanket draped over Lauren's port-a-crib. Smiling politely, I escorted our curious guests back into the living room area. To the best of my ability, I tried to communicate with them, but their French was mixed with a dialect, so I could not understand them. Surely they wondered what kind of missionaries came to live among them that could not even speak their language. Meanwhile, Jeff had a chance to get dressed properly, coming out to greet our uninvited, but perturbed guests. Though, in our American mindset, we felt that it was us who were wronged in this situation, most likely our guests felt exactly the same way about us not properly hosting them that afternoon when they had come to greet us.

A few days later, while preparing supper, the second event happened. I turned around with a smile when I heard a sound that I thought to be one of my girls. Surprisingly, there was an African woman whom I had never met standing at my kitchen door. She was Liberian, because she spoke in English, making it clear what she wanted; "*I say, you may give me $20 work. I need 20 dolla work bad-o!*" (Interpreted: *Give me enough work so that I can earn twenty dollars.*) No *hello*, no introduction of herself, no nothing. Instead of addressing her remarkably blunt request, I asked her why she had walked into the house without knocking. She just stared at me. I attempted to coax her back out on the porch, but she stood firm. "*I say, I may not go until you give me 20 dolla work. I will stand here.*" Her attitude was offensive, but I tried to remain kind and calm while my supper began to burn on the stove.

In our five years of living in Liberia, I had not come across such a blatant attitude very frequently. Later I surmised, it was perhaps because these Liberians came from a different part of the country. On top of that, they were traumatized from war, desperate for even their basic needs. I would love to tell you that in realizing the deep hurts and fears of those whom we lived among drew out my sympathetic heart, but it did not. Survival, that of my own survival, was what became foremost in my mind. I was quite the missionary parody.

Those two incidences of uninvited guests would have turned into dozens of other awkward intrusions if we had not put locks on our doors. Between the surround sounds of activity from every direction, goats bleating on our porch and Lauren trying to crawl out into the yard where *you-know-what* had dropped from the free roaming animals, I knew I had to find a smidgen of solace. If it was as simple as putting locks on our doors, then so be it. Call me callous, call me weak. You can take the American out of America, but it is extremely difficult to take America out of the American. Pehe had already begun to unravel our stamina and fresh calling to ministry in those parts of Ivory Coast. We had stepped into unfamiliar territory.

Muddy Roads

To travel anywhere in that particular area of Ivory Coast was not easy. The road system through and around Pehe was completely dirt. Still trying to decide if we could raise enough money to purchase a vehicle, the missionary team in Pehe traveled just like the Africans. By bus. Near the end of our first three weeks there, our monetary funds were running low, making it inevitable that Mark and Jeff would need to travel back to Abidjan for needed supplies and currency. Before they could leave for Abidjan, they first needed to make a trip to a town on the Liberian-Ivorian border for ministry information. It was a treacherous trip on thick muddy roads, and more times than they could count, the bus struggled in the mire and seemed in danger of tipping over. They returned to Pehe exhausted and flustered by the tedious travels, but even more determined to pursue the possibility of finding our own vehicle in which to travel.

Jeff developed bronchitis immediately after that trip, so our missionary nurse put him on antibiotics. Within that same week, Stefanie (who was four) complained that her head hurt. We watched her closely. Mark, Nancy, Ardith, and I had planned a trip to Toulepleu to buy food and pick up a car which a Lutheran missionary was allowing us to borrow for a few weeks. Toulepleu was a larger town very close to the Liberian border and was the town we had determined we wanted to do ministry from. Soon after arriving in Pehe, we looked into having two duplexes in Toulepleu readied for us. The owner of the duplexes told us that it would be a several weeks before we could move into them, so we had to be satisfied with staying in Pehe for the time being.

When the four of us arrived back in Pehe later in the afternoon, it was evident Stefanie was worse. Her head was hurting more intensely, and she had a rather high fever. For the next twenty-four hours she vomited and cried as she held her head. We gave her chloroquin syrup and aspirin, assuming it must be a bout of malaria. When Stefanie was six months old, she had come down with malaria while we were living in Liberia. Again, I felt vulnerable and helpless as I watched my little girl struggle with that consuming illness in a remote part of Africa. Holding her almost constantly and singing softly to her, my heart was so consumed with fear, I could hardly pray. Little by little, her headache and fever lessened and she ate more. Unfortunately, the severe reoccurrence of malaria left her vulnerable and sickly for the next couple of years.

The borrowed car, thankfully, gave us more leverage in starting up much-needed ministry opportunities, and each family took turns using it to travel to nearby villages. While our living situation in Pehe became more difficult, it was the initiation of those external ministries which held us together and kept us focused. We taught in the refugee churches in Toulepleu often. A thirty minute drive beyond Toulepleu towards the Liberian border were hundreds of refugee villages perched off the roads - waiting for encouragement and hope. We did what we could to visit, distribute food and clothing, always taking time to teach them the Word of God. One of the centerpiece ministries for me personally during that time was walking to a nearby village to teach the local women. My journal of July 21, 1991, reads:

I had told the women who washed our clothes and cooked for us on a daily basis that I would one day walk to their town. It was just the next village from here, but it took about 30 minutes to walk. I walked with them Friday after they finished working. Jeff agreed to watch the girls while I was gone. I really appreciate these African people that walk everyday out of necessity and really think nothing of it. It was a hard walk for me, but very well worth it! Everyone seemed glad to see the white woman come into town. I met with about seventy-five women, teenage girls, and children with a few curious men peeking from around the houses. I told the story of Gideon and tried to encourage their hearts. There was one very pretty Ivorian lady that was fascinated by my teaching. She said she attended the Catholic church but they didn't teach the Bible and asked if I could help her to study the Bible. What an exciting request!

Walking to that village to teach was one of my epic African missionary moments. It took me out of myself, thrusting me into the world of those African women who worked so hard for everything, but yet possessed so little. Sometimes it is in the stepping out of our closets of pity, choosing to look outward and upward that loosens us from the darkness threatening to consume us. Our circumstances *can* consume us. It is true that we can drown in our own sorrow. The American mentality in the past decade has fed our narcissistic tendencies, thrusting more of us into mental and emotional instabilities. As Christians, **God does not propose for us simply to care for our own needs, but also to look toward the needs of those around us**. That is a biblical truth, while certainly not an American mantra.

In Light of Eternity

We spent much time in Kpobli, teaching the people and listening to their desires to see a church established. Jeff had about twenty-five men including the town chief in an afternoon Bible study; I taught at least twenty-five women. After the study, eight older women were saved; six of them were Ivorian women who had never heard of Jesus before! I was so very excited, and even the adversity of living in Pehe seemed to fade away as I saw the glory of God rain down on that seemingly insignificant village. Insignificant to the rest of the world, but indeed important to the One who had providentially placed us together for that time. Oh, how precious those people - and all people - are to Him.

My journal dated July 21, 1991 reads:

> *On Saturday we traveled by car to Kpobli (the town where I had walked to teach the women) and saw a man named Farley become a Christian. We also watched an Awana program. After that, our entire family traveled further in the bush to a youth conference. We spent the night in an Ivorian one-room house. We took Lauren's crib which was very helpful in keeping up with her. The service*

on Saturday night was from 8:30 - 10:30 p.m. On
Sunday morning, I taught about sixty ladies in
the Sunday School hour as Michelle and Stefanie
entertained Lauren. The morning service went for
two and a half hours. No air conditioning, no nursery
for Lauren, no padded pews. There was a 20 minute
offering, a long song service, and then after Jeff
preached, there was a 45 minute invitation. Six people
were saved and there were three recommitments to
Christ. If you look at the service in light of eternity,
the length of the service really did not matter!

I wish that I could tell you from that day forward, I always looked at my circumstances in eternity's light. But, that is not the way it went. Human nature is extremely selfish, forgetful, and demanding. Soon I found myself again completely absorbed in my troubles. But for the greater good of those needy souls around us, we had to believe God had placed us firmly in that oppressed town for three long months. There were still lost souls searching for Him, and since He had promised to always be found by those who seek Him and since we had told Him we were willing to be used.....well, did we mean it or not? Did we really want to be a part of His kingdom work? Anywhere? No matter what? From a human perspective, God asked much of us during that time. But in the challenges, it was divinely refining both in our spiritual and physical lives. Sacrifices? My flesh whined at our plight, but my spirit struggled to see that time through the eyes of the One who stayed by our side and worked His incredible will - despite us.

Black Monday

To all appearances, it was to be a non-eventful Monday afternoon until two men stepped up to our door and knocked, transforming that day into an extraordinary event. John Deah and his son had come for a visit. During our years in Liberia, I had taught John and his wife to read. Somehow, John had *heard* we were back in West Africa, though how the news traveled among the African people without the aid of phones or newspapers, we could never figure out. During the visit, John told stories about what had happened in the three years since we had seen him. Feeling called by God to preach, he had refused to take up arms and fight with the rebel army. He was beaten many times, he shared with us, but plodded on. In my mind's eye, he became somewhat like a modern day Apostle Paul, wandering from town to town preaching God's Word to anyone that would listen - and often, having to flee for his life.

He thanked me again for taking the time to teach him to read so he could be used of God among his people. Later, it occurred to me that while ministering in Tappi, I had listened to the devil's lie which said that *taking care of my girls, my home, my husband, and doing what little ministry I could from my home was not enough.* Today as I write this, I am again astounded by God's amazing power in my life. While living in Liberia, through my tears, complaints, grumblings, and discontentments, He was there. He was working. He was using me in spite of myself. That ministry of teaching Liberians to read on my terrace during our first three years in Liberia has no doubt realized more fruit than I could ever have imagined. God knew that, and despite my doubts concerning my efficiency in His kingdom, He compelled me to take the time to teach others, even when it was not glamorous and especially when it was intense and difficult. I am overwhelmed by the beauty of His orchestrations in my life. **Even in the most simple ministry, much fruit can still abound**. That's just like God. If we are but faithful, small things result in big things in His kingdom work.

It was a sweet afternoon of catching up and being encouraged by John's testimony. But as the sun headed towards the horizon, John and his son walked back to the bus stop on the main road. Within minutes, we heard a mounting commotion and glancing out the window, we were perplexed to see the two men running full force towards us. Jeff quickly opened the door as they dove inside screaming, "*They coming to kill us! Close the door! Hide us! They want to kill us!*"

By the time John could explain to us what had happened, our house was surrounded by nearly one hundred angry Africans yelling for us to kick the Liberian traitors out. John and his son were of the Gio tribe who, at the time, had the advantage in the Liberian civil war. The townspeople (Ivorians and Liberians) in Pehe were of the Krahn tribe, taking upon themselves to declare any Gio person their mortal enemy. At the bus stop, someone *supposedly* recognized John, yelling into the crowd there was a murderer among them. Reacting to the frenzy, another Krahn man slapped John soundly in the face while shouting that his own family had been killed in Liberia that same Gio man. The town residents - already tense because of the present war situation - did not need much convincing for the accusations to escalate. John and his son perceived almost immediately they were in grave danger. That is when they had madly sprinted to our house located ominously in the very center of town.

As the sun flickered and ebbed at the horizon, our lives changed drastically. Thankfully, all the missionaries along with the children where together at our house when this mayhem began. The crowd was growing as was the noise of their disgruntlements. Before long, we saw torches being burned close to the house and decided it would be best to put our children under a bed in one of the back bedrooms. At the time of this sobering event, Michelle was eight, Stefanie almost five, and Lauren a one year old. Along with the three other missionary kids, we desperately attempted to make a game out of the hiding, not wanting them to see our fear.

John stood firm that he had never taken up a gun at any time and never in his life had he killed anyone. We chose to believe him and were resolute in our determination to protect him and his son from the frenzied accusations. The local Ivorian pastor arrived, trying to talk to the crowd but to no avail. The hysteria of the crowd grew as they worked themselves into fits of anger. It was obvious by this point that the entire incident had become not so much an attack personally on John, but a tangible appeasement for the reality of civil war which had affected their lives drastically. John and his son were, in essence, to be sacrificial lambs. And for us? There we were; five white missionaries in the midst of tribal animosity, raw and out of control.

Jeff and Mark quickly decided it would be best to drive John and his son out of town in the Lada (yes, that is the name of the Russian-made car we were borrowing from Lutheran missionaries). The African pastor was going to inform the crowd of the plan while the men worked on getting the car ready for the trip. It took some effort to get the Lada road worthy due to a slack right front tire which needed air - available only by using a bicycle pump. Finally Mark brought the car around to the front door as Jeff walked out with the two emotionally dismantled men. As they headed toward the car, the crowd rushed the group in a way that made our guys feel unsafe. Whisking the two Liberians back into the house, we were forced to come up with another plan. After two more attempts to get the accused men into the car were met with comparable reactions, the town spokesman came to the door with these dire words, "*We want these two men. Give them to us and we will leave you all alone. If not.....*" He dramatically stepped back into the crowd with a pointed look on his face.

As the evening wore on, several town leaders tried to gain control of the situation. This event was unprecedented in magnitude and intensity, so no one really knew what to do other than appeal to the crowd to lay down their animosity, but they remained adamant, continuing to chant, threaten, and rave about how the white missionaries were siding with the Liberian rebels. Quite unexpectedly a few minutes later, the spokesman of the mob again knocked on the door and asked to talk with us. He told us the group had decided we could leave with the two Liberian men and transport them out of town. Everyone just wanted the rebels out of town. In one way, we were extremely relieved, though we thought the change of heart was a little abrupt. We chose to take it as a great answer to prayer. Before leaving the house, Jeff took me in our bedroom, shut off the lights, he went over some *just in case* instructions with me. Feeling the bile rise in my throat and fighting down a raw panic, I tried to listen as he gave me the pouch with our passports (except his) and most of the cash we had left for the month. Lying in his arms for a *not-long-enough* moment, he held me tightly. When had our lives gotten so topsy-turvy?

Opening the front door, we were all surprised to see that the crowd had moved farther away than they had been the entire evening, giving a tangible nod to the plan to get John and his son out of town. We locked the door to the house as soon as the men headed toward the car. Still sensing immense danger and feeling the need to do something besides wringing our hands, the other two missionary ladies and I lay prostrate on the floor in prayer. Sad to say, it was the first time I had ever prayed in a face-down position. We pleaded with God to calm the hearts of the crowd and put a strong hedge of angels around our men.

Meanwhile in the car, another drama was being played out. The previously pumped up tire was flat again, so Jeff went for the bicycle pump as Mark attempted to start the car. It would not start. As Jeff manually put air in the tire, Mark kept trying to start the car. Nothing. The motor would not even turn over. Jeff remembers looking out at the crowd who, by that time, were moving closer towards them. As he watched the tire slowly, *too slowly*, inflate, and listened to the malignant whining of the engine refusing to start, he simply looked up. Being far from city lights, the night was inky black and millions of stars were blinking down at him. His prayer was simple, "*God, there are some white boys down here in trouble. Protect John and his son and please allow this car to start so that we can get them to safety. This is not feeling good, Father.*" Confident, he got into the car and encouraged Mark to turn the ignition again, but still nothing. Complete silence except for the angry shouts of the crowd moving closer and closer. *God? Did you hear me?*

The Ivorian pastor was able to edge the crowd back a little and doing the only thing they knew to do, Mark and Jeff fled with John and his son into the house. It was then that the crowd began to vehemently rant and rave, surrounding the house with torches and rocks in their hands. Not long after, they began to throw rocks at our windows. After Jeff and Mark explained to us the reason for their abrupt return, we all sat in silence and prayed. We knew nothing else to do. Knowing the crowd would soon become even more aggressive, the Ivorian pastor sent his son to bring back a policeman who lived in the next town. Almost an hour passed before we heard someone violently pounding on our back door.

Believing the crowd had finished with their waiting and were going to edge their way into the house, the mothers checked on the children while the men went to see who was knocking so incessantly. A familiar and friendly voice was behind the door. Wilson, one of the Christian young men who attended the local Bible school, had urgent news for us.

Returning from a nearby town on a money bus, the vehicle he was on stopped suddenly because of a large tree trunk in the middle of the road. When the driver asked the reason for the roadblock, the men were told of the afternoon events, how Liberian traitors had been visiting the missionaries in Pehe. Speaking of their devised plan, Wilson heard them say they were going to allow the missionaries to think they were escaping with the two Gio men. At the roadblock, the car would be stopped and **everyone** in it killed! Hardly believing what he was hearing, Wilson jumped off the bus and ran the few hundred yards back to Pehe. Stepping into our house, eyes large with fear, Wilson said, *"Don't go anywhere with the car. Please, don't go anywhere,"* and further explained what he had learned on the bus.

Stunned at how God had so obviously saved the lives of the men just an hour before, we simply stood there listening to Wilson. God had lain His Almighty hands on the engine of that Lada and said, *"No, not now."* **What we perceived as God not answering us was not that at all.** *It never is.* We do not always know what is best for us and He never makes mistakes. When would that sink in? Really, really sink in to the point we stopped accusing God of not hearing us? Not answering us?

The military policeman soon arrived from a nearby town and was extremely vexed at having been awakened to deal with such an embarrassing skirmish. He climbed out of his car wielding a handgun and shot it in the air several times, getting his point across to the astonished mob. Within ninety seconds, the crowd pushed back, but still seemed eager to follow the story to the end. After the policeman heard the complaints from the protestors and listened to our story, he personally put the two Gio men into his car with the promise to take them to Toulepleu, seeing them safely on a bus headed for Liberia. By the time Mark and Jeff went out to check on our car still sitting in the front yard, the crowd had magically dispersed. Just like that. As the women and children stood at the door watching, the key was put into the ignition and turned. The car started pronto. Amazing Adonai!

Exhausted after our seven hour ordeal, we all dispersed to our own beds and tried to sleep. Trauma has a way of weaving its way in and out of our consciousness for days, months, even years after an event. It seeps into every part of our lives. Affecting us slowly or suddenly, but surely. Adrenaline still in my system, I slept fitfully, waking up several times, checking the girls, peering out the windows, walking around and trying to process the episode. Struggling not to project my anger on God, I cried out. Finally, I was able to sleep deeply for a few hours, so desiring to forget all the trauma and fears for a little while.

Early the next morning, everything was quiet except a rapping on our door. Though the knocking was not loud, Jeff and I jolted awake with immediate thoughts of safety and wondering if we were to have a repeat of last night. The purpose of the visit was a stunner. Pehe's town chief (mayor) had sent word that our attendance was **required** at a town meeting at 10:00 a.m. that morning. Leaving us no option to decline the invitation, the courier for the town chief told us that the meeting was to formally accuse us missionaries of disturbing the peaceful town of Pehe. Incredibly, it sounded like the town chief was mandating an apology from us for the pandemonium of the previous evening.

To put it mildly, I can only describe our predicament as a character test, separating the strong, mature Christian desiring to live like Christ from the one still embedded in her pride and selfishness. I must tell you, that if it were a test, *I failed miserably*. Acting out of physical exhaustion and continued fear for my family's safety during the event of the previous evening, I chose **not** to commiserate the townspeople. I was furious at such a request. Jeff, being a wise man, knew it was not prudent for me to go to that meeting. Not with the fire he saw smoldering behind my eyes. Though we all knew the accusations were ridiculous and none of us wanted to relive the incident in front of the town, the men felt strongly they should attend the meeting and give the apology. They cited to us the example of Christ as He was beaten and crucified for crimes He never committed. Why should we live any differently? I was both convicted and astounded at the men's insight.

Though I know it took much denying of self, they went to the town meeting, apologized for something they did not do, and humbled themselves before the very people who had wanted to kill us just a few hours earlier. After the men's expressions of regret, the entire incident seemed to dissolve like snow in a warm rain. During the same day, some townspeople even came to apologize to us. As is the West African fashion, when retribution was made, apologies spoken, and the heat of the moment passed, the two opposing sides always shook hands and seemingly became long lost friends. It never ceased to amaze me...and convict me. For the furtherance of the Gospel **alone** could we continue to live in such a place. I began to comprehend more meaningfully some of Paul's writings. My flesh desperately wanted to flee the town and never look back. Discerning that was not God's plan, I struggled with how to share the Gospel while my flesh screamed for retribution.

Days later, as we still processed the entire event, I was skittish in my reactions to sounds around me and when people approached the front door. We kept our children in closer view and I purposely found things to keep me busy inside our house, so I would not have to face the villagers. Forgiving the townspeople for what had happened to our family was slow in coming, but it gradually came. Overwhelmed by how God so graciously saved the men that night in the car, I bent a little more to His will for my life in that spiritually dark African village. I asked desperately for His love to shine through my tired and bruised heart. *Your love, Father, always give me Your love! I have none of my own to share with those people to whom you've called us,* I cried.

CHAPTER THREE

Hope is faith holding out its hand in the dark. —George Iles

When Missionaries Despair

At the time of the following journal entry, we were so bogged down with our living circumstances, it was almost impossible to see what God was really doing in the lives of those to whom we ministered, even in our own lives. My journal of August 13, 1991 reads:

> *You people need to pray for us. Jeff and I were talking today, and we are even wondering whether we are where we really are supposed to be. We have never been through so much before in our lives. <u>The Lord has used us, and even through the despair we feel day to day, people are seeking God and finding Him</u>. But there is a cold, heavy hand on our ministries, and they do not seem to be able to expand. Our clinic ministry has been hampered through the jealousy of the Ivorians here. We give Liberian refugee free medicine and the Ivorians cannot handle that.*

Our container shipped from the states had arrived, but we did not feel like unpacking anything personal. The bikes we had brought out for our children stayed in the container mainly because some of the town children were becoming more rancorous towards our own kids. For nearly two weeks after the Black Monday event, our children had stopped playing outside. It was just too much of a hassle for them to do anything without being hounded. Disturbingly, our older children resorted to carrying large sticks to protect themselves when they did venture outdoors. Regardless, they were followed, prodded, probed and taunted by the African children. There was no privacy unless they came inside.

Though playing inside was louder and produced more of a mess for us, we no longer cared. We felt extremely sorry for them. My mother's heart fretted at how all of this would affect my girls over the long term.

Though the houses were nice enough, the constant noise, and the peering in our windows by young or old wore us down. I would have sold my last piece of bread for privacy, but it was an impossible dream. We were like the zoo situated right in the middle of the town, and there were many times we felt like caged animals. I am not exaggerating. We felt trapped. Our hearts and minds struggled to remember why we had come there. It is when oppression comes in ministry that we must totally rely on the truth of a calling which may have become blurry.

One bleak morning around 6:00 a.m., we were awakened to a whistle blowing loudly, people shouting, and the sounds of the town soccer team doing calisthenics. Right outside our bedroom window was one of the goals for their soccer field, so you can imagine what happened to the ball if the goalkeeper did not catch it. When we complained to the local pastor in town, he talked to the coach and players. In the end, we definitely felt like we were the ones in the way, out of place. Some days I felt completely crazed by the noise around me because there were no glass in the windows to buffer out any of the noises. Every rooms, except the bathroom, had windows. Dark curious eyes followed us wherever we went. To an African, privacy was not a word to put into cultural context. Most likely, there wasn't even a word for *privacy* in their dialect. They thought nothing of endless noise and having people constantly around them. To an American, it was daunting and more challenging than I could ever had imagined. **Privacy** became an obsession.

When we had been there for a month, Lauren developed a full-blown case of dysentery. It was inevitable because of the living conditions right outside our door. Goats, chickens, and even pigs ventured on our porch. While we had someone clean the porch on a daily basis, still the dysentery got her. She was not walking sturdily yet, so there were times she would fall, hands touching the ground. Before I could pick her up and wash her hands, she put them into her mouth. Dysentery with a baby was a nightmare. If anything, it did help me to empathize with the African mothers whose children lived with those kind of diseases constantly. Some days she would go through five or six diapers *per hour*. You can imagine how red and raw her bottom became. By the way, I am talking about *cloth diapers*, not disposable diapers. Where in the jungle would I buy those? In the city? Yes, there were grocery stores in Abidjan that carried them, but a bag of diapers cost enough to feed our family of five for days.

We hired a couple of women to wash our clothes by hand which helped, but there was no dryer to finish the process. The month of August was the beginning of heavy rainy season in that region. Since I only had a limited amount of diapers, Jeff rigged up a kind of drying process for our clothes....especially the diapers. There was a small wooden shed right outside of our house, and though I do not remember what was in the shed, we gained permission from the pastor to clean it out and use it as a drying house. The men added clotheslines and a charcoal grill to incite the process of drying the clothes. Inside the shed it felt like a sauna without the benches to relax on. Heavy rains splattered humidity through the cracks of the building and the charcoal grill provided the heat. The clothes dried nicely if we constantly kept the grill stoked. I tried to be thankful for dry diapers, but the pungent stench of wood smoke on our clothes and the flecks of black charcoal all over them was hard to ignore. Another lesson in contentment and gratitude was in the making.

And the Beat Goes On and On

Just as Stefanie's first birthday was celebrated in the shadow of our Lassa Fever scare in Tappeta, Lauren turned one in the middle of the oppressiveness of Pehe. Soon after our small celebration of our youngest daughter's birthday, Jeff had to return to Abidjan for supplies. While he was gone, Lauren came down with chicken pox, and because of the African heat, was suffering tremendously with the itchy side effects of the virus. An old Liberian lady who lived across the path from our house had evidently seen the sores on Lauren's little body. One day the old lady's daughter came with her to visit us. She held in her gnarled hand some dubious-looking *country medicine* to rub on Lauren's sores - guaranteed to dry them up. She insisted that I rub the homemade concoction on the baby right away.

Those are the moments which could make or break a missionary in her efficacy. While not wanting to endanger my little girl by rubbing her open sores with unsanitary ointment, there was an abiding confidence I was to do just that. As I put my fingers in the salve, a horrible smell wafted to my nose, prompting me to ask the daughter (who had been interpreting for the older lady who knew no English) what was in the medicine. A particular tree bark, herbs, and cow manure were the main ingredients, I was told. Trying my best not to gag and wishing I had not asked, I knew that I was up against another cultural collision. The two women were not Christians though we had witnessed to them repeatedly. The last thing I wanted to do was to offend them by turning away their medicinal offering. Lauren and I both cringed from the smell, but I decided to continue applying the salve and let God take care of the rest. It was greenish in color, and when Lauren was enveloped with the salve, she looked like a bug-eyed little lizard.

As I wanted to talk to the two Liberian women a little more about their need for Christ, I asked Michelle to take Lauren into the bedroom with her. When Michelle picked up Lauren and got a good whiff of her little sister, she adamantly refused to take her anywhere smelling like that! It was so pitiful that it was funny. After a few minutes, the African women left, and I put Lauren straight into the bathtub to relieve us all from the smell. As does usually happen in cases of chicken pox, within two or three days, the sores started drying up and Lauren was feeling better. The old Liberian woman and her daughter came in the yard to tell us how happy they were that the country medicine had worked so well. I smiled and thanked them profusely for their kindness, leaving out the fact that Lauren had only worn that salve for all of ten minutes. There are some things that just do not need to be revealed.

According to my journals, the ministries continued despite the hardships and oppression which we felt everywhere we turned.

Growth and spiritual revival often emerges off the hem of affliction and tribulation. My journal of August 18 reads:

> *Jeff and Mark have started a Bible study in Pehe every Monday, Wednesday, and Friday. Jeff had 25 men attend yesterday. I have a Ladies' Bible study here on Tuesday and Thursdays, one in Kpobli on Saturdays, and a teenage girls' class on Sunday afternoon. Many of the African Christians are growing. We are seeing fruit. And every Sunday Jeff preaches in a different town in the surrounding area. We see salvations each Sunday for which we are thankful. We want to be faithful, and we choose to live faithfully, but we need strength from our even more faithful Savior.*

It felt like we were plodding through thick mud instead of pure refreshing water. But even in the mud, there were those who needed Christ. Isn't that where most people reside who truly need Christ? **Who said we would never have to get our hands dirty to make a difference in His kingdom**? Ministry in the Pehe area prompted a necessity to totally die to self so that God could totally have His way. Honestly, I only remember many of the results of our ministries there because I have reread my journals. Sadly, most of the memories I carry in my heart about Pehe are the bad ones. The hard ones. That has been a poignant revelation for me, but it has also shown me that God, like the infamous *Footprint* poem infers, carried us through those times when we had no strength of our own and sustained us wherever He needed us to be. I am in awe how He used us - broken, overwhelmed, and floundering - in some of the darkest parts of the country of Ivory Coast.

Seriously, we had always loved living in Africa and had been able to overcome many of the cultural collisions, but with the war raging across the border and thousands of traumatized Liberians living around us, the dynamics were beyond our control. Nothing could have prepared us for that. So we had come unprepared, clueless, and vulnerable to the rotten elements around us. *I Surrender All* became more than just a song. We were called out to truly *know Him in the power of His resurrection and the fellowship of His suffering.* It was not what I would have chosen outside His Spirit undoubtedly guiding me.

Many areas in West Africa have been strongholds of Satan - Pehe was no exception. It surely had become one of Satan's prized possessions in that region. When we stepped into the middle of his very active domain, we experienced the fight of our lives. After a couple of months of living in the spiritual darkness, it became apparent God alone would have to do the fighting. We had no strength of our own. God's promises were true; they NEVER failed. But I will never get over the feeling of dark, Satanic oppression in that Ivorian town. As Frank Peretti's books arouse dimensional displays of spiritual warfare, there were times I could almost hear the fluttering of devilish wings and feel the sharp probe of deadly talons.

As I have mentioned, jealousy prevailed between the Ivorians and the Liberians. Many Ivorians living in Pehe had nothing good to say about us because they believed we were only there for the Liberian refugees. We had a policy that all relief materials from Baptist Mid-Missions were put strictly into the hands of the Liberian refugees. It was necessary, unfortunately, because some Ivorians who were in charge of distributing the Red Cross medicines and responsible for distributing food from the United Nations forced the Liberians to buy their medicines and rice. If three bags of rice were to be distributed to each Liberian family there, the Ivorian workers would give the Liberian family one and give two bags to the host Ivorian family. Corruption was pronounced on all levels.

Our second month living in Pehe approached and still the duplexes we had contracted to be completed in Toulepleu were not ready. Desiring to get out of Pehe and start more relief ministries closer to the border had to be put on hold a while longer. Nothing moved quickly in that part of the world, so we were at the mercy of clothes perfumed with burnt charcoal, Lauren's never-ending dysentery, our older children becoming hermits and playing almost completely indoors, and the maddening noises all around us from morning to night. Every day, nothing changed. We carried on because we did not know what else to do. Quitting was not an option.

Give Me One Good Reason

My journal of August 18, 1991, reads:

> *On Saturday I had the privilege of handing out the first batch of used clothing. After my Saturday afternoon Bible study in Kpobli, I took ten refugee families and gave each family a box of clothes. Tears were in my eyes as I saw the joy particularly in the mothers' eyes. It was one of the most rewarding things that I have done since we have been here. Right now, during all this conflict and struggle of day to day survival, the only time I can really justify being here in this mess is when someone gets saved or I am able to hand clothes to a child who is only wearing rags.*

Jeff went back and forth to Abidjan either to check on paperwork for our container or to work on the logistics of buying and registering a truck in the country. It seemed every ten days or so, he was heading back to the big city and staying gone for at least a week. Even our tenth wedding anniversary passed by while he was in Abidjan. Having no phones in Pehe, I found it so hard when he was gone. So much could go wrong with me or the girls at home while he was on the road traveling. How would I ever be able to get up with him if I really needed him? This thought made me feel so vulnerable. After almost two months of living in Pehe and having Jeff gone more than he was home, I hit a wall one day. My journal of August 21, 1991, reads:

> *This was one of the roughest days I have experienced since living in Pehe. By 10:30 a.m. I had five requests for clothes, food, medicines, and money. They know my husband is not here and they plan it that way. I guess they feel that I am easier to get things from*

when my husband is gone. This past Saturday I gave
used clothing to the Liberian families in Kpobli.
Today I found out that some of the women tried to
cheat and bring Ivorians in for clothing, or use people
who had received clothing before. There seems to
always be a few sour apples in the barrel.

Michelle and I had a big run in last night, and so
when I lay down in bed, I started crying and praying
for wisdom. I was so overwhelmed by the events
of the day (every day is such a strain and does put
unnoticed pressure on the kids) and I probably just
overreacted. Well, within a few minutes, Michelle
came to the side of the bed, and she was crying too.
So she crawled in bed with me and for an hour,
we cried and prayed and talked. It was one of the
sweetest times we have had in a long time and made
me realize how much our kids are trying to be strong
and that we need to be strong for them. It is so hard
to think of all these things when your head is barely
above water.

Taking a Bite Out of My Morning

During one of Jeff's many trips to Abidjan, the girls and I had
visitors. Lots and lots of uninvited guests had crept while we slept. I
woke up one morning and dawdled sleepily to the bathroom. Sitting
down on the toilet with my eyes still closed, it did not take long to
realize something was askew. After being bitten a couple of times
on the backside, I found the problem right away. DRIVER ANTS!
They were on the toilet, parading around the shower, under the
sink. I then followed them into my bedroom where there were three
separate trails under Lauren's bed, but hankfully none had gotten
into her crib. I needed to get dressed, so I put Lauren down on the
other side of the bed away from the trail of ants. She started toddling
toward the kitchen when my mother's instinct told me the ants were
probably in there too. I caught her just in time. The cabinets were

black with the busy critters as was the trash can and most of the floor. There was not a place on the counter uninhabited by ants!

Rousing the other two girls, we rushed quickly out of the house and over to the Sheppards' house. Mark Sheppard and several Africans worked hard to exterminate the ants. It took nearly two hours before the ants were cleared out of the house enough so I felt comfortable going in there. All day, despite the extermination, we were bitten by rogue ants in the kitchen, bathroom, or bedrooms. Finally, at 10:30 that night, Jeff arrived from Abidjan, having completely missed the entire driver ant drama.

A letter arrived from Touleple the next day. It was not good news for the weary missionaries. Any hope of getting into the duplexes and moving out of Pehe soon faded at the news that the truck needed to transport supplies for work on the duplexes had broken down. Since the owner of the duplexes was in France until the second week of September, we knew everything would be pushed back indefinitely. We sank deeper into despondency with the realization that we were stuck in Pehe for an undetermined amount of time. I believed that God knew when we had had enough, but there was part of me beginning to wonder - though I always hated it when I doubted God like that. Could He not see that I was at my breaking point?

Taking It Over the Top

We thought it could not get worse. During the last month of living in Pehe, it seemed we merely existed. Granted, we were in the Word of God, reading it, speaking it, teaching it. But there was nothing else left to give besides that. Why did we think there should have been something else? Was that not enough? We read the Word of God because we knew it was true, we taught it because we knew it was our mandate and the people around us so desperately needed it, and we clung to it like it was the last breath we would ever take. Though we did not *feel* the excitement and joy of ministry, God was still working His purpose in our lives for the sake of those lost in their sin. **Ministry does not always have to *feel* good *to be* right**. God had never promised that. He did promise, however, to enable us and keep us if we chose to stand firm, to remain steadfast.

We were usually quite focused in on things going on in our domestic world, but by the third month in Pehe, we all had become a little slack in our alertness. We simply were not paying close attention to many things around us, and as a result, we got taken. The last weekend we were to be in Pehe and after the news drifted around town we were really leaving, our house filled up with people lamenting our departure. Even the two women who washed our clothes and the one who helped me watch Lauren were acting pitiful. Ruthie, the woman who watched Lauren some in the mornings, insisted that the baby was tired and needed morning naps, and then willingly volunteered to help the two other women wash our clothes. Never before had she done that. She was always so proud that she was the "nanny" for the white people and did not have to wash clothes. **Red alert! Red alert**! It should have been, but our minds were dull.

Who could think at all with the constant activity around us? People sat in our house and sighed, begged, brought letters full of sorrow and great need and other letters containing obvious and blunt requests. The soccer games continued right outside our house, and the kids kept playing inside. I became increasingly numb with noise, requests, and *pretend* sorrow. It was all I could do not to scream in the midst of it. I really felt I would go mad, but God kept His hand on my spirit.

"*Oh, missy, you're coming to leave us. What we will do? Oh, our hearts are so sad...Give me a nightgown!*" or "*Oh, my children will die now. How can you leave us...Give me the toys!*" Constant and uninterrupted begging and pleading. When you have nothing and have hope of nothing, I guess it can happen that way. For five American adults, it was obvious we were drastically outnumbered by the needs and the entreating of hundreds of Liberian refugees. It was not what we had bargained for when we had decided to *stroll in to save the day* for the displaced Liberians. Desperate humans can foster desperate actions. Our expectations and those of the Liberian refugees collided on an emotional battlefield. Who would win? Who would retreat?

The Thursday before we left Pehe, the three of us missionary women took our clothes off the clothesline late in the afternoon. Distantly we were aware that none of us had very many clothes to fold that day. Survival mode can sometimes disallow truth to surface because of the mere fact there are no resources to deal with the truth if it be made known. Reality usually etches itself on someone's mind eventually. The following day, Ardith and I were taking clothes from the line when she noticed that her blue towel and wash cloth were missing. She only had two, so that was easy counting. If the thieves had but chosen to steal my peach or green towel, I would have never noticed - so blitzed was I. But stealing Ardith's blue towel was a different story and strong proof that God does know how to bring things to the surface when He is ready for them to be revealed.

The three of us women started putting the pieces together and realized we were all missing items, especially our children's clothes. After we plunged forward in our investigation, we found out that other Liberians knew of the stealing, that it had been going on for quite some time. The women who washed our clothes been seen stealing plastic bags from our kitchen or even tucking clothes under their skirts. We were amazed at how many people knew and never said anything. When we questioned the three suspected women, they acted appalled at our accusations. Two of them started crying. Stung by our own fresh betrayal, we were not in the mood. As the refugees in Pehe found out about the women from Kpobli stealing from us, they turned on their Liberian sisters, embarrassed and angry because those women had shamed the entire refugee community.

Our last Saturday morning in Pehe, the three guilty women from Kpobli had the nerve to show up for work as if nothing had happened. Realizing the town's disfavor on the three women, we took them out on the back porch and raised our voices so we could be heard by those living in the nearby huts. African women came running to see what was happening - as we knew they would. After we said what we wanted to say, we listened to the Krahn dialect fly back and forth between the accused ladies and the angry refugees. It was evident, early on, that the three African women were holding to their innocence and as all eyes moved back to us, we simply said, "*Bring our clothes back and then we will talk.*" Mayhem erupted between the town's women and those three female thieves as we walked back inside the house, shaken but resolved to see it through.

The rest of the day we received visitors wanting to tell what they knew. Whether they wanted compensation for the information they were giving, we did not ask. We listened, spoke again on the sin of stealing, lying, and pride, knowing quite well we were fighting against ingrained cultural notions. It was the fashion of Liberians not to talk about another Liberian and *spoil* their name, regardless of whether they were guilty or not, regardless of whether someone had seen them in the act. In the Liberian culture, talking about someone's name in a bad way was worse than the crime itself. What a wicked web the Deceiver had woven around the hearts and minds of those precious Liberians.

We knew from experience that the drama was only beginning. On Sunday morning around 8:00 a.m., the three women showed up at our door. When I saw them standing at my door without any bags of clothes, I lost my patience. I said to them, "*How dare you come to my house acting innocent and to continue your lying. I will NOT talk to you until you bring the clothes.*" They were stunned that their normal begging was not working and as I turned to go back inside, Ruthie went down on her knees, grabbing hold of my foot (as is customary in Liberia when one is very serious about their begging). "*I hold your foot, Missy! Please, I hold your foot.*" Tears were running down her eyes and she was sobbing desperately. For the sake of teaching the principles of sin, I held firm against her crying. There was no remorse, no regret, no repentance in the faces of the three women. They had been caught, their names were tarnished, and they were trying to *save face* by having us forgive them without them admitting to the sin or bringing the clothes back.

With all kind of thoughts racing through my mind, I said to them in as calm a voice as I could muster, "*In the Bible when a person sinned, God was angry. It is true. He hates lying, stealing, cheating, and many other wrong things. However, the Bible also tells us that God is very forgiving and will instantly stretch out His arms to someone who truly repents, confesses his sins, and makes things right. I feel like that today, ladies. I am very angry at your sin, your stealing and persistent lying about it. But I promise you that I will be just as quick to hold out my hands to you IF you will come clean with this sin business. But not until then."* I walked inside feeling good for saying what I had said, though I did have to ask God to help me to truly forgive them if they did the right thing. To realize that God would give me victory in that situation was comforting in the middle of a blistering time.

CHAPTER FOUR

I want to be in a place where I have to have God in everything I do,
where God is indispensable to me. — A.W. Tozier

Wrapping It All Up

On the same Sunday morning I confronted the three clothes
thieves, Jeff preached in a town very close to Kpobli. Living there
were about two hundred refugees who begged for us to come
and preach to them....and of course, bring clothes and medicines.
So, Jeff loaded up the car and headed out while Michelle and
Stefanie went to church with Nancy and Ardith in Pehe. I stayed
home with Lauren since her dysentery was acting up again, and
I also had a suspicion our three wash women might return for
another discussion. I spent much time in prayer and reading the
Bible, trying to get a handle on all that had happened in the past
forty-eight hours.

Right before noon, I heard a shuffling noise outside my
door. Sure enough, the women had returned. They told me that
they had decided it would be best to confess and bring back the
clothes. *Well, some of them.* They brought three pieces of clothing,
adamantly insisting it was all they had taken. With a heavy heart,
I went into the house to retrieve the list we had made, asking God
to shine through me even though that was the last thing my flesh
wanted to do. It kept taunting me with thoughts like: *Let me at*
'em! Let me say what you know you are thinking! With a sigh that
embodied a prayer of a thousand words, I walked back in the living
room. The list consisted of thirty-three items, and waving the piece
of paper like a banner, I said again, "*I will not talk until all the*
clothes have been brought back." They left quickly, perhaps stunned
by my coldness. As irony would have it and as was culturally
predictable, the same Liberian refugee women who had sided
with us the previous day came to plead for the three women. The
reasoning went like this: "*Haven't they brought back some of the*

things? It was very hard for them to do that and to have their name spoiled. Can't you just accept their "never minds" (a Liberian term for asking for forgiveness) and forgive them?"

Yes, we could have done that. Accepted their apologies and turned a blind eye to the many things which were still missing. It was not the clothes to which we were holding. Certainly we knew how much more we possessed than they. If they would have only asked for clothes, we would have given some to them. But now, if we did overlooked their stealing, it would do nothing but make us look as if we, too, had fallen into cultural degeneracy. We had spent nearly three months teaching them the strong and unfailing principles from God's Word. All those Bible studies, all those verses rehearsed with them would seem impotent by our unwillingness to see the situation through. We wanted it to end. We wanted to fold because we were almost at the point of being incapacitated with fatigue. But deep in our spirits, we knew there was more on the table than our bruised reputation and tired bodies. Giving in or giving up was the easier thing to do, but it was not the right thing to do. Another cultural collision was staring us straight in the eyes but were we spiritually, physically and emotionally strong enough to withstand it? To stand against it with love, compassion, but also with conviction? I was not sure as I stood at the front door and watched the three woman walk away.

This is probably a good place to talk about the misconception of missionaries attempting to change cultural significance in the midst of our desire to share the Gospel. The opinions are varied and strong. One side believes a missionary should never touch the pivotal nubs of a culture no matter what the Bible may say, surmising there are those cultural traditions which are sacred and foundational. Other missionaries go in with barrels loaded and minds closed, wearing the cloak of Americanism into communities which know nothing beyond their borders. Since we are talking about opinions, I will relate mine here. Both extremes are harmful and do not portray the essence of the Gospel. While working with missionaries in West Africa and the West Indies, I have seen a true and balanced respect for local cultures. Only in those incidences when cultural practices stand directly against the Word of God, do we remain firm.

Even churches in America have watered down the Gospel message with the growing momentum of cultural expectations. Culture is powerful. It defines. It guides. But it can also destroy when it goes against the very nature of God and what He has deemed best. Some Liberians had a strong propensity for taking things not their own and keeping them, perhaps not being taught responsibility toward another man's property at a younger age. But then again, so do some Americans. Every culture has the inclination to be held captive to the very essence of itself.

After Ardith, Nancy, Mark, and Jeff returned from their respective church services and we had eaten lunch, the three Liberian women returned to the house to talk and to *hold our feet*. They held Nancy's foot, Ardith's foot, Mark's foot, and Jeff's foot, and while doing so, our eight year old Michelle walked out of her room and said, "*What are they doing, mommy? What don't they just bring back the clothes?*" As she was talking, one of the women tried to hold Michelle's foot, but she just said loudly and with much feeling, "*No, leave me! I don't want any rogue touching me. Just bring back my clothes!*" What could I, as her mother, say at that point? She had spoken from her young heart and though it was obvious we needed to work on the forgiveness aspect, I could not fault her for her frustrations. It reminded me that this situation was not just affecting us, but also our children. I honestly do not remember if Michelle was rebuked for what she said. It was a tense moment for all of us. My mothering edge had been dulled, I will admit.

On that same Sunday night, we decided to go to Kpobli and talk with the town chief because the Liberian women were registered there. The Ivorian official was very embarrassed and frustrated by the Liberian refugees making a bad name for his town. Surprisingly, the consensus of the other refugees in town was that we were more guilty **because we had exposed the women**. A cultural collision for sure. We knew we were stepping onto unfamiliar grounds by pressing the matter, but since we were leaving Pehe the next day, we wanted it cleared up. There were times we wondered whether we had done the right thing by taking the problem to the town chief. If there had been a pastor in the town, he would have been the more obvious one to present the matter to, but we had been the ones providing English church services during those past three months. Right or wrong, we will never know. But thinking back on the situation nearly ten years later, I do not think we should have gotten the Ivorians involved. It seemed we were airing our "Christian" troubles to the secular world. Oh for hindsight to answer the questions that foresight demands!

During our visit to Kpobli, the women handed over four more items, but we knew there were still at least two dozen still missing. We left Kpobli that evening with heavy hearts, knowing we had to leave behind that situation as we moved to another town. The relentless three women showed up early Monday morning for their final pay. As firm and loving as we could, we said, "*We will pay you when you bring the rest of the things.*" This time they did not beg. They lashed out, threatening us, exposing their true colors. We tried to quietly tell them we absolutely would not reward sin. That if they chose to keep the clothes, that was their payment. There is no happy ending to this story. We can only pray our testimony was a beacon of light into the darkness of where many of these Africans lived.

We had originally told the townspeople we were leaving on Tuesday morning, but by Monday afternoon, the smell of freedom was too much for us. The last box packed, we left as dusk approached - no looking back. I felt my spirit take a really deep breath for the first time in three months as we bounced down the dirt road to a new town, a new place to minister, and duplexes with walls around them. Unfortunately, the only thing I cared about at that moment was to be surrounded by walls. While the Sheppard's was ready for them to move in, our duplex was not. Knowing it was not a good idea to leave his family in Toulepleu as he continued traveling to Abidjan for truck details, Jeff decided that our family would move temporarily to Abidjan. Another *temporary* situation, but at least our family would be together. I had no desire to stay in Toulepleu, yet another unfamiliar town with Jeff being gone so much.

A Village in the Dark

The next morning, we left for the nine-hour trip to Abidjan. The Sheppards and Ardith were also going for a few days just to take a break. It had been three months since any of the women and children had been to the largest city in Ivory Coast. For the men, we knew it was just another trip, but for the rest of us, it was almost like going to Disney World! Well, *almost*.

Since there were too many of us to travel in the one car we were still borrowing, Ardith, Mark, and the Sheppard's two boys were elected to ride the bus. Those of us with smaller bladders needed to go in the car because the buses did not stop very often for potty breaks. Nancy and her daughter, Melodie, and the five Abernethys piled into the Lada with the trailer packed full and hitched behind us. Everything went fine until about 8:00 p.m. that night when we were just an hour from Abidjan. *The infamous flat tire*. After Jeff changed the tire, we drove to a gas station to have the tube repaired. While he was in the shop, we were quickly surrounded by ten African girls who hit at the windows, staring, laughing, and mocking. It prompted us all to feel - as we had in Pehe - like caged animals in a zoo. We had grown desperately weary of the staring, laughing, mocking, having endured it for three months. On the cuff of everything else, it was almost too much to handle. Our kids had meltdowns right in the car, hiding their faces and crying out for the Africans to go away. It broke our hearts to see their pain. In reality I was not too far behind them. As we drove away from the gas station, I was disturbed to see that my hands were shaking and my breathing had accelerated. It was the first time I had come so close to having a panic attack.

A very short ten minutes down the road, the fan belt broke, forcing us to sit for an hour and a half while Jeff walked to find a new fan belt. He then had to get the nuts and bolts from underneath the battery, and after all that effort, realized he was putting a really-too-small fan belt back on. Poor Jeff was doing his best, but nothing seemed to be going right with the repair job. God gave him nerves of steel for the task, finally getting the fan belt to fit. We were back on the road again...for another ten minutes. Close enough to Abidjan that we could almost taste it, but still in the middle of nowhere, the car died. Jeff worked desperately for two hours but the car just would not start. I knew it had to be something more serious because Jeff had aircraft mechanic training at Piedmont Bible College and knew how to work on engines of airplanes as well as automobiles The car was Russian-made, so maybe things were put in a different place under the hood? I didn't know. I just felt immensely sorry for Jeff and deeply concerned for us sitting on the side of a dark and deserted road.

The blackness of the night revealed nothing to us except that we were truly stranded. Thankfully, we had water, but the food we brought on the trip had since been consumed. It was soon apparent that one fifteen month old, a four year old, six year old, and a seven year old all needed to find places to sleep. It was getting urgent by the whiny sounds they were all making, so we had to come up with a plan. I put baby Lauren in the floor of the back seat, Shell and Stef shared the back seat, and Nancy and Melodie did their best in the front seats. For a while, Jeff and I stood behind the car on the grass futilely trying to flag down buses or trucks when they whizzed by, but none stopped. Many buses traveled with only one headlight burning. We were indeed in a precarious position, but knew of no alternative.

Numbness set in. I sensed total and utter helplessness rising again from our months at Pehe and was unsure how to process all the emotions welling up inside me. One saving grace was that Lauren kept waking up, which kept my mind occupied for a bit. Her clothes were wet and dirty, but my mind could not fathom where I had packed more. Probably in the trailer buried beneath the other luggage. Feeling like the worse kind of mother, I wrapped her in a large white blanket, walked and cuddled her, singing from the depths of a broken and tired mother's heart. While holding my sleepy baby girl, somewhere from the murkiness of the night came a man. He startled us because we did not know if he was part of a group of bandits or not. We had heard that bandits often worked those highways, and we had made that a specific matter of prayer. The man was gentle and kind but spoke a dialect we did not recognize. I tried communicating in French, but he did not speak that well either. After realizing we would not be able to communicate verbally with him, Jeff went to the glove compartment of the car and gave him a French tract. The man waved and quietly walked off into the night.

At one point, Jeff thought perhaps we could flag down the bus which was carrying Mark, Ardith, and the boys. It would have to come right by us. We knew the letters were clearly displayed on the side of the bus, so with his flashlight, Jeff walked about a quarter of a mile from where the car was stranded. The plan was if he could see the Toulepleu bus pass by, he would wave his flashlight towards me; then I was to wave my flashlight and try to stop the bus. Eventually, the first part of the plan worked. Jeff saw the letters on the bus distinguishing it as the one from Toulepleu and urgently flagged me with his light. Desperately waving my flashlight, I hollered, jumped frantically, and had to dispel the urge to throw myself in front of the bus. It plowed on.

Watching the taillights grow dim with distance, my despondency increased. Fighting physical and emotional fatigue, we both lay down on the edge of the road. Praying that a snake or some other kind of animal would not find us lying vulnerably on the side of the road, we tried to rest. I thought of my parents and family back in the States as I searched the sky and saw a distant star. I asked God to let my parents think of me and to pray for me that morning. Later that week I was talking to my dad and he told me that he woke up early the very morning of our breakdown feeling a strong urge to pray for us. This was before I even told them the story of our breakdown. Don't resist those urges to pray for others when they come to you.

We were jolted out of our stupor by a very loud rumbling sound coming down the road. Blinking, trying to focus, we could see nothing; but the sound got closer. Jeff, realizing it was most likely some kind of vehicle traveling with NO lights, moved quickly off the road just in time to see the shadow of a log truck barreling past us. To realize there were vehicles traveling in the thick darkness with no navigational lights was alarming. Knowing that, there was no more rest for us that night. I paced, prayed, cried, and lamented. It was a long dark night. The stars seemed to mock me. *God, what have we done wrong? Why this?*

As dawn moved slowly but surely towards us, we were surprised to see the outline of a small village only about three hundred yards away. The entire night we had been close to other people and had no idea! Four men eventually approached the car, one appeared to be the man we had tried to communicate with during the night. He was holding up the tract, smiling, and touching his heart. Who knows? Was he the reason God allowed us to stop at that precise place? It was a warming thought that I allowed to supersede the misery of the long night. When we tell God we are sold out to Him, assuredly, there will be those times when He may ask us to go into the darkness, the uncomfortable, the unknown in order to find the seekers of Truth. We don't know where they are, but He does. Who knows what happened in that village because of that one tract? That is God's business. Mine is to be faithful in whatever situation I find myself, but how often I stumbled in that faithfulness.

One of the men was Liberian and interpreted what the other men tried to tell us. Thanking us for the *God paper*, they suggested we move our vehicle off the road before the police came by and charged money for towing fees. They then helped us to push it to an embankment near the village. Still knowing we needed to get to Abidjan and because I had a better handle on the French language at the time, we decided that I would take Lauren with me and flag down a taxi, ing travel to Abidjan to find Mark. Meanwhile, the girls all woke up with little more than four hours of sleep, but were troopers. There was no whining or complaining. *God bless missionary kids, and thank you, Father, for giving them what it takes to be able to endure things they are sometimes involuntarily required to face!*

Standing alongside the highway to Abidjan with a baby on my hip, my glaring whiteness in a predominately cocoa-color world, it did not take long to flag down a taxi heading towards Abidjan. Crawling in with my soiled but adventuresome baby girl, I said a quick prayer for God to go before us. Struggling with every French word which I uttered, I gave the driver an address and brief description of the area. He nodded his head with a slight jerk and turned the radio up to the loud, clanging, rhythmic music of West Africa. Playing patty cake and other lap games with Lauren, I was fairly surprised when we arrived at the home of our missionary friends in less than thirty minutes. *We had been so close.* The

Bassetts were missionaries with BIMI (Baptist International Missions, Inc). After meeting them several times, we found we had quite a bit in common. There was much relief as I wearily climbed the front steps of their home with an antsy Lauren struggling to get out of my arms. I arrived unannounced during breakfast, but they were wonderful, so helpful and welcoming. The Bassetts displayed the beautiful gift of hospitality extolled in the Bible. I saw it clearly. Weary travelers going from one place to another in an unfamiliar city. But yet, when welcomed into the home of another Christian, the feeling of belongness often lingered.

The first item of business was to call Mark Sheppard who was staying at a nearby guest house to tell him of our plight. Mark, who had been wondering why we had not already arrived, came immediately by taxi to the Bassetts. Mark, Jeff Bassett, and a trusted mechanic went to pick up the tired, stranded group only thirty minutes out of town. Meanwhile, Karla gave me some clean clothes for Lauren and fed us breakfast. After that, I hopped into another taxi and headed over to the guest house where we had previously made reservations. Lauren had no choice. She had to sleep because her mommy had to sleep. I was completely spent. Safe, but spent.

After tinkering with the engine for a few minutes, the men discovered the timing belt had messed up. It took a mechanic to get it fixed properly. Thankfully, we were all reunited at the guest house by noon. It took us two days to recuperate from that trip. On that Friday, we spent time in a pool at a local hotel. A nice break, it was soon time to move on to another phase of our adventures of being missionaries. We could only pray the next few months would be a reprieve from the intensity we had experienced since we landed in the Ivory Coast.

CHAPTER FIVE

*Keep seeking the things above, where Christ is seated at
the right hand of God. Set your mind on the things above,
not on the things that are on the earth.* Colossians 3:1,2

Another Place, Another Bed

Our family settled into a rented apartment in Abidjan for a few
weeks. Our purpose for that was two-fold. Our duplex in Toulepleu
was not ready and it was presenting quite a challenge to get the
right papers to bring a vehicle into the country. We had no idea
how long we would be involved in what we affectionately called
"our Abidjan ministry." It had always been our desire for God to
use us no matter where we found ourselves, and though it did not
seem like we could be used in Abidjan like we could if we were
working with the Liberian refugees seven hours away, those two
and a half months were exactly what were ordained for us. Often
in Christian service, we fixate on the right *location* and the right
time far more than we should. How can we know what is right for
us? Even Isaiah struggled with this when he finally conceded that
God's ways were much higher than his, God's thoughts far beyond
his own.

I mentioned in my first book *In This Place* that we had
assumed at the onset of African ministry in 1985 that we would
minister to the same group of people for decades. That was our
thoughts, our desires, but not what God had planned for us at
all. Missionaries which we had known in the past seemed to be
more stable and settled in one particular ministry. Comparing our
humanly unstable ministries with the seemingly stable ministries
of others took much energy and is a road that leads no where. We
had to learn to accept it was how God ordained us to use us. ***Our
lives, our calendars, our days, our choices in where we made our
home were swept away by our prayers that asked God to do with
us what He wanted.*** And so He did. But, often when He did, I

struggled, I bucked, I complained, I whined. Then I would collapse in His arms, rest awhile, and then get back up to the work.

Our Abidjan ministry started out as an adventure of sorts. Jeff and I were able to cultivate our French, as well as making it possible for the girls to pick up more French vocabulary from the children they played with. We ate fresh meats, fruits, vegetables in abundance (one of the major things we missed while living in Pehe), and made many new friends. It was during that time, our middle daughter Stefanie accepted Christ as her Savior during a Bible class I was teaching the girls. She was five years old and so ready.

One of the biggest interpersonal relationship conflicts I had during our Abidjan time was when we were scolded by missionaries for not keeping our concrete steps swept clean. Though it was a beneficial lesson, the *always had been city* missionaries did not take into consideration that we had always been "bush" missionaries. The thought of keeping our stairs swept was not uppermost in our minds. Perhaps the scolding could have been done a bit more gentle by the other missionary, but you can rest assured that I dwelled on it frequently. I ricocheted from insulted, to angry, to hurt, to paranoid. One day, I swept the stairs three times. The missionary lady who had pointed out my lack of neatness in the stairwell was the same person whom I paid to use her washer and dryer three times a week to do our laundry. Awkward? Yes. But God humbled me, took me out of myself, and grew me through that whole experience. If I could have had my way, I would have taken my laundry services somewhere else. I would have shown her. But there was no where else. How I longed for the day when we would have our own things again and not have to borrow everything we needed. Such hard lessons for an independent woman to have to be dependent on others. God knew what He was doing in my life. Every step. Every place.

A Loss In the Midst of the Madness

For some reason, perhaps because of a stray cat I was feeding outside our apartment, I contracted a pretty hard case of mites, having to take strong medicine to get rid of them. Why I was the only one who got the mites, I don't know. Within a couple of days of ingesting the strong medicines that would kill the disgusting parasites ravishing my body, I started bleeding and my abdomen was in severe pain. In my heart of hearts, I knew what was happening. Jeff took me to a small French medical clinic where a doctor told me that I had been about four weeks pregnant and had lost the baby. Not exactly knowing how to deal with the loss of a baby I did not even know about, I stayed busy with teaching my two oldest girls and nurturing baby Lauren.

At the risk of simplifying this loss, at that time, I did not know what else to do. I had no support system except my husband and he, too, was living on the fringes. We were far away from our family in America. We were living in a rented apartment with borrowed furniture. Nothing was ours. Nothing felt comfortable. Everything became slippery. Losing a baby was just part of all the other discomforts we were experiencing. I tried to feel deep sorrow from the loss, but was only able to draw a faint tinge of something. I dreamed that it was the son I had always thought we would have. I conjured up a face and name. I forced myself to mourn for the baby who had left us before we even knew he was there.

Jeff continued to pound the pavement at various government offices, constantly needing to check on the status of our truck's paperwork. It was true, the truck still had not arrived in the country, but he wanted to have all the paperwork in order. No officials in the Ivorian offices moved quickly, and sometimes it took several visits to one office to procure a necessary stamp that would then require a visit to the next office. There was a 100% duty tax on vehicles brought into Ivory Coast, which meant that if we registered the truck in Ivory Coast, we would end up paying for the truck twice. So, Jeff's plan was to drive it to the Liberian border and register it with the rebel government. Amazingly enough, Ivory Coast was recognizing both the official government still in place in Liberia's capital city and the government formed by rebel dictator, Charles Taylor. It was a complicated ordeal but would save us thousands of dollars.

If I knew then what I know now about the effects of long-term stress on a person, perhaps I could have recognized the signs of us entering a crash and burn mode. Since we were in Abidjan where communication to the U.S. was more reliable, we were blessed to have several long conversations with our pastor, Dr. Bradley Price. He was so good to take time to check on us and pray with us concerning our struggles. Because we did not know how to voice all that we had experienced in the past months: our disillusionment with what we *thought* was supposed to be happening in ministry, how it was affecting every aspect of our lives, and how we wished to know what to do next, we kept fairly quiet when communicating with our family. The previous year, while still in the U.S., our family and friends had heard nothing but our desire to return to West Africa. That had happened, but we were finding it nothing like what we expected it to be. Our expectations had turned to shambles. Telling them of our struggles would only seem like we were volatile and inconstant. Writing prayer letters at those times were exceedingly difficult. Saying just enough for prayer support, but certainly not painting the total picture. Missionaries in the trenches often do not believe people in American churches really want to know the whole truth of what we are facing in our ministries. That may be an unfair assumption, but it does weigh on what we put in prayer letters sometimes.

Jeff and I did not recognize the fallout we were dealing with from those difficult months in Pehe and the uncertainty of future ministry in daunting circumstances. None of our thought processes were normal or healthy. We assumed every missionary dealt with the same kind of vulnerable feelings, so we struggled quietly. Wouldn't exposing our weaknesses, our struggles to our family, our mission administration, to our supporting churches make us sound weak? Look inadequate for the task? We felt hemmed in by the trauma behind us and the uncertainty ahead of us.

By Thanksgiving, our new truck had still not arrived, but it was necessary to travel to Bouake (a city to the northeast of Abidjan) for a Thanksgiving field conference with other BMM missionaries who had recently arrived. It was an enjoyable time of reunion and a solace to my soul in many ways. It brought a little normality in the middle of the madness. We shared some of our experiences from Pehe and our ideas of what ministry realistically looked like on the

Ivorian-Liberian border. After that week together, our family of five traveled back to Abidjan to pick up the Mitsubishi truck which had finally arrived. Ready to be out of the city and on to the new ministries in Toulepleu, we packed up the small apartment, handed in the key, swept the stairs one more time, and took the nine-hour journey back to Toulepleu.

Our kids were excited to be reunited with the Sheppard kids, and we all hoped that perhaps some routine could be found in our lives. The day after we arrived in Toulepleu, Jeff was required to take our truck to Liberia's border to register it. A man from the truck dealership had traveled with us from Abidjan to witness that Jeff was indeed taking the truck across the border into Liberia. So, like it or not, I was left with the unpacking and the necessary acclimating to another strange house, another bed, another town without Jeff as he traveled into Liberia. It was either that or pay a huge sum of money. I understood why he had to go, but I could not seem to shake the vulnerabilities that flagged me. I would not have traded places with him for anything because traveling into Liberia was so difficult those days. I tried reading Proverbs 31, hoping it would encourage me to be a faithful wife that my husband could trust in. It was a daunting proposition and only made me even more despondent. Who could ever measure up to that Super Woman?

Checkmate is Not Just for Chess

When Jeff took our new truck into Liberia that first time, Chick Watkins traveled with him. Since they were already at the border, they felt it prudent to visit our previous home of Tappeta. What would normally have taken three hours to drive took them almost ten hours because of about two dozen military checkpoints between the Ivorian border and Tappeta. Occasionally, it would take more than an hour to talk through one checkpoint without handing out the requested money from the soldiers. *What can you give me?* a coltish soldier wearing sunglasses would ask as he pointed his gun into the vehicle. For those young misguided boy soldiers, Jeff and Chick had loaded up the truck with pens, tracts, and candy, since it was a known fact that anyone traveling into Liberia needed fodder for those stops. Checkpoints were not for the weak - taking great stamina and a few bags of tricks to get through.

After finally reaching Tappeta, they were greeted by many of the Christians still living in the area. On the following Sunday morning, while Chick and Jeff were at church, someone came into the house and stole $1,500 from Chick's room, plus food, clothes, and toiletries. It had become so desperate in Liberia that stealing was happening in broad daylight. Many of our bigger pieces of furniture were still in the house, but the smaller things were gone. While that particular trip was mainly to assess the possibility of moving back to our Liberian compound, neither Jeff nor Chick had good vibes about that happening for quite a while, especially families with children.

Jeff was able to bring a few of our things back to Ivory Coast when they returned six days later. The two biggest blessings to me personally were the baby crib and half of a Christmas tree he found in the attic. Since we had been in Ivory Coast, Lauren had slept in a portable crib. At 17 months, she was tall enough to rock the flimsy crib over on its side when she wanted to get out. Long had I lamented that Lauren would probably never sleep in the sweet Jenny Lind crib my mom had bought before Michelle was born. We had brought it out to Liberia so that I could also use it for our second child, Stefanie. Jeff deduced the only reason the crib was still in the house at all was because it was too wide to move through the bedroom door without tools to take it apart. God and His mercy. He created my mother's heart and He protected that crib. That breathed refreshing winds into my soul. Never did I dream I would see that crib again. Today, it is in our home here in Charlotte being used for our grandchildren. What an unexpected blessing.

Another missionary family newly arrived to Ivory Coast moved in with us until a decent house could be found for them. We were glad to invite them into our home because the only other place this family could have temporarily stayed would have been Pehe - which was not an option in our book. The missionary family with their two boys and a baby girl a little younger than Lauren integrated nicely into our home for almost three months. Jeff and some of the other men were constantly in and out of Liberia, so it was pleasant to have another adult woman around the house.

As we settled into this new region, we were able to experience some unbelievably fruitful meetings in churches in the border towns. The week before Christmas saw nearly two hundred professions of faith, many of them Ivorians. It was wonderful to see how God had used something as terrible as civil war to bring lost souls to Himself and strengthened many Liberian pastors to remain faithful through it all.

Celebrating Christmas Halfway

I previously mentioned that along with my prized baby crib, Jeff brought back from our home in Tappi *half* of a Christmas tree. Well, half is better than nothing, right? He decided to climb into our attic to see what might be left up there. That is when he found half of our Christmas tree with no clues as to where the rest might have been. Seriously? In the middle of a civil war and someone wants to mess with half of an artificial Christmas tree? Still, he was my hero for bringing what he could find. We have sweet pictures of the girls sitting beside our rather strange looking Christmas tree sparsely decorated with ornaments special enough that they always stayed with me. Handmade from my grandmother, most of them were crocheted. That Christmas of 1992, the girls and I baked cookies with shaped cutters and sprinkles I had brought out earlier. In the midst of our chaotic surroundings, those times in the kitchen with Christmas music blaring and flour on all our faces are highlights in my mother's heart. Because of our industrious families who sent our Christmas packages very early in the year, we had several gifts to open that Christmas morning. If you were to see pictures of the girls standing in front of the tree that particular Christmas morning, other than the strange half tree and the metal barrels setting around, all would look *somewhat* normal. I longed for that. For my girls. For my family.

Some of our African Christians told us there were wild turkeys in the bush near the border towns, so one morning the men took all of the older missionary kids and went hunting for a Christmas bird. What an adventure that was for big and small kids. Dreams of bringing two or three dead turkeys back for us to roast was the talk for days. But, if I remember correctly, the great white hunters ended up having to buy a couple of turkeys from someone in a nearby town. That was perfectly fine with us women, who could not imagine how we would clean and prepare a turkey that still had its legs. The outing was a release for everyone. Just the idea of going turkey hunting was enough to get the kids all worked up and excited. Celebrating Jesus' birth in Africa had always been something I enjoyed. Forget the commercialism and the empty jangling of the season you find in America. In Africa, Christmas took on more of its true essence. It was easier to imagine the humbleness of the manger, the potent quietness of the moment of His birth.

Face to Face With Our Humanity

Every week fresh reports came out of Liberia, and most of them were enough to discourage us from ever planning to return. During those five years of in Liberia, we worked predominantly with the Gio and Mano tribes who were intrinsically involved in the Civil War. On the other hand, our ministry to the Liberian refugees in Ivory Coast were to the opposing Krahn tribe also fighting in the Civil War. We walked a continuous tightrope as we attempted to show fairness to Liberians caught up in unnecessary tribalism. The Christians in Liberia constantly pleaded with us to return to Tappeta. The Christian refugees in the Ivorian border towns became extremely attached, demanding more of our time and resources and energies. Within a month of moving to Toulepleu, the front door of any missionary abode constantly revolved as the desperate refugees were told of our stockpile of medicines and monetary aid. The lines of needy humanity was seemingly endless, from early morning until the sun went down and the night air forced them to find shelter. As we missionaries started comparing stories the refugees were telling us in order to receive help, we began to see a pattern in the pleas. Sometimes we were alerted to a genuinely sick baby being used by multiple families in order to swindle money from us. It was hard to fathom that parents would allow their ill baby to be passed around as a pawn. As I've said before, desperate times produces desperate measures.

Just after Christmas of 1991, a veteran missionary couple moved back to Tappeta as a trial run before any other missionaries followed. Having no children living at home and being twenty-year veterans in Liberia, they seemed the logical ones to *try the waters*. Not just once, but two times during that stay, *rogue* government soldiers came to the house and taunted them. The soldiers accused them of hiding rebel warlord Charles Taylor inside and demanded they come out and face the consequences. During the second visit from the same soldiers, the assault went on all night. Enduring fire balls to deafening gunfire to pieces of metal being slung through screened windows into the house, the couple determined to stand firm inside. The soldiers then started breaking glass out of their car windows, punching air out of the tires with sharp objects, and violently denting the car doors.

Thankful the missionaries did not sustain serious physical injuries, but the obvious mental strain was unnerving. God used this incident in a concise way to show us it was not time for any of us to move back into Liberia. We were living on a constant, emotional roller coaster. *Yes, maybe we can go in next month. No, it is definitely not time. Yes, maybe. No, not now.* It was exhausting. We tried hard to lean heavily on the Everlasting Arms during those times and to be faithful to the many ministry opportunities around us. But the incessant demands of the refugees bore down mercilessly on us all.

We left the uncontrolled deviance of Pehe and came to Toulepleu where, though people had to travel farther to reach us, there were also many more concentrated needs with which to contend. The shadowy incessant level of relief work fast became distasteful, especially to the original five missionaries who had been doing it for almost a year. Interestingly, the United Nations only allowed relief workers to remain in an intense refugee situation for no more than three months at a time. I am inclined to believe that just our three months in Pehe would have been considered extremely intense. By the time we moved to Toulepleu, most of us had surpassed the healthy emotional and mental limitations of relief work. But we did not know all of that. So, we did our best to push through and keep working.

The needs of the refugees in the border towns of Ivory Coast and the desire of missionaries to contribute to the massive relief effort all sounded good on paper. True, it was a plan devised by passionate missionaries in a sterile conference room on the other side of the ocean. But living smack in the middle of the rancid effects of war, being consistently bruised by the pounding needs of those caught in the middle never formulated into anything glamorous or productive. It was hard. Energy drenching. Impossible. Heart breaking. Endless. Exhilarating. Heady. Extreme. Emotionally draining. Disillusioning. Impossible to grasp. Impossible to fix. Impossible to describe. Impossible to anticipate. However, God is never dormant.

Around the first of March, 1992, our BMM field administrator, Evan Gough, came out for a visit to discuss the logistics of moving families back into Liberia and to get a bird's eye of the relief efforts. Each time the men would go into Liberia, they would file a report and send it back to Mr. Gough, so he had a relatively good idea of how things were shaping up ministry wise. But, he soon discovered that there was so much not in those reports. It took Mr. Gough only a few minutes to assess the evidences of heavy stress in Jeff, Mark, Nancy, Ardith, and me from nine months of refugees ministry. By the end of his visit, he gave an unexpected mandate to the five original relief missionaries, "*I am strongly recommending that the Abernethys, the Sheppards, and Ardith, take a six-week sabbatical in the States. You are quite obviously in need of it and I don't even think you realize it.*" We sat in stunned silence while his words sank in. I honestly do not remember what took place after that, but I do know it ignited feelings I had not dared allowed myself to acknowledge. I believe most of us felt somewhat vindicated by the inner struggles we were dealing with but were too exhausted to voice.

By March, Jeff and Mark had grown weary from traveling into Liberia once a month and trying to maintain refugee ministries near the border with seminars, Bible conferences, and such. The trips inside Liberia were grueling, because of all the checkpoints and tension. Frankly, our guys were just tired of going and coming, going and coming, hassling with soldiers, listening to needs one side and then again on the other side. Expected to be the saviors of the incessant civil war, it was closing in on all of us. The needs were unceasing. The pleas louder and louder. Our hearts hurt constantly.

The Trip of a Lifetime

I wanted to visit Liberia at least once, but it never seemed safe enough. Finally in April, Jeff felt it stable enough to allow me to go into Liberia for a visit. A couple of the other women had already been with their husbands; I so badly wanted to see Tappeta again. To try and connect with some of my Liberian friends there. In the back of my mind, though I never voiced it then, it was a type of closure for me. Deep in my heart, I did not imagine we would ever live in Liberia again though I certainly did not voice that audibly to anyone. How traitorous it may have sounded, though I was sure that others wondered the same thing.

Jeff and I had already determined we would not travel into Liberia **together** for the sake of our children. Michelle, who was eight at this time, was fully aware of all the hushed conversations about conditions in that country and had heard the stories. One night, after we assumed everyone was sleeping, Jeff and I were lying in our bed talking about the day. Michelle quietly opened the door and came in. Asking her what was wrong, she stood as still as a statue for a moment. Then we heard the sniffing as she attempted to hold back the tears. She admitted that she was afraid we would both go into Liberia and never come back. Crawling in the middle of the bed with us, she begged us to never again. The fears of her young heart were founded. She fell asleep in my arms that night. My oldest daughter trying to be brave, but with so many unspoken fears with which to deal. It broke my heart to realize that I should have been doing a better job listening to what my children *were not saying*. There is often a multitude of emotions in their silence.

With the two oldest girls, I talked about my desires to see Liberia before we left for the United States, and I feeling they were content to stay with their daddy while I traveled with Chick Watkins, his wife Joan, and their daughter, Becky, I packed my bags. It was a unique experience in so many ways. I will start out the story by quoting from my journal of April 14, 1992.

> *It has been two years this week since we evacuated Tappeta. We never dreamed it would be so long before we could return. We have just arrived at Komplay and we are sitting at a mechanics shop. The car hit a rock and knocked the muffler loose. We have already passed at least five or six checkpoints. General Musa was there and was glad to see Chick. He is a 4 Star General and the Chief of Staff for Charles Taylor. He helped Chick complete our papers to enter Liberia. At the fourth checkpoint, a Private Jackson told Chick that he wanted to only talk to me. He said that I was his long lost sister. Anyway, he insisted that I find something for him. I finally gave him a pen and he seemed happy. I was not a happy camper by this time. The strain of these checkpoints washed over me.*

Several of the checkpoints took half an hour or more to get through mainly because the soldiers loved to hear us beg to pass. Even more unnerving was that a majority of the soldiers were nine or ten year old boys holding machine guns, probing them at the car, and taunting us with their "authority." There was no question they had already been involved in killings, so we had no desire to test their sincerity at what they said. Part of me was so very afraid by the temperamental attitudes of these little boys with real guns, but on the other hand, I wanted to scold them like a mother would. "*Get that gun out of my face, son; go home, play with your toys, and go to school!*" But, war had scripted its own warped and unpredictable rules.

Already a very long day, we still had a couple of hours to travel before reaching Tappeta. My nerves were stretched to their limits; I was shocked by the abhorrent conditions I found the country in which I had once lived. All this turned me into a wound-up plucky missionary woman just waiting for a reason to expel my feelings on anyone that asked. The opportunity came at the next checkpoint. As we pulled up to the gate and Chick searched for someone that he might know, three different soldiers shouted out three distinctly different orders. Waiting until we could find some semblance of order in the confusion, a fourth soldier, obviously with more authority than the other three, came to the car. I alone was told to bring my bags inside to be searched and instructions were given to Chick and the other women to stay in the car. As I pulled my suitcase out of the trunk, I thought one of the men would help me carry it inside, but there was no gallantry. As I entered the small wooden building decorated with nothing but peeled paint and makeshift desks and chairs, the first wave of ire was swallowed down. However, when I saw the soldier in charge leaned back in a chair with his feet propped up on his desk looking condescendingly at me, I had to breath deeply and try to smile.

"*Open your bag and show me the contents,*" he barked at me as if I was condemned already. I first tried to make conversation, told them how long it had been since I had been inside Liberia, and asked if any of them knew my husband Jeff, since he had preached several times in a church there in Ganta. A couple of the soldiers did acknowledge they knew him, making me feel a little better. However, it was evident the majority of the soldiers were bored and ready for a show. I suppose a white woman with a suitcase provided a distraction from the humdrum of the day. As I opened my suitcase, I tipped it so that the soldier in charge could see inside. "*What else do you want to see?*" I carefully asked. "*No, you must show me everything. One by one. Perhaps you have something hidden in the bottom,*" the soldier taunted with a haughty lilt to his voice. There was snickering from around the room. It was more than I could take. The unrealized pressures of coming into a war-torn country for the first time rose up in me.

Without another thought at the consequences, I took a jar of peanut butter out of the side of my suitcase and flung it toward the desk of the head soldier. I do not remember all I said, but I know it was loud and provoking. After the soldier dodged the peanut butter jar, I started slinging clothes everywhere as the tears edged down my cheeks. Fear, frustrations, sorrow, and blatant anger at the ugliness of war and the crassness of the soldiers accelerated both my tears and the tantrum into which I had worked myself. In the middle of my conniption, the soldier in charge no longer lounging in his chair, jumped up on his feet as did the rest of the soldiers in the room. They were quickly picking up clothes, shoes, shampoo bottles, and a hair brush, saying over and over, "*Don't feel bad! Don't feel bad!*"

All the same, I didn't stop until every last item was dumped out, and then I took the empty suitcase, shook it vigorously, and flung it at the feet of the commanding officer. I cried through my pique. "*There! Are you satisfied? Do you see that I am who I said I was? A missionary woman who wants to live here and love you people and teach you of God's ways? And you want to accuse me of what? How can I ever live here in this kind of mess you have gotten yourself in?*" So much for my Christian testimony. It was a bust.

By the time my tirade was finished, my suitcase had been packed, zipped up, and was being carried back out to the car. Several of the soldiers took me by the arm and escorted me outside while they continued saying, "*Oh missy, don't feel bad! This t'ing called war is too bad for all of us. You may come and live with us and teach us. Don't feel bad! A-ya!!*"

It was a lame apology, but nonetheless, it was an apology. Even I recognized that. By then, I was spent and climbed into the car quietly, still shaking and no longer smiling, as the soldier in charge personally came and talked to Chick Watkins. I heard Chick telling him how bad it was that they had treated me, a missionary wife, with no respect, and especially since, it was my first time visiting since the war had begun. They opened the gate quickly and we drove toward Tappeta as I cried quietly in the backseat. Our dear beloved Liberia had changed and I was afraid.

My journal of April 1, 1992 reads:

This is no April's fool! I am sitting at my dining room table with the chairs and cushions still on! I am the only one in my house right now. Other than the absence of my husband and my children's voices and the realization that some of the items in the house are not mine, I would say that everything seemed normal and I was really home. But, in that blissful revelry come the soldiers walking around the compound and the used cars parked everywhere in our yard. It doesn't take looking very far to see that this is not the same place that we left some two years ago.

It was so good to visit Tappeta. For the first three hours, my heart was full as I hugged, held, and talked with some of my dearest Liberian friends. It is a complex thing to describe - all the varying emotions I felt that day. What a hard and sudden way to have left our home, our friends, our ministry two years before - and then being able to go back and reconnect was such a blessing.

We stayed in Tappeta for four days, but honestly, by the last day, I was emotionally exhausted from the traveling, dealing with the realities of what had happened to Liberia and to our home in Tappeta, and hearing the stories of my friends. Stories that I could not comprehend. Horrors that I could not protect them from. I just wanted to be with my own family so badly. I desperately needed some soothing order in my life - whatever that looked like. Our return trip did not seem as dramatic. When we arrived at the Ganta checkpoint where I had my meltdown a few days before, we were whisked through so quickly we hardly had time to greet them. Well, perhaps my emotional collapse had done more good than bad, especially when other missionary women passed through that checkpoint - perhaps they would receive more respect. Even in the midst of war, there was something to be said for the powerful vulnerability of a woman under pressure.

CHAPTER SIX

God has no afterthoughts. Every plan is Plan A. If he reverses a trajectory, that was the plan. —John Piper

And It All Came Tumbling Down

I came from a family who has always been strong, determined, and of a hearty nature. We are survivors. Over the years, alongside our dramatic missionary journeys, my brother's twenty-seven year battle with chronic kidney disease, my dad's battle with diabetes (losing both of his legs in a ten-year period), we were and still are not quitters. There is a quiet resolve, a spirit of purposefulness, a strength of character in all of us. In that light, the last two months of living in Toulepleu were agonizing for me. Why couldn't I hold up? Why couldn't I keep going through those difficult situations?

I felt myself slipping into an oblivion which seemed to have no bottom. Homeschooling both Michelle and Stefanie had ceased except in a cursory way; I could no longer answer the door and hear the needs of the myriads of desperate people lined up outside. There was a desire to just find solace in sleep. However, with a child under two and the nature of our African household, that was not possible. Jeff was not home much of the day, so I was compelled to put one foot in front of the other. To make life happen for my family. Thankfully, tickets for our return to the States were already purchased. We would be leaving sometime near the end of June. That became my focal point. My escape.

Jeff stopped going into Liberia those last couple of months, trying to concentrate on ministries in the Ivory Coast border towns where we had invested so much time and effort. The relief money was quickly ending and with that knowledge, there was much pressure to make the last penny count. There were so many places still needing help, and disturbingly, we started believing we were the only ones who could help them. That thinking formulated because of the knowledge that there was not exactly a huge parcel of relief workers in our area of Ivory Coast. Even our African Christians were pressing us as they knew we would be leaving soon. It was a dangerous place to abide. Anytime we see ourselves as indispensable or as the only solution to a problem, we set ourselves and those whom we are trying to help up for emotional and perhaps even physical disaster.

It would have been easy for us to beat ourselves up when faced with our failed expectations concerning the relief ministry. "*Well, if I had not stuck it out, if I had not endured, if I had not dug in my heels and did what needed to be done, nothing would have gotten done.*" That, in itself, is a matter of pride. There is a definitive line between having faith in ourselves in difficult situations and simply being a part of God's plan so that He may ultimately receive the glory. Too often our plans and decisions are really about us and have nothing at all to do with God.

Forgive my digression, but it has everything to do with what happened in the next few months. Time was short, our energy depleted, and the Africans, instead of being appreciative of our help, became more ungrateful, more demanding, and more desperate. For a girl who was naturally drawn to words of affirmation, it was like walking in a dry desert with an empty bottle. A few weeks before we left, the officials of the Baptist churches in the border towns asked to meet with us. There was no precursory appreciation for what had been done over the past few months, only the underlining of all the things we had failed to do for them. As they pulled out a thick catalog of ongoing needs, it became evident it was all out of control. Listening to some of those African pastors drone on about our failures and angling their dire circumstances to make us feel sorry for them, I could no longer keep silent. The internal snap should have signaled me to retreat to a quiet place and call out to God, but I had yet to choose to deal with life that way.

It came from deep within me...this anger, this desperation to make it all go away. I had reached my saturation point. Honestly, I do not remember what I said, but I know it was not laced with Christian love. I spoke loudly and harshly to the men who dared to press us in such insensitive ways. Embarrassing to admit how it played out, Jeff literally had to take my arm and lead me into our bedroom. He, too, was feeling the pressure; it was perceptibly written all over his face as he soothed me and then prescribed I stay in the room until the pastors left. Shaken from the shame I had caused my husband and the scalding reaction I had allowed to surface in front of the pastors, I sobbed into my pillow as the darkness enfolded me. I tried so hard to stay above it, but it had captured me, pulling me into its clutches. I was lost and did not care if I was ever found. Until the day we left for the United States, I only put one foot in front of the other and subsisted. Turning inward and concentrating only on the care of my children and packing for our trip, I refused to think any more of the refugee needs around me. I had allowed the vines of self and bitterness to take over my heart. I was, at that point, a servant unfit to be used for my Savior.

Without a Glance Back

As we boarded the plane taking us back to America for our recommended six week sabbatical, I felt emotionally crystallized. Busying myself with making my children comfortable at the beginning of the trip, I pushed aside feelings I did not want to acknowledge. It was only when Jeff and the three girls were sleeping, in the depth of the night, somewhere over the Atlantic Ocean, that I opened the floodgates and stared straight into my soul. What I found was a war zone. There was no place inside me which had not been touched by the residue of the year behind us. I felt drained, bitter, angry, and lost. The tears came uninvited but yet unavoidable. Jeff woke up in the midst of my emotional collapse and held my hand tightly. As often happens, anguish can quickly turn toxic as a person attempts to protect herself from the overwhelming sense of self-destruction. I caved to the bitterness that spewed from my soul, allowing it to consume me, lashing out at the people God had called us to serve. Turning to Jeff with my tear-stained face but with flint in my eyes, I regretfully spewed, "*I **hate** those people! Hate them! Don't ever ask me to go back there..... ever!*" Jeff looked away, lay his head back on the seat, and said nothing. Thankfully, he kept holding my hand for a very long time which penetrated my heart like words could never have done. He knew me well. Any words spoken would have been diced in an instant. Such a mess, this missionary woman gone awry.

I have to admit I struggled with whether to share that very raw, personal time in this book. Forgive me if you felt I was too candid. Fully aware there are those who place missionaries on high, though fragile pedestals, disallowing us from entering into the land of humanity, to you I do apologize. Please note, missionaries struggle with anger, bitterness, depression, discouragement, disillusionment, and temptation of all kinds - just as anyone does. But then, there is God's beautiful mercy and the revealing of the true condition of our hearts through His Spirit. As painful as it can be, I am thankful for the convicting power of the Holy Spirit. Difficult to acknowledge, but I have regretted the use of the word *hate* and know that deep in my heart, it is not what I meant. Sadly, my flesh had risen up and grabbed at the opportunity to reign, my spirit too weak to combat it.

In retrospect, at the beginning of our six-week sabbatical to America, we probably should have been immersed in some serious debriefing. Just as military soldiers arrive back on American soil in need of a listening ear and a guiding word, so it should be for missionaries. We had been in a strong spiritual battle and it had taken its toil. Regardless of those inward struggles, we enjoyed our time in the states, rested, ate wonderful American food, and were strengthened by the love of our family and friends. For the first three weeks, Jeff and I hardly talked of Africa, not with each other nor with our family. Anyone close to us *assumed* we were fine. We gave them no reason to contradict that assumption.

Time zoomed by as it always does, and one day about halfway through our stay, very nonchalantly, Jeff sat down to start making a list of things we might want to take back to Ivory Coast with us. Even writing this some years after it happened, I find it difficult to know how to describe to you what happened to me. With the reality of preparing to return to Ivory Coast, I completely shut down from the inside out. For two days, Jeff attempted to talk to me about our return, and each time I would look at him with blank eyes and say nothing. It felt as if a massive concrete wall slammed in front of me every time *Ivory Coast* was mentioned. It overwhelmed me, but I did not know how to speak of my fears. For my sanity. For our ministry. For me as a person.

In The Potter's Hand

I must preface this next section by saying it was one of the most delicate of times in our marriage and ministry and remains extremely personal. We refer to this time as one of the greatest pinnacles of our spiritual growth - individually and as a missionary couple. If you are a man, you *may* sympathize immensely with Jeff and have an understanding of what must have been going on with him. If you are a woman, you *may* concur with my actions and reactions with great compassion. I am asking for neither. No sympathetic nods are necessary. We have shared this story with many couples and in different scenarios throughout the years. It perfectly portrays the vast differences between men and women in processing life while emphasizing the unequivocal importance of love and respect in a marriage.

For the third straight day, Jeff persistently attempted to engage me in a "return to Ivory Coast" conversation. As he pressed me, I finally said out loud what I had been thinking deep within me for weeks, "*I cannot go back there. Please don't make me.*" If you know Jeff very well, he has immensely beautiful brown eyes that grow larger by the degree of surprise before him. His eyes were huge with disbelief, as he said quietly, "*What will our churches say? What will we tell them?*" I was beyond caring what anyone would think about me. I was lost in a world turned upside down.

As we were staying at the home of his parents' during that stay, any of our disagreements had to be quiet ones. That momentous day was no different. We said things to each other during the next couple of hours, most of which I do not even remember. Though married and supposedly one in Christ, we were never farther apart than we were at that point. Two souls floundering in profound emotions. The pun *on the same page* could not have been further from the truth. We were not even in the same *library*! As Jeff struggled with the reality of what this would mean to our ministry, to our churches, to our family, and other missionary friends, I retreated further and further into the inner world that had become my home. The concrete wall of my soul slammed soundly and I refused entrance to someone such as he who seemed to care more for the feelings of others than what I was going through. He, as the head of our home, grappled with a proper course of action, trying to find some guise of normalcy in a situation where there was none. He did not know the person whom he had called his wife for ten years. She did not know herself.

We went days without talking, without even the fundamental goodnight kiss which had always been paramount to our bedtime routine. We played the sweetheart game in front of our family, while slipping away from each other on the inside. Finally, Jeff decided we needed some help - a fresh perspective of our dilemma. He called our pastor of Northside Baptist Church at the time, Dr. Bradley Price, and scheduled an appointment for both of us. Jeff has told me since then he really felt like Dr. Price would side with him and persuade me to return to Africa. Deep inside I also believed that would happen. However, I was determined absolutely no amount of persuading could make me return to such a wretched, dark place. Some of you may be wondering about the *submitting* issue of my wedding vows. Though, I have struggled with that biblical command, the resolve not to return to Africa went much deeper than that. I was fighting to regain the strength to ever want to be a missionary anywhere again. Retreating is often negated as weakness, but as humans, sometimes can be used in order to eventually rebound. Tucking those feelings deep within me, I went with my husband to the counseling session. Our marriage was fragile, our ministry was in grave jeopardy, and neither of us knew what to do. I had no words to describe the need deep within me to save the very core of who I was. The only way I could see to do that was to retreat. And be silent.

Being a home pastor to missionaries cannot be an easy thing, especially when a pastor does not live in the same "world" in which we live. While gauging our uniqueness as a married couple, he must also attempt to understand the unique struggles and circumstances we missionaries might call "normal." Honestly, from conversations with other missionaries, there are not many American pastors who are willing to even try to *shepherd* missionaries - maybe they just don't know how. However, God was merciful and gracious to give us a pastor who chose to rise above the daily etchings of his own American ministry and embrace our unorthodox, but serious situation in light of our exclusive needs. We will be forever grateful for Dr. Price's willingness to invest in our lives during that crucial time. Even before that particular counseling session, we had talked with him numerous time in Ivory Coast when he would call and check on us. Perhaps one of the fundamental reasons why we turned to him in our great time of need was because he had built a bridge for us to cross over.

Following Without Understanding

After we were seated in his office, Dr. Price prayed a powerful prayer for wisdom...for all of us. He then prompted us by asking questions, clarifying things we had said, watching us closely. He did much listening those first few minutes. I have often wished we had recorded what he told us that day. Though it shocked us both, it was also very compelling and enlightening. Sensing I was in no shape to return to an African ministry right away, he also affirmed that he understood the hard place that Jeff was in. He expounded on how God gave men their wives for many wonderful reasons, one being the ability that women have to discern things more acutely at times. Men focus more on the situation in front of them as women struggle more with all the peripherals. Worked out with mutual respect and trust, those differences could produce a more well-balanced couple when needing to make hard decisions.

The bottom line of our meeting was that Jeff should not urge me to return to Africa right then. Dr. Price did not believe my refusal to return to African ministry had anything to do with submission. I was spent. Injured emotionally. Physically depleted. A classic case of carrying unresolved stressors for way too long. Perhaps God was using my weakness, my inability to take that next step to get Jeff's attention; to turn us toward something else He had for us? That had honestly never crossed our minds and I squirmed against the thought of it.

Jeff avowed he believed I was a godly woman and also vocalized his memory of me saying I had promised God even before Bible college that I would never run from His will again. He asked me about that in the pastor's office that day. I spoke instinctively from my heart. Honestly, I never felt like I was usurping or running from what God had for us. I just felt frozen and unable to move forward. That's what I told them both.

That whole conversation with Dr. Price knocked Jeff for a painful loop, and it took him several days to pray and assess what we needed to do based on what he heard our pastor tell us. Still disappointed and not exactly on board with the delay in returning to Africa, he contacted BMM. If I remember correctly, Dr. Price had already called our field representative, so Mr. Gough was aware of the evaluation our pastor had made during our counseling session. We agreed that BMM could help us mull over alternate ministries as a temporary measure. I use the phrase "mull over" purposefully. It would take time to warm up to and find sweetness to any other ministry that might be presented to us.

A couple of days later, we received a call about a Jamaican ministry opportunity. At that time, there was only one BMM missionary couple on the island, and they were overdue for furlough. For several months Jim and Bonnie Storey had pleaded with the home office to help find a replacement for their ministry. Bonnie was having severe problems with her back and the medical care in Jamaica was not up to par. Given this information, we were asked to visit the Storeys and see the ministries in Jamaica. So we booked our flight.

For Such a Time as This

Having never visited Jamaica even for pleasure, it felt a little strange knowing we were traveling there for a ministry possibility. Of course, you can imagine the badgering from our family and friends who knew about us investigating a ministry in a tropical paradise. Little did most people know that West

Africa has a tropical beauty much like the islands, so we were already used to that. But to our American friends, it seemed like we were going on holiday and getting paid for it. Honestly, my heart just did not feel like going on a holiday, or meeting new people, or assessing a ministry. I took cues from my husband, whose own heart was torn between his desire to return to West Africa and his need to care for his broken wife. I felt so badly at times when I thought of how he must have been feeling. Feeling like a complete failure, I knew I was standing in the way of Jeff's happiness. Those misguided, sulfurous thoughts come from Satan himself.

Living out our faith often means we keep doing what we know is right without seeing how it all will come together. Beyond that, I think it also means we have to walk without necessarily *feeling* anything. Often we think that we need to *feel* something in order for it to be the right thing to do. It is in that thinking where we can stumble into spiritual murkiness. If we followed our hearts on everything that felt right, where would we be? Living out our true depravity and making excuses for the messes we would make. We get all worked up and excited about doing something that certainly *feels* right. Then when it all goes wrong and the happy *feelings* aren't there, we blame God. Incredibly, God wants more than that for us and has enabled us through the Holy Spirit to live above and beyond our *feelings*. **Living in the truth of God's will is *sometimes* a quiet place.** I had never been there before by choice. The essence of Kim had always been loud, passionate, emotional, and impatient. Quiet was not where I resided. Not *feeling life* was foreign to me. There was no other way at this point in my life. I had no strength to experience anything beyond what God brought to me day by day. That simply had to be enough.

Recently I was counseling a college student, who was struggling to tie together her willingness to do a certain thing with the teachings in God's Word. God gave me this thought: *A God transformed mind can walk safely in rhythm with a God delighted heart.* (based on Romans 12:1,2 and Psalms 37:4, 5) So, you see, I do not think feelings are all bad. Totally delighting in God, Who

He is and what He desires to do with us; that simply must be foremost. I know this now experientially, but in the summer of 1992, I was living this out by the seat of my pants. We packed our bags, left the girls in capable grandmotherly hands, and boarded the plane to Montego Bay, Jamaica.

Upon meeting Jim and Bonnie Storey, we instantly fell in love with them and the Fairview Baptist Bible College compound. There were classrooms, dormitories, kitchen facilities, water cisterns, two residential homes, dozens of citrus fruit trees, and innumerable cows roaming the fenced hillsides, indeed a peaceful and beautiful place. From the beginning I felt myself relaxing and my spirit awakening. In the following days, Jim showed us much of the western side of the island; Bonnie was not able to travel with us very much because she was in such pain with her back. It was evident they needed to be able to return to the States quickly to get medical care for her. Lying in the Storey's guest bedroom on the last night of our stay, I remember Jeff and I talking about what we were sensing. I saw hope and passion reignite in Jeff's eyes and knew Jamaica might be a place where I could heal, renew my spirit, and watch God work out His purposes in our family's life. To us it was a *Yes*, but we still needed to seek counsel from BMM and gauge the response of our supporting churches about the interim ministry we were purposing.

It all fell in place. BMM gave their blessing and helped us with logistics of transferring to the Jamaican field in an *On Loan* status. Our churches and families were excited. God had gone before us. This was what we were supposed to be doing...for now. After committing to relieve the Storeys for at least a year so they could return to the States for their furlough, it was a madhouse getting everything ready for our next move; though the complexity of the move certainly was not on the same scale as when we moved to West Africa. Homeschooling materials needed to be purchased for Michelle and Stefanie. On the other hand, being so close to the States, Jamaica had many of the amenities we felt necessary. To bring a container into a port on the island was very expensive, and so was out of the question. We had to consider air transportation cost in everything we wanted to bring with us. The Storeys would

leave their home mainly set up for our use - all the furniture
and kitchen supplies and appliances. It was necessary for us only
to pack in Action Packers those items that were personal to us.
Perhaps this was like a holiday?

Before we could move forward with this new opportunity
placed before us, it was first necessary for Jeff to return to Ivory
Coast and deal with our belongings left behind there. He never
asked me to go. I was glad that I did not have to make that
decision though I felt for him having to do it all alone. It was an
arduous trip for Jeff. He sold the things we were willing to part
with, packed up the few things in a wooden crate that we wanted
to ship back - which did include the baby crib. Saying goodbye
to some of our Liberian Christians was one of his hardest tasks
during that trip. I know it hurt many of our missionary friends
as we were unwilling - at that time - to give them the real reason
for our change of ministry. We felt fragile in what we were feeling
though not confused in what we knew to be true. Copping
out on our ministry partners in Ivory Coast only heaped more
pressure on us as we tried to make sense of our future. Jeff was
not completely on board with Jamaica, his heart still immersed in
the Liberian ministry. How sad he must have felt as he flew away
from that continent towards an unknown future. I wrestled with
guilt and sorrow many a long night about what my incapability
to return to West Africa was doing to my husband. At least I was
feeling something. And I did care deeply about our ministry. I
really did.

Doing our best to turn our hearts and passion toward the
interim Jamaican ministry, God bonded our hearts with Jim's and
Bonnie's. More than anything we felt sure that we were being used
to minister directly to them. There was no way for us to understand
- upfront - the perfectly structured plan of God which was weaving
itself intricately through our lives, but we knew He was able to
make all things beautiful **in His time**.

When Jim and Bonnie returned to the States, it was
immediately determined her back pain was much more serious
than originally thought. Inoperable, cancerous tumors were
found on her spine. She was given a mere four to six months to

live. We could not even imagine how this news affected Jim and the Storey family. To us, it was a compelling affirmation that we were where we needed to be *for such a time as this.* We buckled our spiritual seat belts and started forward in the next journey with God. Like it or not, we were right where we were supposed to be.

CHAPTER SEVEN

He has made everything appropriate in its time. He has also set eternity in their heart, yet so that man will not find out the work which God has done from the beginning even to the end. Eccl. 3:11

Life On An Island

We arrived in Jamaica on November 17, 1992, and after five months of being in limbo, had fun settling into our own place. The mission compound was located about eighteen miles from Montego Bay, approximately 2500 feet above sea level, with a beautiful, mountainous view from our front porch. It did not take long to see the exquisite timing of God's plan for both the Storeys and the Abernethys. Jim and Bonnie desperately needed someone to take over the work, and God brought the need before us as we were exploring other options. It was such a peaceful feeling to know we were in the middle of one of God's masterpieces.

Michelle was nine years old and in third grade when we moved to Jamaica. Stefanie was just starting 5K, and Lauren was 2 1/2, so my days were obviously full with the needs of our daughters. It did not take us long to formulate somewhat of a routine to our weeks there. Since the house had three bedrooms, Michelle was able to get a bedroom to herself. The larger room was used as part bedroom for Stefanie and Lauren and part schoolroom. Jeff built a divider in the middle of the room, leaving a fairly small area for bunk beds and toy chests for the younger girls. On the other side of the divider was a compact but organized academic haven. Desks for Michelle and Stefanie, a teacher's desk for yours truly, bookshelves packed with intriguing school stuff, and bright posters decorated the walls.

I always felt productive and teacherly when I crossed the portal from the bedroom into the classroom. It was unfortunate that the girls did not experience the same transformation into scholars as I would have hoped. But fun we had! Art, music, math drills, science projects, and of course, recess, where they would head straight to the tree swings beckoning them. Some of my most treasured moments as a mother are those days spent with my girls in our makeshift classrooms - in Ivory Coast or Jamaica. Granted, they were also some of my most frustrating moments, at least in their younger years. Parenting has many dimensions, and it is a wise parent who will embrace them all.

One of our highly anticipated weekly trips as a family was the trek to the bustling farmer's market in Savannah La Mar. The girls loved the excitement of the little town and being able to help me choose fruits and vegetables to buy. Our little side of the mountain was so peaceful and quiet most of the time - and for me that was needed - but for little girls, they did like to explore and see new sights. Very soon after settling in our home in Jamaica, we had the privilege of meeting David and Anita Fenley, hailing from Georgia and missionaries with another Baptist board. They became dear friends and confidantes as we grew in our knowledge and love of the Jamaican people. It was wonderful to have missionary camaraderie and our girls quickly grew close to their two children, John David and Melissa. To this day, we stay in touch, attending weddings, sharing sorrows and joys. God indeed gave us forever friends with the Fenleys.

An extremely challenging and rewarding outreach during our two years in Jamaica was to host high school and college mission teams from the States. In West Africa, we had the occasional short-term mission teams, but never in the quantity we saw in Jamaica. It was not just mission teams that visited; because of the close proximity to the States, many of our pastors and friends came out for *work vacations*. During one particular fifty-two week period, we had visitors (ministry or personal) for forty-four of those weeks!

Close Enough To Hear God Speak

My journal from March 1993 reads:

> *What a privilege to SOW the seeds of salvation! From March 11-22nd, we hosted a dynamic team of 15*

*college students from Liberty University. Through
the avenue of puppets, skits, dramas, singing, and
testimony, we were able to SOW seeds of the Gospel of
Christ to some 4,000 Jamaican young people in those
twelve days. Even though it was extremely busy, the
results were well worth the effort!*

*We told you in our last letter about Bonnie Storey and
her plight with cancer. The Lord graciously restored
Bonnie, but not in the way we would have desired. He
gave her a new body! She passed away from this earth
filled with suffering and pain on February 26, 1993.
God was gracious to take her quickly and quietly. She
had already suffered so much. Her husband, Jim, has
resumed his furlough schedule of visiting his supporting
churches and plans to return to Jamaica in October.*

There is an amazing story that accompanies the above journal
entry. About a thirty minute drive from our home was a small
community called Bird Mountain. Perched on the top of that
mountain was Bird Mountain Baptist Church. Once a month,
following in Jim's footsteps, we would travel up this mountain
and Jeff would preach to the warm, hospitable folk. Nestled in
the crevices of the mountainside were dozens and dozens of
houses and some of the nicest, happiest people we ever had the
opportunity to meet. One particular woman was Sister Murray.
A pillar of the community and the church, spiritually delightful,
refreshing, and strong in her Savior, she so inspired me. It was
evident she was a powerful prayer warrior, and because of that,
God was etched all over her face. Jamaica, as well as many areas
in West Africa, was extremely oppressed by Satanic powers. But
not on top of that mountain. God Himself seemed to reside there
in a way I have seldom experienced anywhere else. I know that
may sound dramatic, but I am serious. She was an incredible lady
who chose to live her physical existence meekly and humbly on a
rural Jamaican hillside. Her house was small, her decor far from
metropolitan, but it was a home of peace and strength.

Each time we would visit, she asked about the health of Bonnie Storey, giving us messages of encouragement and affirmation to relay to both her and Brother Storey. On the Saturday night before we were to again travel up Bird Mountain for Jeff to preach, we received the call from Jim telling us of Bonnie's passing. The following morning, it was with heavy hearts we took the sad news to the church on top of the mountain. Driving our little red micro van around the final turn, we were met by a breathless and exuberant Sister Murray! Before we could even get out of the van, she surprised us with the words, *"My brother and sister Abernethy! I just know that you are bringing good news about Sister Bonnie Storey, aren't you? Last night about 7:30 I was praying for her healing when the Holy Spirit told me that I did not need to pray anymore - that she was **healed**!!! This is true?"* Our mouths and eyes wide open, we told her of Jim's phone call to us the night before. For a fleeting second, there was pain and sadness in her eyes while she allowed the humanness to have its moment, but only a moment. Then she said with the same buoyant confidence, *"Well, then, praise our Father for He has indeed healed her perfectly! I will sing praises to Him for His goodness! How is Brother Storey?"*

You have to love this delightful story of how a seemingly insignificant island woman living on the side of a mountain rocked our world with her faith in God. I aspired so deeply to be like that. To become more in tune with God's leading and prompting in my life. Not too often in life are we blessed to meet the kind of person who definitely exudes an otherworldliness in everything she said or did. Inspiring. Even still.

Respect, Sir, Respect

In March 1993 I wrote in my journal: *Nestling....just as a seed will nestle into the rich, warm, moist soil, so has our family settled into Jamaica! The girls are thriving off all the very fresh vegetables and fruits at our fingertips.* My mother's heart was content. After living in West Africa, living off canned meats and vegetables for such a long time, it was a blessing to be able to eat such succulent fresh foods. I renewed my love for cooking and preparing well-balanced meals, also learning how to prepare some of the exclusive island fare such as breadfruit, ackee (the national fruit of Jamaica, resembling clumps of scrabbled eggs when cooked), beef patties (spice meat pies that look like a calzone), coco bread, callaloo (a rich and nutritious green vegetable), and rice and peas. It took a while to realize how much I had physically and emotionally shut down during those last few months in Ivory Coast. I enjoyed baking with my girls, even making Christmas cookies to hand out to some of the children in nearby towns.

In our efforts to continue the momentum and customs the Storeys had with the churches and the neighbors, I continued having eggs delivered to our house, just as Bonnie had. Mrs. James, an older Jamaican lady, trekked across a rocky hill to our house each week to sell her fresh eggs. There came a time when I did not see Mrs. James for a couple of weeks, but really needed quite a few eggs, so I bought three dozen at a grocery store. As Murphy's Law would have it, Mrs. James showed up the very next day with two dozen eggs and beads of perspiration on her wrinkled brown face. She had to be in her seventies, and since she lived on the other side of our hill, it was quite a challenging walk even for a younger person. She told me she had been sick and that is why she had not brought the eggs sooner. When I - unwisely - told her that I had recently bought eggs and really did not need more at that time, I received an unexpectedly curt, "*Well, Miss, **you can do NO betta**!*" Another lesson learned in the peculiar Jamaican culture. It was her way of saying, *Okay, well I am very disappointed, but if that's all you can do...*

To me, it sounded very intimidating, and admittedly, I was a little afraid of her for a while after that incident. Trying to appease her, I offered to have Jeff drive over and pick up the eggs from her house once a week so that she did not have to walk. She condescendingly told me that there was only a path to her house, way beyond the cisterns on a hill above our property, through the fields, and she said that she seriously doubted we as Americans could walk there easily. So, stoically, she continued to come with her eggs each week, and determinedly, I worked my charm on her until she softened. I invited here in for tea and cookies during her weekly visit and learned so much about her family and the

Jamaican culture. My biggest lesson? Having too many eggs is better than an offended the elderly Jamaican egg deliverer. Little by little, I was gaining a respect the Jamaicans and their way of living life. A Liberian would have appreciated the offer for us to pick up the eggs. A Jamaican would not. Slowly but steadily the differences of the two cultures came to light and I began to respect what I was learning. My journal entry about "respect" says it all.

> *The neatest word used here in Jamaica is **RESPECT**. It is used in place of "excuse me," "pardon me," "listen to me," etc..... A man bumps into you at the grocery story and he says, "Respect, ma'am, respect." Interesting? However, the place where **respect** means nothing is on the Jamaican highways. Please pray for our safety as we travel from place to place.*

There were two reasons why we had bought the red Suzuki micro van: less expense and it was small enough to dodge the larger vehicles sometimes dominating both lanes of the highways. Learning to drive on the left side of the road seemed to come pretty easily to Jeff; however, for me, it took a good three months before I was ready to actually put my hands to the wheel. Not wanting to be limited to one place for very long, I knew that I would have to face my fears and take the car for a drive. In order to safely drive on the roads in Jamaica, one must remember, that though the steering wheel is on the right side of the car, one must drive on the left side of the road. One must train the mind to completely think the opposite way from American driving rules. There were scores of driving stories where we had to run off the road to miss an oncoming truck who was taking up both lanes. Ivory Coast travel had been treacherous enough, but any trip on Jamaican roads raised the word perilous to new heights!

When Ministry Takes On a Different Face

For ten weeks during our first summer in Jamaica, we hosted a young man from our home church in Charlotte named Colin.

Our family bonded tightly with Colin that summer and consider him one of our own to this day. Planned also during that time was a two-week missions trip by two teenagers from one of our supporting church. They had their own puppets and desired to put shows on for some of the Jamaican schools. It took quite a bit of planning and prodding since schools were still in session through July, but we were able to schedule evangelistic outreaches in eight different schools during their daily program.

Our plans were in place, but then again, so were God's. Just a few days before the two teenagers with their puppets were due to arrive, Jeff was brought to his knees - literally - with a pain in his lower back that radiated to the front. Thankful that we could leave the girls with Colin, I drove Jeff from doctor to hospital and back home again without any solid answers. While we suspected kidney stones, we could not find any medical personnel during those first two days who would give a particular diagnosis. The only doctor who seemed to know what he was doing prescribed a sulfa antibiotic - thinking the pain was coming from some kind of intestinal problem. The antibiotic did nothing except confirm Jeff's low tolerance for sulfa drugs. Added to his excruciating pain from the kidney stone was a relentless burning in his stomach. He stopped taking the Bactrim after only eighteen hours of ingesting it.

Between our missionary friend David Fenley and myself, we must have driven Jeff a couple of hundred miles around the western end of the island trying to find someone to treat his pain. Meanwhile, he was not sleeping and was becoming erratic - which is never a word I would use to describe Jeff. On the fourth day, his parents called to check on him and I buckled under the sympathy I heard in their voices. Sniffling on the phone, I told them that I did not know what else to do for him except to drive all the way to the other side of the island to the city of Kingston, which in his condition would have been horrific. The roads in Jamaica were dangerous, as I have mentioned, but they were also rough and filled with potholes in many places. Jeff continued to writhe in pain, getting up to walk and moan loudly. It was unsettling, not being able to do something to help him.

Late in the evening of the fourth day, Jeff's dad called back. His news was like a breath of fresh air. He told me he had gotten Jeff on a flight to Charlotte which left early the next morning. Their thoughtfulness and care for their son (and me) was so touching. One of the biggest concerns at that point, besides the fact he would have to travel alone, was that he needed to change planes in Miami before heading on to Charlotte. Jeff seemed almost disoriented because of his pain and I knew it would be a long trip for him. I stayed up most of the night, packing his bags and soothing him as much as possible. Silly perhaps, but I even tucked a large piece of paper in his shirt pocket stating who he was, what we thought his condition was, and where he was going. I also included our telephone number in Jamaica as well as his parents' in Charlotte. Who knew if he would pass out with the pain? I felt better about knowing at least someone would know what to do with him if they found the piece of paper.

As I dropped him off at the airport the next morning, it was very bittersweet. I was torn between wanting to go with him, to care for him, and to see that he got the proper care, but I had to let go. Back on the mountainside were three sweet little girls who were worried about their daddy and a very capable young man who was fast becoming a big brother to our girls and would be extremely helpful in Jeff's absence. Besides, in just two days, I would be right back at this same airport to pick up two teenagers for a demanding couple of weeks of ministry. I cried all the way home. I cried for Jeff. I cried for me. I cried for how scared I knew the girls were and how I would have to be mommy and daddy to them for a while. It wasn't refugee work in a remote hotspot in West Africa, but it was going to be a different kind of challenge.

Our three girls were so well-behaved during their daddy's absence and during the puppet ministry with the other two teenagers at the local schools. They went with us to every school, singing the songs, helping with the puppets and talking with the Jamaican children. I was pleasantly surprised by their helpfulness during meal times, their willingness to do their school work with minimum protest, and their love shown to me in unexpected ways. I was convinced those two visiting teenagers had indeed seen our "best foot forward." It was a good feeling. Thankful to know, I had overcome most of the fears of driving our little red micro van on the Jamaican roads. It felt great to again be productive in ministry - that my husband's trust in me had been honored in his absence. My heart was healing in the midst of the challenges and opportunities before me.

Upon arriving in Charlotte, Jeff was admitted straight into the hospital. A couple of substantial kidney stones were found in his left ureter. Thankfully, Jeff was able to get exactly the medical care that he needed, be relieved of most of the pain, and spent most of the time at his parents' home until the stones finally passed. He felt like a new man. I could not help but think that if we had been in Ivory Coast living in the remote town of Toulepleu, he would have most likely suffered even more. Most likely, we would have been able to find a hospital in Abidjan to treat his stones, but the long nine hour trip by car would have done him in. Though Jeff missed the two weeks of ministry with the visiting teenagers, when he did return, he was back to his sweet, even-keeled self. How we had missed him, but we had survived. Somehow I was surprised by that fact - still rather vulnerable about my capabilities to do ministry. God has His ways...His wonders to perform.

Like a Boomerang

We enjoyed being able to minister with our home church, Northside Baptist, for a week in July 1993. Getting to reconnect with some of the kids - now teenagers - and pour into their lives was amazing. There was a particular young man named T.R., who was really struggling during one of that trip. He rode with me back to the Bible college to pick up something one day. We had a heart-to-heart talk about what was on his heart. I smile when I write this because neither of us can remember the details of the talk, but he still remembers how I took the time to invest in him and care about his struggles. We can never go wrong by giving attention to those whom God has placed in our peripheral or direct view. "*A word fitly spoken.*" My journal of September 1993, reads:

> *Utterly awesome! That's the only way to describe the*
> *months of July and August. One week in July our*

home church in Charlotte sent a 39-member mission team! They held week-long Bible clubs in three different areas, plus three street meetings, and two services on the Sunday they were here.

The results keep coming back like a boomerang! A couple of weeks after the team went back to the States, Kim and the girls did a week of VBS in the same area in which the Northside team ministered. The following week Jeff preached a whole week of meetings in a church there. Sunday through Thursday nights NO ONE came forward, so you start wondering, hmmm....But, strangely, every night there were at least 12 young men standing outside the back of the church laughing, snickering, being loud. Later in the week, we knew they were listening when 9 of them came forward for salvation on Friday night. We praise the Lord for the seed sown and the victories won for His glory!

I mentioned before that there was tremendous demonic activity in Jamaica. As lovely an island as it is, Satan had his footstool in the heart of its lush beauty. During one of the evangelistic street meetings, a mongoose ran suddenly through the crowd, hedging under benches, and interrupting the preaching to the point that order was never really restored; another time a jalopy with a loud muffler kept driving back and forth during the invitation. In another place, a deranged man jabbered and interrupted nearly the entire service, walking back and forth at the back of the crowd. Laughing. Spouting profanities. Completely distracting some from hearing the precious Gospel message. Evident that Satan was not happy, it was good to know that the Gospel was still permeating many of his strongholds. Like sunshine seeps into the cracks of sewers and dungeons. Light trumps darkness - though at times we may wonder.

Before any group arrived, there were weeks of preparation on our part. We had visitors in Liberia, but never on the scale as we did in Jamaica. A group of twenty or more took much planning, lining up schools for outreach, scheduling churches for programs, finding the right kind of transportation, hiring the cooks, buying the food, cleaning the dorms. But it was worth it. Our girls loved it when the visiting teenagers took time to play with them or just hang out or when the teenage girls would invite them into their dorm rooms.

There is a ministry opportunity anywhere you turn. Whether it be to those without Christ or those who love Christ but are struggling in which direction to go. It is important to be available and willing to make a difference. Sometimes it may only take a few seconds or a few words. You may think what you say is insignificant, but in fact, may touch someone's life and change the course of that life. Over a year ago, Jeff received a letter from a young man who happened to be on that particular 1994 Liberty missions trip. He thanked Jeff for telling him that he had what it took to be a good missionary somewhere in the world. Fifteen years later, Glen located Jeff and told him that he and his family were now in Asia as missionaries. Jeff honestly does not even remember this conversation with a Liberty student named Glen. It doesn't matter. Glen did. And now look at him.

CHAPTER EIGHT

Faith does not operate in the realm of the possible. There is no glory for God in that which is humanly possible. Faith begins where man's power ends. —George Mueller

Plodding Through Some Murky Waters

By our second October in Jamaica, Fairview Baptist Bible College had opened its doors again with five young men enrolled for classes. Both Jeff and Jim Storey would be teaching in the college since Jim was returning a few days before classes started. He did not want to move back into the house he had shared all those years with Bonnie, but instead, chose to live in the small apartment attached to the main house. While Jim obviously loved the Jamaican people, he was still grieving deeply from losing his life's partner. Coming back to where he had spent the last "healthy" years with Bonnie must have been extremely difficult for him. Our girls, sweet and sensitive, somehow picked up on his struggles. While I did not want them to be a bother to Jim, they visited him frequently in his apartment, ministering to him in their own ways. The girls soon made it mandatory that Uncle Jim join us for pizza and movie nights. He later told us it was exactly what he needed. He truly became family. A brother, an uncle, a dear friend. We blessed him and he blessed us. Christian camaraderie at its best.

After our second Christmas in Jamaica, I received a call from my brother, Eddie, who was physically declining quickly and would soon be in need of another kidney transplant. He had been fighting a terminal kidney disease since he was thirteen, and when he was fifteen, my mother gave him one of her kidneys. Because of the nature of the disease and how it traveled destructively through the blood stream, it was inevitable the disease would, at some point, destroy the transplanted kidney. True to its prognosis, in late 1985, just a few weeks before we were to leave for Liberia for the first time, he received a second kidney from a deceased donor. It had served Eddie well until just a couple months prior to his call to me in January, 1994.

Back in 1976 when we knew Eddie would need his first transplant, I had just graduated from high school and was ready to start college. The summer before my freshman year, my mother, father, and I went to Duke University Hospital to be typed as potential kidney donors for Eddie. There were several complicated tests to determine whether a person was a good match or not. I matched my brother perfectly in five out of six of the necessary prototypes. My mother matched four of them and my father less than that.

Since I was not a mother at the time of the testing, I could not understand how my mother rejected my willingness to give my brother one of my kidneys. I wanted to do that for him so desperately, but my parents were adamant. Now, after being a parent for more than twenty-five years, I completely understand and would have done the same thing. My mother gave her son a kidney. How well I remember that long six-hour surgery at Duke Medical Center. My father and I were surrounded by our pastor and a dozen of our closest friends, but I felt so alone. So afraid. Thankfully, they both recovered beautifully. In the ensuing years, I kept telling Eddie if he ever needed another kidney, I would be there for him. Partly joking, I said that I would be old enough to sign my own papers.

So, in January of 1994, when Eddie called asking me if I was still serious about giving him one of my kidneys, I lunged toward the affirmative but then stopped. I now had a family of my own and could not make this decision alone. I knew I needed to talk with Jeff and to Michelle, who was ten at the time. Though we did include Stefanie (age 7) and Lauren (3), I was not sure they would completely comprehend the situation. Receiving unanimous affirmation from them, I called Eddie and told him the good news. He then booked a flight back to the States for me. When I saw him, it seemed we would need to act quickly. He looked older, sicker than when I had last seen him. There was certain criteria for being able to receive a kidney, and when a person's health deteriorated past a determined point, no medical facility would

94

dare do a transplant surgery because it was extremely taxing on the entire body.

Many people were praying for God's will to be done in that situation. We asked for God to make it clear whether I was to give my brother a kidney or not. Soon after my stateside arrival, my mom and I traveled to Duke Medical Center where we met with its legendary kidney transplant team. After a battery of preliminary tests, they were ready to do an ultrasound on my kidneys. It was during the ultrasound that God spoke loudly and clearly. An almost inaudible grunt from the technician was heard as he shifted his feet and sighed. The probe hovered over the same spot for another minute before he lay it down, telling me to lie still; he would be right back. He left me reclining on the white sheets with medical equipment humming softly around me. I had no understanding of what he had found that would send him to find one of the doctors.

Eventually, two surgeons came in, looked at the ultrasound monitor, spoke quietly to each other as they took pictures from several different angles of my left kidney. Before long, all three men exited the room; I was again left alone. After ten agonizing minutes, the door opened and an entourage of white coats took up every space in the small room. *This is a teaching hospital*, I kept reminding myself - to dispel the panic I felt running through my bloodstream. They spent about four minutes pointing at the screen and fielding questions from some of the other *white coats* in the room. Intrigued that my kidney would be getting so much attention, that quickly switched to concern when I was asked to have a CatScan performed on my left kidney. A suspicious spot had been detected on the ultrasound image, and they wanted to see it more clearly. They told me that I should not worry. At all. *Yea, don't they always say that?*

Of course, I agreed to do it, and was promptly wheeled into the CatScan area. After all the procedure, I met with two of the surgeons in a generic office as they described what they had found. My right kidney was very healthy, but on my left kidney was a *slight* 9 millimeter benign fatty tumor. Most likely it would never give me trouble and probably had been there for some time, nonetheless; because of it, I could not give my brother a kidney. Not understanding why, if the tumor was benign and probably harmless, they were rejecting me as a candidate to give my brother a kidney, I kept pushing for more clarification. They explained it was because of medical ethics. I honestly had quit listening to their technical explanations and could only see my sweet brother's face. In a last ditch effort, with tears in my eyes and a tremble to my voice, I pleaded, "*Well, just give my brother the kidney with the tumor! He doesn't care! If it's not going to bother me, then it shouldn't bother him. Please, doctors. Don't shut the door on this. Please.*" As soundly as I was begging them for a reprieve, they did shut the door on our hopes. They gave me all the patented answers. I wanted to hurl the closest potted plant at their faces. Blame them for the disappointment. Eddie's future looked bleak without a transplant. Could they not see that? Did they not care?

Walking blindly out of the office, I found a bathroom, needing some time before I would have to face my mother and tell her what they had found. I felt like a failure, like it was totally my fault for harboring the ridiculous tumor and chiding myself for not taking better care of my kidneys. Grief and loss brings all kind of emotions and irrational thoughts. Denial. Anger. Disillusionment. Bargaining. *Where was God? He could take this silly fatty tumor away! He could. If it was part of His plan.* Yes, He could. But He did not...and that was also part of His plan.

As I found my mother flipping through a magazine in the waiting room, she looked at my face. Before I said a word, she knew that the tests had not gone well. I fell into her arms and blubbered my way through the explanations though I could not look her in the eye. I felt so ashamed for letting her and Eddie down. After gaining my composure, my mother and I walked quietly back to the car; each lost in her own thoughts about what had just happened and what it meant for Eddie's future. God had answered. He had said **NO**. We called my brother, telling him everything. He honestly seemed to take it better than either of us. Eddie had given God his life many years ago and was determined to live smack dab in the middle of the faith God was teaching him to embrace. I was not feeling too spiritual at the time. Disappointed with God's clear answer, exhausted from the surging emotions of the day, I slept most of the way back home. Within a few days, I flew back to be with my little family waiting in Jamaica. Life, though, had changed. Without a transplant, Eddie had very few years left on this earth. It took me a long time to let go and believe it was not my fault. That God was good all the time. *All the time, He was good.*

A Time To Come and A Time To Go

If Jeff and I had learned anything in the topsy-turvy life we had lived, it was this: just as there is a time and purpose for being in a specific place, there is often a time and purpose for leaving that place. Too many of us try to hold on to ministries which are not ours to claim. We think because we have invested a few hours, a few months, a few years in a ministry, we have the right to own it. To control it. Many a ministry has shriveled and died sorrowful deaths simply because the minister did not know when to let go. It is true that God has ordained some missionaries and pastors to stay in one particular harvest field for decades, but it is not true for all. Discerning the call of God and knowing when He is redirecting is difficult to recognize if we are only embracing our personal feelings in a situation and concentrating on our investments. It is all God's, never ours.

We knew it was right when we arrived in Jamaica. Everything fell into place. For Jeff and I, when we think of Jamaica, we do not think of the same thing. For me, it was a place of spiritual and emotional healing, the purposeful restoring of a broken and disillusioned servant whose heart so desired to serve God, but had lost the will and know-how. For Jeff, it was a place of learning to be obedient and accepting that he would not be one of those missionaries who would remain in the same place for forty years. We both learned, however, that God was alive and in full control no matter where or why He moved us. We do not, as humans, have the ability to fully gauge eternal value in a given situation. Usually what we do in ministry, at least in our minds, is either way too large or too small; very significant or painfully insignificant. But God does not work in specific degrees. He is not limited to our humanly off-kilter meters. If we tell God that our lives are His, it should mean He controls the timing, the place, and the results. We are simply to be faithful. As a united missionary couple once again, that is the one thing we brought out of our Jamaican ministry. Going forward, we desired to be faithful no matter what. In any place. In every place.

So many things were happening. Excitedly enough, other missionaries were being brought into the rich ministry opportunities of that beautiful island. In the two years we spent in Jamaica, God had never given Jeff and me a specific, long-term plan for the ministry there. After the arrival of two missionary couples, and as we sat in a "field meeting" one afternoon, we heard the enthusiastic blueprints for future ministry being laid out. Later that night, Jeff and I dared to be honest with each other and found we were both feeling the same thing. *The Jamaican ministry was no longer ours.* We had carried the bulk of it for almost two years and had seen much fruit. Encouraged by the enthusiasm of the new missionary team there in Jamaica, we listened to the plans *even as we knew they did not include us.* We were learning that was okay.

Euthanasia: Never Easy

During our two years in Jamaica, Michelle became interested in guinea pigs, so we bought one for both her and Stefanie. Michael (Michelle's) and Leah (Stefanie's) were the first of many guinea pigs we would raise in the years to come. After we had the two guinea pigs for a few months, Stefanie and Michelle were playing with them in the yard. Ready to put them back in their cage, Stefanie's pet Leah decided to play hide and seek with the girls. One of the girls accidentally stepped on her hind leg and broke it. We tried putting a splint on it, wrapping it, and cleaning it, but because she was a rodent, she just chewed off the splint or the wraps. The area around the break became severely infected. It soon became obvious Leah's body was septic.

If you have a weak stomach, do not continue reading this paragraph as I describe Leah's condition. Jeff and I saw maggots crawling out of the poor guinea pig's ear one afternoon and talked about our options. All she could do was lay on her side writhing in pain. The sore oozed and smelled putrid. Michael, the male guinea pig, had been put in a separate cage when the maggots around Leah's broken leg first appeared. Knowing something needed to be done, I asked Jeff to take the girls with him on an errand one day, deciding to euthanize the poor creature. Starting the process by putting a small amount of Benadryl in a dropper, I gingerly fed it to Leah. Over the next hour, I gave her three doses, watching her relax more and more. Coming out with a fourth, and what I hoped would be the last dose needed, I observed her breathing was very shallow and her eyes were glazing over. I stayed there with her, crying, and talking to her. Within a few minutes, Jeff and the girls drove up and found me sitting there with the dead guinea pig. I had discreetly tucked the dropper full of Benadryl in my pocket. It was quite a while before I told the girls I had actually accelerated Leah's death. I was their hero, but certainly not my own. I never wanted to do anything like that again.

The Faith of a Child

As it became evident we would be leaving our island ministry early in the summer of 1994, Michelle asked to take her guinea pig Michael back to the States. Not knowing exactly how to go about it, I called the airlines and got quite a runaround. No one knew what to tell me. The conversation went something like this: *"Excuse me, sir, I have a question. We will soon be buying tickets to return to the United States. My daughter has a small guinea pig that we would like to transport back to the States. What is the procedure for that?"* A long pause, a *professional* clearing of the throat, and then, *"I'm sorry, ma'am, what kind of animal did you say that you want to transport?"* I braced, *"A guinea pig. It's a rodent of sorts, but is a family pet, and my daughter really would like to bring it back to the States."* The airline official, *"I see. Well, this is a very unusual request, ma'am. I am not sure what the procedure is for this kind of animal. How big is it?"* And on and on we went. It took several days of persistent calling, petitioning and explaining before we finally got permission to transport the guinea pig. Even after all that, I had to go through the same thing with our connecting airline in Miami. It was quite funny listening to myself explain about wanting to take a rat-like creature on the plane with us because my daughter really was attached to it. What mothers will do.

Speaking of mothers, my very own sweet mother, who cares nothing for flying, hopped a plane and came out to help us pack up the house in Jamaica. It was so wonderful to have her there with us, taking time with the girls, prodding them to finish their packing in an awesome grandmother kind of way. She cooked meals and soothed tired nerves. She was truly a blessing at that transitional time in our lives. It was also very fun to have her traveling back with us to the states. Almost giddy, I gave the entertaining of Lauren into her capable and creative hands.

When we arrived at the airport on the day of our departure, we had Michael all squeaky clean and shiny white in his little green cage. Michelle proudly held him up at the checkout counter to show him off, but only received wrinkled up noses of disapproval and a firm request to please put the animal down on the ground. After we were cleared to enter the boarding gate, we were told Michael could not accompany us, but would need to be put on the conveyor belt which carried baggage. As hard as we argued that the animal in his very flimsy plastic cage would not be a problem for us to carry on and citing the poor animal might be crushed by the baggage, our pleas fell on deaf ears. If we wanted to transport the animal, it would need to follow airline protocol. *Oh, now there was protocol?* A great test of Michelle's faith, she prayed right there at the counter that God would care for her sweet little guinea pig just as He did for her. The airline official look chagrined.

God does hear the prayers of our children. Often, their keen but simple prayers must please God much more than our sophisticated, *is-there-something-in-it-for-me* prayers. When boarding the plane, the flight attendant asked if we were the family traveling with the *small white animal.* Michelle quickly said yes, affirming we were indeed the family strange enough to travel with such a small animal in a green plastic cage. As we walked through the first-class section, to our utter surprise, there perched high on a comfortable leather seat with a seatbelt strapped around the cage, was Michael, the regal guinea pig. The flight attendant explained that since there were no first class passengers traveling on that flight, and not really knowing what to do with so small an animal, the crew had decided to place the animal there. We stood with our mouths hanging open until Jeff, shaking his head, walked to find his seat in economy class, saying something about never having liked that guinea pig anyway. Michelle, with tears in her eyes, thanked the attendant. The scenario had God written all over it. Michael, a little white guinea pig, hailing from the country of Jamaica sat in a first-class seat munching on greens and carrots which someone had thoughtfully given him. What an awesome God! What a sense of humor! What delight He has in the prayers of our children. I shivered with amazement as I, too, walked back to economy class to soothe the feelings of a husband, still scowling about the rodent sitting in first class while he sat in coach. I suggested that perhaps we should have our children pray for first-class seats for all of us next time. That got a smile out of him.

As funny as that story is - even now - it helped to diminish the sting of yet another major transition. Though we had only been involved in the Jamaican ministry for two short years, we left pieces of ourselves there. The memories of our children's birthdays, our entire family learning to snorkel, solid friendships established, and the awesome ways we saw God use us in a part of the world where we never would have imagined we would live. We saw God heal, strengthen, refresh, renew, and knit our hearts together again in pursuing His purpose for our life. For the next phase. For the next step.

Into the Future

Leaving the Jamaican ministry in God's Hands, we had no choice but to turn our eyes toward America for a year's furlough and, at the same time, seek God's will for future ministry. After being in the states for three short weeks, Jeff was asked to go on a survey trip with a missionary appointee to one of the South Pacific Islands, helping to evaluate the needs for an aviation ministry in that part of the world. Also a possibility was that God would lead us to minister in those islands as a result of the survey trip. We were trying to be open to any possibilities put before us. Jeff and the other fellow flew to Honolulu, then taking another flight toward the South Pacific, crossing the international dateline (where today is actually tomorrow). Surprisingly enough, even to Jeff who had traveled to very remote places in Africa, the South Pacific islands seemed much like *the uttermost parts of the world.*

Back in the states, I was struggling with the fact that I had no inclination to live in the South Pacific and learn to live in another new culture - the third in less than ten years. It drained me and overstimulated my mind to think of ever *settling* in another part of the world so different from West Africa or even Jamaica. Clinging to the fact God wanted me willing to be used - no matter where - I tried to remain open. Feeling strongly the South Pacific islands, even though I had never visited, were not for us. In answer to my ponderings, God used that vulnerable time to gently turned my heart back to West Africa. For the two years we had worked in Jamaica, I suppressed any insurgent sentiment that made me think fondly of ministry in West Africa. During the weeks of Jeff's absence, those feelings toward Ivory Coast emerged again. I cried, complained, bargained, made excuses, and then just told God the truth - as if He didn't know it in the first place. I was still angry at the Africans who had used us, pushed us to our limits. In addition, I was genuinely frightened to take my children back. *There.* After admitting that, it seemed to free me a little. The truth always does - even if it is not pretty. Looking deep into my fears about Ivory Coast, I little by little gave them to God. *Is that what you want, Father?*

It was not an easy thing as God worked, softening my heart towards the West Africans. I would wake up in the middle of the night and cry with the realization that God was asking me to be willing to return to the very place that had undone me spiritually, physically, mentally, and emotionally. *How could He?* Did He not care about me? Oh, you know how the conversation goes, don't you? We make it all about ourselves, don't we? What we will lose. What we will struggle with. We, we, we! Then the Holy Spirit mercifully intervenes and gives us a snapshot of the true deal. Lost souls. Dying. Hell. Thy Kingdom come. Thy Will be done. **I did not want to run again**. I had promised God and then later my husband that I would never run from God's plan for my life again.

When Jeff returned from his trip, I surprised him with a two day getaway - just the two of us. We needed to reconnect, talk out the madness going on in my heart and mind. I desperately needed his full attention for that to happen. I was so worked up I could hardly breath. You can imagine how much courage it took for me to finally say to him, "*I know this might surprise you but I feel I can go back to West Africa and work with the refugees if you feel that way, too. I don't want to and I'm scared, but I will do it.*" Shocked and **never** expecting to hear those words out of my mouth, he held me while we both cried for a long time. He shared about his trip, telling me all that God had spoken to him about during those two weeks, relaying how he never felt the South Pacific was where we should be. His heart always went back to Africa. He desired so much to return to West Africa, but he assumed he would need to give those desires up. After I told him I could go back and after he told me what had been in his mind while he was on the trip, I cannot explain to you the metamorphosis in my heart. Hatred, bitterness, unspoken fears, and apprehension all were swept away in the wake of God's unfaltering, powerful love that filled my heart for the Africans again. *Only God can make a heart brand new and create a beautiful song.*

Of course, Satan certainly knew how to throw a damper onto a fine party, and within a couple of weeks, my fears of taking my children back to West Africa rose to the surface. I almost buckled under the unexpected trepidation that consumed me. Without even realizing it, I emotionally bolted and ran the other way, becoming irritable and volatile at the mention of Africa (again). Confused and concerned, Jeff forced me to talk about it one night and it all came spilling out. What if Stefanie got malaria again and died there? What if Michelle was raped by unruly soldiers? What if Lauren had no friends to play with? What if? What if? What if?

I've mentioned it before, but it is not always easy living with an ordained minister. He spoke candidly and to the point and was exactly what I needed. He held my hands tightly and said, "*Kim, look at me. These are not our children. Whose children are they?"* He asked me over and over until I finally said, *"GOD'S! THEY ARE GOD'S, but I can't help it. I am still scared. I can't do it."* With deep sorrow in his beautiful brown eyes, he said, *"You must. He gave them to us. He can take them away. But I believe it is His plan that we trust our children to Him and be faithful to do His will. They are made to take whatever God puts in our lives and theirs."* Struggling well into the night, the stronghold finally came crashing down. I would choose to trust Him, believing Him to be as faithful in the future as He had in the past. With my children. In Every Place.

CHAPTER NINE

Now to Him who is able to do exceedingly abundantly above all that we ask or think, according to the power that works in us. Ephesians 3:20

Africa Again!

We spent the following year visiting churches and being involved in stateside ministries in Charlotte. Expressing our desire to return to the work in Ivory Coast with BMM administration, we then met with our former African co-workers, Mark and Nancy Sheppard, strategizing about where we should settle for the next great African adventure. Because of the plans to re-open a missionary clinic in the town of Blolequin, it seemed perhaps that might be the right town for our families. The men would be instrumental in helping Dr. and Mrs. Burrows getting the clinic buildings operational. Though there were Liberians located in the area, we felt they would be more settled and self-sufficient than the ones to whom we ministered in Toulepleu some three years before. We felt wiser, more cautious, but also more optimistic about having fruitful ministries in a town further away from the Liberian border.

If you remember, we still had Michelle's guinea pig who had traveled with us from Jamaica the year before. Not believing the guinea pig would have lived through the transition to the states, I started making phone calls trying to glean permission for transporting him to West Africa. Oh, you should have heard the conversations and the "tongue in cheek" remarks from some of the airline officials. I almost relented on the project. There were so many other things that needed to be done. More important things? Not to Michelle. I tried talking Michelle into leaving the guinea pig with a friend, because it was a long trip to travel with such a delicate creature. She cried. She dug her heels in. I caved. I pleaded with her daddy. I made the phone calls for the sake of my sweet girl's heart.

A few days before we left to fly back to West Africa, we were enjoying a cookout at Jeff's parents. Michelle had brought Michael, her guinea pig, over to her grandparent's so that her cousins could play with him. Placing him under a plastic clothes basket which I adamantly warned her was not a good idea, she soon was caught up in playing in the swimming pool with her cousins. In a flash, a random dog ran into the yard, overturned the basket, and carried Michael off in his mouth. Oh, the screaming and yelling that ensued. The commotion was so disturbing, it actually scared the dog, so he dropped the wounded guinea pig soundly into the grass and ran off. Paralyzed by both fear and because of a puncture wound to his spine, it was evident that Michael only had a few minutes to live. Jeff sat with Michelle as the sweet little creature took his last breath while I stayed on the porch bawling like a baby. At least I would not have to pull out my syringe of Benadryl, I thought, as daddy and daughter went to bury the little creature.

Cleaning our house and packing all our belongings for the trip took much of our energy. My parents drove up from Delco to spend the last couple of days with us - playing with the girls and helping with some of the details. Michelle still mourned the death of Michael, but we promised all the girls that we would see about getting more guinea pigs when we settled in Blolequin. We said the harrowing goodbyes to our family and friends, ate our last American steak and baked potatoes, and boarded yet another plane. Flying off into an unknown, but ordained ministry.

We landed in Geneva, Switzerland, and, just as we had done four years before, we met the Sheppards and Ardith Maile. All twelve of us boarded a smaller plane and flew to Zurich where we planned to spend a couple of days sightseeing. We took a train ride to the French border and then a cable car straight up the side of an exquisitely detailed mountain. While exploring the hillsides that connected France and Switzerland, we found a well-laid out playground tucked away on the side of a hill. We stayed there for several hours enjoying the last of cool air. West African tropical weather never produced that kind of freshness.

Don't Send In the Clowns

We flew into the large city of Abidjan, Ivory Coast, and stayed in guest housing for almost a week. Before leaving the city to travel the seven hours westward to Blolequin, we celebrated Lauren's fifth birthday at a small pizza restaurant. Wanting it to be a fun experience for Lauren, everything did not go according to plan. If you know Lauren very well, you may be aware of her extreme phobia of clowns. It was that fifth birthday party which instigated the deep rooted fear. At the pizza place, built in the middle of the restaurant, was a small playground and also a little dance floor. Though we did not ask for them, African guys were paid to dress up as clowns and play with our kids. Sing, making silly noises, and trying to dance with all the kids, it became too much. We asked the proprietor to have the clowns stop because it was scaring our children. He only laughed and told us to enjoy; that there was nothing for the children to fear. Within a few minutes, Lauren came crying to us about the clowns, telling us she was very scared. They simply would not leave our girls alone. A Michael Jackson song came on, and they said in broken English, "*Come dance Michael Jackson.*" A gyrating clown is not a pleasant thing to watch and was the prompting for us to leave, continuing the party at our guest house apartment. Unfortunately, for Lauren, the damage had been done.

The next day we visited a small mall which had recently been built in Abidjan. Lauren was walking with her sisters on the second floor when, from below, we heard screaming sounding much like our little five year old. Sure enough, there was a clown chasing our terrified baby girl. Making what he must have thought were cute "clown" noises, he would not stop until the two older sisters took the matter in their own hands. Michelle scooped Lauren up, bringing her downstairs to us while gutsy little Stefanie started chasing the clown, yelling for him to stop scaring her sister. We definitely had the attention of the mall crowd at that moment. To this day, Lauren will have absolutely nothing to do with clowns of any sort. No kind of masked or dressed up character - not even Disney ones.

Back to the Bush

Purchasing a car in a foreign country always such a risk, we actually found one which we felt would serve us well. There was just one small problem: the car had no registration papers. No title. Stolen perhaps? After informing the guys who were selling the car that we were not interested unless they found the papers, we left it in God's hands. About four days later, they came back with the car and the papers, or at least what we hoped were the real papers. It was a light blue Mazda 323 station wagon. The air worked well and it had a tape deck which was a big deal in 1995. What else could we want? So we packed up all of our belongings and headed West.

Blolequin was a small town located almost two hours from the border town of Toulepleu where we had last lived in earlier years. We were part of a team helping to set up a six-bed clinic and work towards reopening a medical ministry for Dr. and Mrs. Gene Burrows, scheduled to arrive a few weeks after us. The possibilities of evangelistic outreach were numerous because of the hundreds of surrounding villages which needed both medical care and the Gospel. If they came for medical care, we felt it would give us openings to visit their towns and preach Christ to them. As people had donated puppets for our children to use in their very own ministry, we saw going into towns, doing puppet shows, watching our children serve Christ also.

Because we had to wait in Abidjan to deal with the car issue, the Sheppards and Ardith Maile left for Blolequin a few days ahead of us. By the time we arrived, the Sheppard family had settled in the house on the compound where the medical clinic was also located. Ardith Maile had traveled to San Pedro, choosing to wait down there until her housing in Blolequin could be worked out. Not having a better plan at first, the mission house became home to both the Sheppards and Abernethys for a time. Though Blolequin was much larger than any other African town in which we had lived before, the choice of housing was still not impressive. In the mission house where we lived were three bedrooms, a large living room, and one and a half baths. We put a triple bunk bed and a double bunk in one of the rooms for the five older kids. Lauren slept with us in the second bedroom. Nancy, Mark and their nine-month old daughter slept in the third bedroom. Nancy and I worked out a kitchen schedule where she would be responsible for all the meals one day and I would take the next. We had done this before with other missionary friends who lived with us in Toulepleu for three months, so we knew it was doable for a short amount of time.

The day after we arrived in Blolequin, Nancy and Mark took us to see the *Grand Maison, (*meaning *large house,* in French*)* which is the term we affectionately called our future two-story home. Mark Sheppard and one of his sons had found the house on a survey trip a few days after we all arrived in Ivory Coast. Driving down a side road looking at some duplexes that might work for our families, they spotted a zinc roof high above the trees. Odd. That would have to be a two-story building. Interest piqued, they turned down an isolated narrow side road, and there in the middle of grass fields and surrounded by huts, was indeed a two-story house. They found out later that the house had been started back in 1989, but was never finished. That would be about the time right before the Liberian civil war started. Had God started preparing that house for us long before we had any idea we would be living in Bloelquin? Indeed He could have. I love how He engineers things down to the finest details. He already knew six years later that two missionary families would need a place to live as they lived out the plans He had for their lives. Marvelous He is. So precise. Don't ever doubt it.

When we first saw the house, the floors were dirt and the walls needed to be plastered and painted. The plumbing had been started, but it still had a long way to go before it was operational. Despite all the needed work, both families that it would work for our needs. The only two-story house in Blolequin, it was an oddity in comparison with the huts and smaller mud brick houses. Interestingly enough, it was owned by a Muslim town leader who had the idea of constructing it as a rental property. It had the potential of two upstairs duplexes and two downstairs. The Abernethys would take the entire upstairs and the Sheppards would live in the two duplexes downstairs.

We lived together with the Sheppards for almost two months while still looking for other temporary housing. The Burrows were scheduled to soon arrive, and the mission house had already been promised to them. The Muslim owner of the Grand Maison told us that it would take about three weeks to get the bottom part of the house ready for occupation, and for some crazy reason, we chose to believe him. Of course, we should have known better, but it helped with the living situation to think it would only be a short amount of time before we could move into our own housing. One of the biggest blessings, while living on the medical mission compound, was finding a wringer washer in a shed behind the house. Seriously, we thought we had struck gold to find the washer. Cleaning it up and making sure it was in working order, we were so thankful to be able to wash our own clothes. After our ordeal in Pehe with washing ladies stealing from us, we were all unwilling to repeat that scenario.

Pink is Not Always the Color of Love

The first deadline for the Grande Maison to be completed passed with hardly a thing being done. Closer and closer to the arrival of Dr. and Mrs. Burrows, we needed to find another place. My journal of August 18, 1995, reads:

> Well, news gets around town quickly, and within a few days, a man who works at a local pharmacy came to see us. He wanted to show us a house that he was trying to rent for his brother. It is very close to both the Grand Maison and another house they were working on for Ardith, completely fenced in, has a very nice yard, an outbuilding for storage, and a huge thatch hut with a cement flooring for the kids to play under, or even for hanging out clothes if it rains. The house is small, even though there are three bedrooms. There is only one bathroom and you would die if you could see it.

Really, I cannot even find the words to describe the bathroom to you. Tucked inside its own small space connected to the small bedroom where the girls slept, it was a narrow, rectangular room with peeling bluish-green paint. High concrete walls bare except for the chipping of paint and dirt. Lots of it. One small window was located almost at ceiling level behind where the toilet sat. No dividers of any kind, the shower head was located right above the frying-pan size sink. One yellow light bulb dimly lit the deplorable space just enough...to see roaches, many roaches milling around. Doing our best to scrub the room with gallons of bleach and cleaner, we felt better about using it even though it did not look much different when we had finished. Everyone was mandated to wear rubber flipflops when using that room for any reason.

We affectionately called the house *The Pink House* because the outside was crudely painted a very bright pink. It was in this house, God humbled my American mindset once again and stretched me more than ever. The house, previously lived in only by Africans, had no room resembling a kitchen. The only running water was in the very small bathroom, so there was no way to wash dishes in there. We had to become creative. Jeff built narrow, long wooden tables to create a kitchen work space. Those tables became my kitchen counters. No tile, no granite, marble, or even simple laminate. Just stained wooden tables set up in a room that probably had never thought of itself as a kitchen. When we moved our gas stove into that room, it had no choice but to become a kitchen. I was determined to persuade it to believe it was indeed a kitchen.

After each meal, we put our dirty dishes in a red Igloo cooler. Twice a day, a young Liberian man named Aaron washed our dishes under the thatched gazebo in the yard. He used water drawn from a well in our back yard. Because of that, I had him boil the water, adding tons of bleach before washing the dishes. He smiled at my instructions, but wisely said nothing. I would not let my mind dwell on the parasitic passengers in that bucket of water coming from the well. When the dishes were clean and dry, we stored them in another cooler with a tight fitting lid. All our food items, pans, and bowls were kept in a clothes basket under the work table. I remember little five year old Lauren saying very unexpectedly that she really liked the *Pink House* kitchen, how it was a really nice, fun kitchen - challenging me to think of it the same way. Sometimes it worked, but most of the time, it did not. I prayed to keep a good attitude while living in this very *African* house, and in that, showing my girls that our joy does not come from our outward circumstances, but in being thankful for where God puts us.

Right beside the makeshift kitchen was our little sitting area furnished with two Lazy Boys, the TV/VCR combo, and a table with a lamp. The only place in the house that looked familiar, cozy and inviting, it seemed entirely out of place with the rest of the house. One priceless commodity from the *Pink House* experience was the empathy I developed for the West Africans. Our previous homes in Liberia and Ivory Coast were set up marginally "American" in nature. But the *Pink House*? There was no template for how it should look in my world. I had never lived so elementally in my entire life. There were nights I cried softly in bed from the hardness of living in such a place.

Into the already tedious days of living in the *Pink House* entered another notch to challenge our resolve. We found ourselves without running water for five days, which was precursor to many such times while living in Blolequin. Electricity and water were not things you could ever stake your life on in that town. Fortunately, the girls thought it was great fun to draw water from the well in dented, metal buckets. During the three and a half months of living in the *Pink House*, the two older girls got pretty agile in filling buckets with water anytime we needed it. Looking back on those seemingly endless months in the rudimentary dwelling, some of the best times as a family were lived out there.

The girls were troopers, enjoying the novelty of living in a true African home. They all slept in the same small bedroom furnished with only three simple, bamboo bed frames draped with three army green mosquito nets. There was no room for anything else. No matter, almost every night we heard the sweet, cordial chatting of our awesome missionary daughters, living life, exploring the shadows with their flashlights, and making the best of their tiny place in the world. The Pink House's third bedroom was our *whatever* room where Jeff's tools, the girls' toys, bikes, and some of our cleaning supplies were kept. It also had to be used, on occasion, to actually house guests. Every time I prepared that small room for a guest with the simplest of commodities, it reminded me of a prophet's chamber. I determined to think of that room as being a blessing to others no matter how stark. How plain. How small.

Missionary Stuff

It is never an easy task to ship a container of personal and ministry items to a mission field, especially not to a third world country. Waiting on a container to arrive in a foreign country and then playing the games the government forces you to play just to have the container released can be exhausting. We were having our container shipped to the port town of San Pedro instead of the bigger city of Abidjan, since we now had missionary co-workers who lived in there. They had told us it was much easier to have a container released in San Pedro. Hearing our container had arrived, we traveled to San Pedro with an itemized list of every packed box. Thankfully, we had learned that valuable, but time-consuming lesson from the first two times we had shipped containers to Africa. If a custom officials checked the contents of a box and found an item **not** on the list, it could jeopardize the entire shipment. Thankfully, some missionary friends living there opened their home to our family for the four days we were in San Pedro. Since the town was located on the ocean, we took time to enjoy lounging on the beach one of the afternoons.

We had previously hired a "transeteur" (French word for *a middle man* who could do all the running around for the container business, procure the paperwork, and talk to the officials for us). If the officials were satisfied with the itemized list we had made, we were told, the container would be cleared by noon on the following Thursday. That given day came and went, still not hearing from the transeteur we had hired. My journal of August 23, 1995 reads:

> *Jeff went to the hotel where he knew the guy was staying. The man at the desk could not get an answer at the transeteur's door. Finally Jeff went down to the room and knocked on the door. No answer. He went*

back and got Nate Watkins, a fellow missionary, to help him. Nate went back to the hotel with Jeff and banged on the door until someone finally opened it. There sat the transeteur on the bed with a half-nude woman and another man in his underwear all eating bread and looking at Jeff and Nate like they were the problem. The transeteur's eyes were red, and it was obvious he was struggling with a hangover. The day before, when he came to the Cuthbertson's to see us, I had smelled liquor on him then, but I didn't say anything. Jeff was madder than anything, especially when he realized we were paying for this guy's liquor. Nate and the guy worked it all out and it was taken off the bill in the end.

Because of that drama, we were unable to get the container out of port until Friday. Nate Watkins went down with Jeff to talk to the customs general. It was obvious Nate had a great testimony with the general and other officials at the port, because when Nate vouched for the container and its contents, the guy waived the search. It was not opened at all.

Mark and Jeff had already done their homework on how to transport the container back to Blolequin. A few weeks before, they had visited a huge lumberyard in the nearby town of Guiglo, asking the French owner of the company if one of his trucks could bring our container back. Nearly all lumber, after it was cut, was transported to San Pedro for shipment. The trucks traveled back to the lumberyard in the western part of the country empty. *"Ask not....and you have not."* So, they asked. The owner of the saw mill gladly worked out the details to have our container brought back on one of his empty trucks, charging us nothing. What a blessing.

Celebrating Life and Family: No Matter What

Positioned around the Pink House was a slatted wooden fence. Though the fence prevented stray animals or people from just wandering into our yard, the wooden slats were spaced far enough apart for curious eyes to peep in, leaving us very little privacy. Anywhere you turned, if you looked hard enough, you could see dark eyeballs peering from between the thick strips of wood. It must have been entirely too fascinating to watch the "white" people do whatever they do behind in their yard. We had a Liberian build a car gate which opened to the small two-track road passing in front of our house. Before that, there was a huge gaping area - about twelve feet wide - where the children of the neighborhood could watch our comings and going freely. Anytime the gate was opened, we were never disappointed. The children, mesmerized with the fact that white people had come to live among them, were always lined up to take a peek inside our yard.

When the container arrived and we had unloaded some of our things, the girls were excited to take off down the dirt road on their bikes. I will never forget the string of African children who followed in close pursuit. Our children could never walk or ride anywhere in town where they were not an anomaly. Some of my daughters' most vivid memories are of opening the wooden gate at the Pink House to the laughing and good-natured bantering of at least two dozen children wanting to touch them and their bikes. Missionary kids. Gotta love their stamina and acceptance of living in glass houses - sometimes tinted with a little *pink*.

While living in the *Pink House*, Michelle turned twelve; six weeks later, Stefanie turned nine. Our living conditions, not exactly the kind of environment I thought could make a nice birthday, was the site of parties put together with creativity and love. God taught me so much about living in the moment, not in the circumstance. For Michelle's twelfth birthday, we woke her up to breakfast in bed - taking time to roll her green mosquito net up and propping her comfortably up in the bamboo framed bed. We served her an omelet with bacon, two pieces of toast, coffee, and a flower that Jeff picked from our yard. Later that morning, while Michelle and Jeff went to Guiglo to find a part for her bike, Stefanie, Lauren, and I made cupcakes and a sheet cake for the party. We decorated the thatched gazebo for the party which was set for later in the afternoon - when hopefully it would be cooler. Using balloons and crepe paper as decorations, I also made a banner which said, *Shell is 12*. The Sheppards, the Burrows, and Ardith Maile came for the festivities along with a couple of the African friends we had made.

Later in October we had the same kind of festivities for our little Stefanie who turned nine. She had french toast, a fried egg, and hot chocolate which, at the time, was her favorite breakfast. That afternoon we baked Stefanie's cake, but then Stef, Nathan Sheppard, and Lauren wanted to decorate it. I showed them how to make some colored frostings with food coloring and the cake turned out really cute when they finished. Festively decorating the outdoor gazebo again, we had quite the party. Stef got her own banner declaring she was NINE. I am a sucker for birthdays any time or any place - no matter what. No matter if the house is *pink* or has no kitchen. Some things are important. Birthdays are celebrated all over the world in some form or fashion. Who said they can't be memorable no matter where you are.

An All Day Nuptial Event

We had been involved in a few African weddings during our African ministries, but Jeff was invited to officiate one in a nearby town that put cultural differences in definite perspective. Jeff left Blolequin at 1:00 p.m. with a car load of things to transport to Guiglo for the wedding, including the wedding cake that a Liberian woman in town had baked. At 9:45 p.m. he returned home with an amazing story. My journal of September 30, 1995, reads:

> *The church was packed with people by 2:30 when the wedding was scheduled to start, but a few minutes later he saw the bride, groom, and others pass by the church on their way to the bath houses. About 3:15, the groom entered the church and sat down with his father. No worries, no hurry. Everyone was talking congenially as if everything was going according to plan. About 4:00 p.m., the bride and the others in the wedding party came in. All well and good, except for one small detail. The bride's family had not arrived yet. After some talking, the bride and groom decided*

to go on without them. Two and a half hours after the service was supposed to have started, the mother-of-the-bride entered the church. About 30 minutes later, the bride's father slipped in the back and sat down. Three hours later it was Jeff's turn to preach.

The entire ceremony lasted five hours. Can you imagine? Jeff said there were probably 500 people at the ceremony, and after the ceremony, everyone remained seated as the reception was brought right into the church. One crate of Cokes, a three-tiered cake which would normally feed fifty guests actually fed all 500 people! Rice and soup was brought in with an assortment of cups, plates, and spoons. As soon as someone finished eating, the dishes were taken, washed, and refilled for another guest. Rest assured, the whole wedding affair was deemed a success and everyone's heart was satisfied.

Another wedding which we all attended during our time in Africa was also quite unique. From my quickly written notes about the event:

The bride had her regular clothes on. Before she came in, one man ran in, sprinkled rice around the groom, then ran out. He did this twice. Then some women walked with the bride down the aisle, holding colorful cloth over her head. The pastor's message to the couple was this: "If you marry an ugly woman, stay with her. If you marry a woman that won't cook for you, stay with her. If the woman gives you a hard time or is not good to you, still stay with her. Because you will get a new bride in Heaven when we have the Marriage Feast of the Lamb. And if a woman gets a man that is lazy and doesn't want to make farm, stay with him anyway. There are better things in Heaven when we get there."

No reference to love or respect; just how to endure the marriage. I could not believe what I had heard. Another cultural collision, for sure.

CHAPTER TEN

The Lord is gracious and full of compassion, slow to anger and great in mercy. The Lord is good to all, and His tender mercies are over all His works. Psalms 145:8,9

When Life Throws You Lemons, Find the Sugar

Compared to the three months of living in the spiritually oppressed village of Pehe, our situation in Blolequin was workable. Still, within a few weeks of living in the Pink House, I succumbed to my prideful self again. During the sultry tropical afternoons, when the unbearable heat inside the small house would force us outside where it was actually cooler, we would do small projects or catch up on our correspondence under the shade of the thatched gazebo. Having frequently speculated why the Africans congregated under shade trees in the afternoons, I wondered no more after that experience.

One afternoon while working on a construction project, a bamboo bed frame fell on the back part of Jeff's leg, right above his ankle. It scrapped off the skin and caused a bruise, but it was not until a few days later, we saw the real problem. After the bruise healed, the skin around the injury took on a dark hue and remained raw, oozing. Dr. Burrows, the missionary doctor we were ministering with, called it a type of *jungle rot*. It literally took a couple of months before the sore began healing well. There is an old medical missionary adage about how to treat sores in tropical areas. If a sore is dry, add wet antibiotic cream, but if a sore is wet or oozing, apply only a powdered antibiotic ointment. At night, he would soak his foot for a few minutes, and then apply the powdered antibiotic medicine directly on the seeping, black wound. Michelle told me later she was really worried that her dad's foot would rot off. Honestly, I thought the same thing several times. To this day, there is a slight discoloration on his ankle where the jungle rot prevailed for those months.

Every day brought more complications and delays that kept us waiting to move in the Grande Maison. The owner demanded more money from us for little things, and we struggled with the right thing to do. He seemed to come up with all kind of excuses for why some part of the construction was not pushing forward. It was hard not to be disheartened by the delays. After three months of living in Blolequin, when we assumed we would have been in our new home, we had to accept the fact that we were not even close. Regardless, we pressed on with ministry, especially on the weekends when we traveled to surrounding refugee villages. It was during the days when our ministry had not yet defined itself that the puppet ministry launched.

The thatched gazebo in the middle of our yard was the perfect place for a backyard Bible school complete with coloring books, crayons, music, flashcard Bible stories, and puppets. One notable day, fifty-five kids showed up for our two-hour program. At the end of the program, nine kids believed in Christ as their Savior! It was wonderful to know our own children were being used in such special ways, including our little five year old Lauren who had to stand on a chair in order to raise her puppet over the top of the curtain. During the time we lived at the Pink House and held Saturday Bible clubs, we saw a total of 26 kids come to Christ. Jeff and I often wondered if perhaps it was because of the thriving puppet outreach to the neighborhood kids we were kept in the Pink House longer than we expected. *Not our timing, but His. Not our plans, but His.*

God was definitely doing something far beyond our temporal discomforts of living in an intolerably hot house, with no kitchen, a scummy bathroom, and having to draw water from a well. Our physical inconveniences were indeed trifling as He reached down His redemptive Hand, using us in spite of our human frailties, drawing needy children to Himself. Through the ministry to those kids, we were able to reunite an orphan boy with family members in a nearby town and helped get another little boy out of an abusive situation at home. Today, I cannot even remember the names of those precious young people who are now adults, but I pray they are continuing to follow Jesus, making a difference wherever they are. Yes indeed, it seemed that *perhaps* our extended time in the Pink House was for eternal purposes and nothing at all to do with providing us with the personal comforts we thought needful. *Not about me. Not about me.*

One particular day near the end of September as the thick humidity of rainy season settled upon us, God asked me again to completely get over myself, to die to all that my flesh was crying to fulfill, and be used in a soul-stretching way. Coming off a wonderful puppet program where we had witnessed eleven African kids saved was one of my biggest personal challenges while living in the Pink House. I was in the middle of cooking dinner for both my family and the Sheppards, since they were moving into temporary housing that day. Not being of sound mind, I had chosen to fry a couple of chickens and make potato salad. As the heat of the day sizzled its way through the concrete walls, permeating my feet and pores, the chicken popped and splattered fragrantly in a large frying pan. Feeling literally sick from the heat and physical exertion of the day, I was not sure if I would be able to finish the meal.

It was during the hectic supper preparation and while I was trying to *beat my body and spirit into submission*, that Jeff came in and told me he was bringing an American young woman to our house that evening. Evidently she had gotten stranded in town overnight because of bus troubles. *We could put her up and feed her, couldn't we?* He asked with not a clue of what was already churning inside me. I stabbed pieces of chicken and turned them over in the bubbling oil which was keeping cadence with my spirit - willing this husband of mine to go away and not talk of such nonsense. He explained that on his way home from doing work on clinic building, he saw a white woman standing at the bus station. Not used to seeing other Americans or caucasians in town, he stopped to greet her, finding out the bus she was taking to Toulepleu was being repaired. She was a Southern Baptist missionary on her way to visit her sister who worked in a town by the border. After telling me the story, he looked at me with his compelling brown eyes - which were looking a little skittish as he recognized *that* look on my face.

There we were, two families, eating in shifts in a house that had to be at least 100 degrees, and now we were to make room for one more? If pinching myself would have helped me be able to see the situation more clearly, I would have done it. *But I knew.* Deep down, I knew the test was mine. My flesh wanted to protest, to lament the imposition. To focus on the thankless job I was doing. I blinked back tears of pity and begged God to help me. *Yes, bring her here. We can't leave her on the streets, can we?* I said those words softly without looking him in the eyes. When I finally looked up, he had left the room. Quietly. Smart man. Taking a deep sigh, I left supper preparations long enough to tidy the tool room/storage room/guest room. Setting up the roll-away cot, I cleared a small area for her luggage. *Of course, we would keep her.* My gift of hospitality emerged bright and beautiful, though my flesh was not at all happy to be dominated. We all know how that battle goes between our flesh and spirit. I asked God for mercy and compassion which would stem from His love, not mine.

The young missionary woman was very nice and so grateful for us taking her in and giving her a place to sleep. She told us that while she was standing at the bus station praying for God to intervene in her predicament, she had no idea there were American missionaries in Blolequin. But God did. The house was packed full of kids, mud, heat, noise, and the languorous smell of fried chicken. It was a substantial test of what I was allowing God to do with my life. That night, the battle between my flesh and spirit continued. Thankfully, I did survive the evening despite the whining of my flesh. My spirit was strengthened a little more. Squeezing those sour lemons, I dumped in a heap of sugar, stirred vigorously, and drank heartily of the lemonade God gave me that day.

Another Sweet Deal

Abidjan was a seven hour drive from Blolequin, so it was no small thing to travel there as a family. However, it was where the main grocery stores and all government offices were located, so it was imperative we make at least monthly trips. Piling our blue Mazda with luggage and school books to keep the girls occupied, we usually tried to leave early in the morning. Two girls would sit in the back seat, and usually Lauren, being the youngest, made a small indentation with her blanket, pillow, and some books in the very back of the car with the luggage. Jeff had been affected by some kind of allergy, sneezing along with a runny nose since we moved to Blolequin. During one of our monthly trips to Abidjan with the entire family, Kleenex was on our grocery list. Always trying to save money, I had bought the *Sweety* brand because it was about *fifty cents cheaper* than the brand we normally bought. Understanding that Jeff was always extremely frugal, much more so than I, makes this next story even funnier. My journal of September 24, 1995, reads:

> *Jeff is very thrifty and all about saving money. Well, he has been extremely generous with these Sweety tissues for some reason. The first time he blew his nose into a Sweety tissue, everything (that came out of his nose) went through the tissue and on to the floor. Then when he removed the tissue from his nose, little bits of it were stuck on his chin and eyelids. Soon he was volunteering to use them for napkins at our meals. Everyone would find a pile of Sweetys by their plate, but with one wipe of the mouth, they would just disintegrate into white flecks of paper that went all over the table! Finally, he put them in the bathroom to be used as toilet paper. They wouldn't even flush down! With little over half of a box left, he finally gave them to the girls to play with, use for the guinea pigs (whatever a guinea pig would need a tissue for, I don't know) - ANYTHING! So, this afternoon, we went back to the grocery store to buy our monthly groceries. While Jeff was down another aisle, the girls and I piled the shopping cart full of Sweety tissues and went to find him. We casually pushed the cart up beside him and he looked down. He stood frozen in the middle of the aisle until he realized **surely** we were kidding and we all laughed*

*heartily about the look on his face. It was so much
fun teasing him about those blasted Sweety tissues!*

House Party

Around the middle of October after reviewing how much
was not getting done on the Grand Maison, we decided that Jeff
and Mark would personally need to invest a good amount of
time and effort to help the process along. We really wanted to get
into our houses before Christmas. My nesting instincts were in
high gear, and in my mind, the stifling hot Pink House was not
a place Christmas could happen like I envisioned it. Adding the
construction projects of a house to their already maxed schedules
which included evangelism outreach, setting up the medical clinic,
and discipleship opportunities seemed a crazed idea, but both
families were so tired of living in limbo. We vowed to make the
Grande Maison construction project a family affair. Doing what we
could help get it done.

Most often, right after lunchtime, we would take an hour or
so to rest. Thankful to have a small window air condition unit in
our bedroom, sometimes when the house was at its hottest, our
family of five would pile in our bed to cool off. One such time, Jeff
had dozed off, when Michelle heard a knock at our front door. She
came to tell me that it was one of our Liberian workers coming to
tell us there was going to be a strange kind of party at the Grande
Maison that night. My journal of October 19, 1995 reads:

> *The Liberian worker said that he had just come from
> the Grand Maison and there were about 25 people
> preparing a big "fete" (party) that evening. They were
> bringing firewood and pots inside the Sheppards
> downstairs kitchen area. When I went back to the
> bedroom to wake Jeff up and give him the news, he
> must have been sleeping hard, because he just looked
> at me for a while like I was crazy. He told me later
> that he really thought he was dreaming. That surely
> someone would not be having a party at our house.*

Jeff and I hopped on his moped and went over to the house to see for ourselves. Sure enough, it seemed to be true. Piles of wood were already stacked on the floor of the Sheppard's kitchen. Pots and dishes had been placed in one of the back bedrooms. A woman was sweeping out the rooms just like someone was getting ready to move in. It was like something out of the *Twilight Zone*. When we asked what was going on, we were told the patron (the Muslim man who owned the house) had decided to bring his three wives and eighteen children plus other relatives to celebrate the completion of the downstairs house. Without telling us about the plan, they had come onto the premises and were going to actually build a wood fire in the Sheppard's living area to sacrifice a lamb. Never mind that the living room had just been painted the day before and was not dry.

With that information, Jeff sent for the patron to come for a discussion. Upon arriving, the patron was quite surprised that his *fete* would cause such strong disapproval on our part. He told us that it was simply a little party with his family to celebrate the completion of the downstairs house. Completed? Never mind that the bathrooms were not plumbed yet, half of the house had not been painted, and the roof was not finished over the kitchen; but to the patron, I suppose the house was livable. Beyond the celebratory meal, they were also going to dedicate the house to Allah, asking him to bless it. A futile gesture, we knew, but it gave us a wonderful opportunity to share the Gospel with the patron and those standing around. The missionary men explained in clear terms about Jesus Christ, who is One with His Heavenly Father. The Muslim entourage listened politely, but then just clicked their tongues and mumbled something in their dialect that we probably would not have wanted to hear.

Finally, it was decided that *if* they felt a party was needed, all the cooking would need to be done outside. No fire wood inside the house. I know, picky Americans! Of course, the patron's family could tour the house and do whatever they felt necessary to celebrate the house. It broke our hearts to realize they rejected the One true God and His Son Jesus Christ. However, it was the patron's house, so we felt it best to stand back and let them do their prayers. They did not understand that there had already been many prayers over this house to the One and Only True God. During the night of the party, we thought about the dedicatory feast going on over at the Grand Maison, continuing to pray for the patron and his family at our missionary prayer time.

A few days later, the patron told us the party went very well and that Allah was well pleased. *We held our tongues.* He informed us that he would do the same celebration when the upstairs house was finished. We told him politely, *No thanks.* I did invite some of his family members for a meal after we moved in, but told him that we would prefer no prayer mats. He just laughed at the silly white woman and mumbled in dialect to the men with him. Regardless, there never was a Muslim dedication for the upstairs before we moved in. We had our own celebration as a family, setting up our Christmas tree and decorating, singing carols about God who came in flesh to redeem us. Ironic, really. Jehovah God! The Ruler of the universe reigned supreme in the Grand Maison owned by a Muslim man who desperately needed Jesus. To God, who is All in All, we prayed to be a light of His redeeming power to those around us and all over that town.

The Beginning of a Church

As the months passed, we noticed growing animosity between the Ivorian and Liberian Christians in the local Baptist church in Blolequin. When Liberians came to church, they wanted to worship in testimony and song, but some of the Ivorians accused them of trying to take over their church. Technically, it was more a matter of the philosophy of worship, not control. The Liberians came out of more evangelistically assertive and passionate churches; the Ivorians did not. The longer the Liberians stayed around, the harder it seemed for the two groups to worship together. There really never had been any symbiosis - even though as Christian brothers and sisters, there should have been.

We heard disturbing stories about how the Liberians were being treated by the leaders of the church. One of the biggest things was when the Lord's Supper was celebrated, the Liberians were asked for their baptismal cards before they were allowed to participate. For a Liberian Christian to simply say they were a baptized member of a Baptist church in Liberia was not enough. Seriously, how many Liberians had thought to grab their baptismal card as they were fleeing civil war in their towns? While we understand the Ivorian church's desire to be careful about bringing disorder into the church, the struggles were animated pages right out of I and II Corinthians.

Soon after these things were brought to our attention, Jeff was invited to preach in the church. He accepted and asked God to give him the wisdom to penetrate the resentment that prevailed. He preached on jealousy and division in the church. One church member actually stood up and apologized during the message for some things he had said. Jeff made another point by reminding the Ivorian church members that he, the missionary, had taken the Lord's Supper with them twice since we had arrived in Blolequin, and never had anyone asked to see his baptismal card. Why? Was there a *respecter of* persons issue? He tried lovingly to reveal some of the ugliness on both sides of the issues.

Rising partly out of those mounting concerns, some of the Liberians Christians asked Jeff and Mark to help them start a Liberian church in town. Theyndesperately missed their churches back in their war-torn country. We began to pray as a missionary team, seeking God's will concerning the request. Coming to Blolequin to evangelize the surrounding villages, help with the medical clinic, and encourage the Liberian refugees had been our mandate. None of us had really thought of establishing a church. Was helping the Liberians start an English-speaking Baptist church a way to encourage them? Or would it draw deeper lines in the sand with the hosting Ivorian Christians? God answered those questions in vivid ways as He continued to unfold His perfect plans for us and as we began to lay aside some of our own aspirations. *His ways are higher than ours...*

Ending In a Song

As painting began in our second floor house, we began to gather our things and make ready for the move. The last weekend we were to be in the Pink House, the girls surprised me by saying, *"Mommy, we are going to miss this little house. The Grand Maison will be really, really nice, and we're very excited, but this has been our home. You have made it as nice as possible, and we'll always remember that!"* What a blessing to have girls who could see sunshine passed the heat and small spaces and dingy bathroom. Thinking back on all the times I had complained about the little, hot Pink House, I am amazed it still held such good memories for my daughters.

Then, there was the devil, menacing and persistent. He was obviously at work trying to discourage us as the final touches were put on the Grand Maison. A few days before we moved in, the electrician finally showed up, but it was quickly evident he was drunk and stayed that way all day. By the end of the day, we still did not have any electricity which was no surprise to us. We suspected the patron of the house was keeping us from having current until the last minute, because we had told him that we were not pleased at the pace of the painter whom he had contracted. We vowed to complete the rest of the painting with our own Liberian guys. Because of our forthrightness, there seemed to be a conspiracy to keep us from having lights - to keeping us from finishing the painting.

Four of our faithful Liberian men went with Jeff over to the house and painted the ceiling. The Sheppards, who had moved into their downstairs house a couple of weeks before, provided light by running a drop cord through one of our upstairs bedroom windows. That night singing and laughter was heard coming from the Grand Maison, so much that the unsaved Ivorians who lived around the big house came over to see what was going on. The devil was clearly defeated and a powerful testimony of God's love was shown to the community. It was an encouragement to Jeff and me of friendship, Christian endurance, and just a touch of heaven perhaps. No matter what else our closest neighbors thought about the Grand Maison and its Muslim owner, we wanted, above all, to proclaim the name of Jesus loudly and clearly as the One we served. As paint covered bare walls, God's name was sung loudly, in every dialect possible. Let the redeemed of the Lord say so!

A Leaky Start

Knowing that most of the men contracted to do the electrical work and plumbing stayed drunk while working, we were not really surprised when serious issues came to light even after we moved in. The one that disturbed me the most was when my sweet little nine-year old Stefanie wanted to be the first to open the refrigerator after it was plugged in. Upon touching the handle, she was literally knocked across the room, stunning her for several minutes. Jeff checked the voltage on the refrigerator handle and found it was 220 volts. There is <u>never</u> to be voltage on the handle of a refrigerator. This mama was livid at the drunken men who put my child in danger, but at the same time, very thankful that God protected Stefanie from severe harm. Though shaken from the incident, she was fine. He reminded me again whose sovereign Hands held our very breath.

More benign, but extremely frustrating, were the plumbing problems in every room where there was a water hookup. Our bathtub had to be extracted and some of the walls around it torn out to find the leak. The girls' bathroom was usable, but barely. Water was running into Lauren and Michelle's rooms from the walls and the floor, so we had to cut off the water to our house except when flushing the toilet or washing clothes. After a heavy rain, we discovered numerous holes in the roof by the telltale dripping onto our tile floors. Plastic buckets were placed strategically to catch the dripping water. Despite all that, I tried my best to live beyond the repair needs and count my blessings.

Christmastime Again in West Africa

To me, there was nothing like truly enjoying the meaning of Christmas in a unfrequented West African town without loud, holiday commercialism. Because we lived on the second floor of the Grand Maison, we decorated our house by stringing lights around as many windows as we could. It was a way we could share the Christmas spirit with our neighbors who lived all around us. A couple of nights during the holiday season, we invited some of our neighbors into our home to celebrate with us. Granted, some of the Ivorian neighbors were too leery to actually enter our house, so we determined to keep trying to win their trust. Most likely, there had never been white people who lived in town before, so we were an enigma.

The week before Christmas Day, we hosted a Christmas party for all the Africans who had helped us complete the work on the Grand Maison. For the first of many times, our schoolroom was turned into a banquet hall. Over the next three years, we entertained scores of Liberians and other guests in that multi-purpose room, decorating it for whatever celebration was on the agenda. Everyone loves a gala, no matter where you lived in the world.

Another Lamb Enters the Fold

From my journal of December 27, 1995,

> *Lauren asked Jesus to come into her heart during our family devotions tonight. She had been under strong conviction for a couple of weeks now and was asking many questions. I did help her pray, but she really knew what she wanted to say already. A little later, after the prayer, we were all just quietly sitting and thinking about the beauty of what just happened. Lauren piped up and said,* **"Hey I feel like a new person!"** *What a testimony to God's saving grace! As she prayed at the end of the devotional time, she said, "Thank the Lord for a good day. It is a very good day since I got saved. I know I will go to Heaven and not to hell. Thank you for a good day. Thank you that I could get saved and mommy helped me and daddy didn't do nothing to help me."*

What a classic coming from a five-year old. Never mind that daddy had been the one to give the devotion and then the one who asked Lauren if she wanted to pray. It was just so cute. That night all three of our girls slept together in Michelle's twin bed to celebrate. The growing sisterhood was only beginning for my girls.

CHAPTER ELEVEN

It was the best of times; it was the worst of times. —Charles Dickens

From the Inside Out

We knew the rule by heart. You take a big risk to eat fresh salads served in restaurants in West Africa. If we wanted to eat uncooked veggies, we did it at home where we knew they had been washed in salt water, soaked in a lightly bleached solution, and then rinsed twice more. It was a process, to say the least, but we all loved salad, so the only fail-proof way to make sure that deadly parasites were purged from the vegetables was to do the wash, soak, rinse, rinse method. During our family's December trip to Abidjan, I must have eaten something that harbored amoebas. Within days of returning to Blolequin, amoebic dysentery had taken over my body like a person possessed. Those parasites, found in contaminated food or drink, enter the body through the mouth and then move through the digestive system, taking up residence in the intestine and causing an infection that can cause other complications. It was relentless and painful, but I will spare you the disgusting details. The word *dysentery* should be visual enough. Desperate to stop the unhealthy purging of my guts, I took some medicines which should have killed the parasites, but did not.

By December 18th, my body was so chemically imbalanced, I began to have literal attacks on all parts of my body. My journal reads, *Jeff and I were watching a video before we went to bed that night. All of a sudden, I felt like I was going to pass out. I felt really faint - not dizzy, just weird. I told Jeff he needed to get me to Dr. Burrows because I knew that something was not right. I was really afraid. I walked downstairs to the car, and by that time, was feeling somewhat better, even though a really severe burning in my stomach had started.* On Christmas Eve, I had an attack very similar to the first one. We had eaten lasagna that night as was our Christmas tradition when not in the states with our families. Four days later, we had Liberian friends visiting us from the town of Pehe with their two children. I sprinkled cayenne pepper on my soup and rice and had just started eating when the attack happened again, only more severely.

My veins felt really warm, I would feel as if I was going to pass out, and then as if I could not breathe. A fiery heartburn ensued - in that order. Each time I had an attack, it would be exactly in that order. It baffled Dr. Burrows as it did the rest of us. On January 2, 1996, I wrote:

> *I was sitting down reading a book, waiting for the rest of the family to get ready for a celebration of the medical clinic opening we were attending. My left hand started going numb and tingly, then I got a really bad heartburn. I stood up and walked around trying not to panic and told Jeff what I was feeling. We went on to the celebration dinner at the Ivorian church, but my left arm hurt for hours. After the program was finished, Dr. Burrows took me inside his house to check my blood sugar. As I walked in the room, my heart started beating extremely fast and from there went into tachycardia. Mrs. Burrows had me put my head between my knees and told me to breath slowly and deeply. My heart rate was well over 130 beats per minute when she checked it.*

After that event, Dr. Burrows advised Jeff to take me to Abidjan for further medical evaluation. Because our car was already in Abidjan for major repairs (CV joints, steering, clutch, etc.), we had to hitch a ride with Lutheran missionaries who worked in a nearby town. Strangely enough, after riding seven hours in an air conditioned car, doing nothing but sleeping, eating peanuts and bananas, I felt better by the time we arrived in the city. I mentioned that to Jeff, but within a day or so, the symptoms had returned. Though I knew some French, we felt it would be best to find a doctor who could speak good English. God directed us to a Ghanaian doctor who had studied in Scotland and recognized the name *Abernethy* as being Scottish. He did blood tests which showed I had severe depletion of both calcium and magnesium in my body, most likely caused by the malabsorption of nutrients which were blocked when the parasites invaded my intestine. Dr. Baddock suspected, by studying my symptoms, there were probably bacterial lesions on the wall of my stomach causing something like esophagatis.

What we were looking at was a very complex problem. My heart was strained and not working properly because of the lack of magnesium and calcium. That, in turn, was causing my left arm to ache and tingle, and subsequently, the heart to jump into tachycardia. For that, he put me on a regiment of liquid magnesium twice a day. The mineral was golden in color and came in a glass vial that could be broken at the tip. I was instructed to mix it with juice or water. I kid you not, it felt like a calming drug as it went into my bloodstream and traveled to my tired heart. I always felt so relaxed and would sleep like a baby right after I drank the *golden heart nectar*. For that stuff, I could easily had become a drug addict. My body was so deprived of the essential minerals.

For the stomach issue, he sent me for an endoscopy which turned into a nightmare for both Jeff and me. The French doctor who spoke no English abruptly lay me on a table, quickly gave me some gel stuff to gargle which numbed my throat. She turned me on my side and without any other sedative at all, began babbling to me in French as she attempted to ram the tube down my throat and into my inflamed stomach. I heaved all over the place, and she became very angry with me. She had her assistant hold my head very tightly as she thrust the tube further down my throat. In French she was telling me to breathe through my nose, but I had forgotten any French. When she accidentally must have touched one of the lesions on my stomach wall, the heaving became wretched and involuntary. As I attempted to tug at the tube around my mouth, she kept telling me she was finished. But yet the torture continued for at least five more minutes.

Jeff was standing by the bed, his own heart racing, watching me flail on the bed like a fish out of the water. He did not know what to do, but came very close to pulling the tube out himself a couple of times. I was slapping the side of the table so fiercely at one point, he thought I was dying. I remember looking briefly into his beautiful brown eyes and seeing turmoil. Before long, he put his hands on the doctor's arm, ready to rescue me from the torture. Then we heard the French doctor look at the monitor showing her the condition of my stomach, and say, "*Oh, Madame!*" Poor Jeff was ready for his own hospital room for a couple of days after that. The horrible seven-minute test did reveal two bad lesions on my stomach along with several smaller ones. She told me to drink no coffee, no soft drinks, no tea, and eat no hot peppers, spaghetti, or spicy food. She then gave me two very strong drugs for the parasitic damage. Still it took almost two weeks before I started feeling like myself again. We were in Abidjan for three weeks trying to solve the debilitating physical issues I was experiencing. Our family was glad to return to Blolequin, though I was a shell of the woman I had been in the past. My body was exhausted in every way. The drugs to kill the parasites seemed also to kill my fervor, my spirit and love of life. The next three weeks went at a snail's pace, painful and blurry.

The Mind Game

Satan took advantage of the amoebic experience and used it to attempt to defeat me. Even after I was feeling better, if I felt one twinge in my heart or stomach, I would work myself up into a full panic attack. For the first time in my life, I had tension headaches. As soon as the invisible band wrapped tightly around the top of my head, my left arm would start hurting again. It went from one thing to another, though I thought physically my body was healing. Emotionally and mentally I was caught in a slimy, dark cavern desperately looking for a light, and Satan did his best to block any light from my view. For days, I battled headaches, a tingling arm, and heart palpitations. I prayed, I tried to praise the Lord through song. One night my arm hurt so badly I thought it would fall off. Sleep had become a thing of the past. If I had to give my ordeal a name, it would have been my reactive nature to past stress factors. Though the crisis of my health was over, my mind still held on to the fears it had invoked. I was quickly become fearful of *fear* itself.

God spoke to me and urged me to leave my fears with Him. I listened intently to His voice as I tried to sleep, wanting so desperately to leave it with Him. Little by little, I was able to live above my fears only through God's amazing grace. Satan continued to play mind games with me and vowed to take me down, to render me useless in ministry. He placed in my head the desire to flee and head back to the States. With my nod of approval towards that plan, he would also remind me that we had left another ministry after just a year in 1992. It seemed to be happening again - *all because of me*. I cried out in the name of Jesus. My spirit was determined only Jesus would decide my future, not the wicked deceiver. So, I kept trying to look up and let God completely have my life. But the past haunted me and my body caved to the fears too often. When I felt the band wrapping itself around my head, I would go in my room, lay down and talk to my Savior. Several times I became weak and bent my ear to hear what Satan had to say. I felt like a failure, but God.......so great in mercy would reach down and give hope in the midst of my confusion. At those moments of physical and spiritual crises, when the flesh desires to trump the spirit in every way, God is there to perform an incredible work. He knows the deepest desires of our hearts even when we can no longer express them clearly. And one word will fell the deceiver of our hearts.

Before We Knew To Ask

A couple of weeks after returning from Abidjan with my health issues, we received word our car repairs were finished, so Jeff took a bus back to the big city to retrieve our car and pay the large repair bill. We had no idea how we were going to make it all work financially, especially since we had recently spent quite a bit of our monthly income on medical procedures. While Jeff was gone, our financial donor statement from the previous month arrived, but I did not take time to open it. Three days later my tired and frazzled man drove up in front of the Grand Maison - honking the horn at the gate to announce his arrival. As I always tried to do, I breathed a prayer of thanksgiving for his safety on the long seven hour trip.

The car was in good shape, running well as it should have been after $1400.00 worth of repairs. Later that night, when we finally went to bed, our pillow talk was about our financial predicament. We concluded it with a prayer that God would provide as He saw fit. As I was in the schoolroom side of our house with the girls the next morning, the door swung open and I was met with the excited brown eyes of my husband. He waved a paper in front of my face and said, *"Do you remember how much I told you the repairs for the car cost? Exactly how much?* I gave him the number of fourteen hundred dollars, and he nodded animatedly as he thrust the donor statement for December in my hand. Halfway down the sheet was a name which I did not recognize and the donated amount to our ministry was $1400.00. It had been received at the mission office more than six weeks ago. *Before we know what to ask. Above what we ask or think.*

God is not kidding when He put those truths in His Word. We were exactly where we needed to be - in spite of the physical struggles, spiritual and emotional setbacks, and financial deficits. Though we had seen God provide for us time and time again, it was the exact amount provided by a donor - to this day - we have never heard from again. That's just how God works. He owns the cattle and the checkbooks of those whom we may never meet in this life.

Home For a Season

In the middle of active ministry, still setting up our new home, and soon to be starting a Liberian Baptist church; I continued to struggle physically. The symptoms had changed. I could not sleep at night or if I fell asleep, I would wake up suddenly, always exhausted, jittery, sweating profusely, with headaches which seemed different from the ones before. I wrestled with the physical plight, but by the first of March, my symptoms became more widespread and I began to feel I was making life difficult for Jeff and the girls. Dr. Burrows concluded either I was going through early menopause or perhaps on the verge of a nervous breakdown. We honestly did not know. Neither of those sounded like something I wanted to claim but none of it could be ignored.

Homeschooling three girls was nearly a full time job, and I remember well the struggles I had every morning to get myself into the frame of mind to teach them. I was tense and on edge and hated that my life felt out of control. Had I not wanted to help Jeff with establishing a Liberian church and even teaching English to some of the Liberians? There were so many ministry plans in my heart, but I could not force myself to fulfill any of them except to teach the girls. One day at a time. One course at a time. One page at a time. It took formidable effort not to snap at them for the smallest things. Who was this person?

One night Jeff talked candidly to me and shared his desire that we find out exactly what was wrong with me. He wanted to send me to the States for a few weeks and let me see a doctor there. Well, of course, a trip to the States would be a wonderful thing, but I was also concerned because it felt like I was failing God, my family, and the ministry. Did this mean that Satan would win if I stepped away for a while? Jeff and I talked for many nights, prayed, and both felt at peace that it was the best plan for all of us. Jeff prayed that I would only have to see one doctor and that he would be able to diagnosis my problem easily.

A trip to the States meant I would have to leave my girls in West Africa with their daddy because tickets cost too much to take them with me. The reality of that was so painful! Again, God called me out to trust Him with my family and with my health. I felt so out of control of everything. When we lose control of our lives, it is wise to admit we never had control of it in the first place. Hand it over to our Savior. He knows what He is doing. He never loses His head. He never acts on emotions. He never tires.

I spent six weeks in the States and will not deny how wonderful it was to see my parents, other family and friends. Thankfully, just as we had prayed, the very first doctor I saw was able to pinpoint my condition, finding nothing life threatening like I assumed. I was diagnosed as having a severe case of reactive hypoglycemia most likely brought on by the parasitic trauma my body had gone through a few months before. Any time there is a chemical imbalance, blood sugar levels can also be knocked out of whack. While in the States, I was given a book and some great advice about how to eat to maintain healthy blood sugar levels and break free of the debilitating symptoms which were consuming me. After the six week sabbatical, I was excited to return to the ministry in Ivory Coast. Nothing like stepping away from a situation to give you a fresh perspective. Being in the states only made me realize my heart was truly wanting to delve deeply into the ministry opportunities awaiting us in western Ivory Coast.

The Birth of a Church

It started subtly in the simple, mud brick home of a Liberian believer. A Wednesday night prayer meeting was planned by Liberian Christians who sought God's will about establishing an English-speaking church in Blolequin. The first prayer event was in February of 1996, and in the following two months, attendance grew so much that we were forced to move to a larger house. We could have offered to hold the prayer meetings in our home; but from the onset, we desired that the Liberians own the process of birthing their church. That also would allow us to watch the natural African Christian leaders come forward. Let leadership rise to the top - if you will. It was a little more difficult to explain to the Liberians what we were trying to do.

In years past, the American missionary had cared for most details when establishing churches in Liberia. But we felt the organizing of a church in Blolequin must be something the Christians wanted enough to walk the talk - learning to live by faith. It is true, that such a plan would not have worked if there were no strong Christians to train. But while living in Blolequin, we had already seen leadership potential in several of the Liberians. It was the right time to teach them to listen to God's leading and to see the immense provision God gives all of us when He calls us to do something. With the civil war still raging inside Liberia, we had no guarantee that we - the American missionaries - would ever be able to return and minister in the same capacity. Our mandate as missionaries was changing before our very eyes.

Our prayer letter of May 1996 reads:

> *Every missionary in Blolequin has felt compelled by God to pray for revival in this region, and for hundreds, yes, even **thousands** to believe in Jesus Christ. This was the prayer of Nancy Sheppard during a missionary prayer meeting. "Why are we only praying for hundreds? Why not thousands?" During our Wednesday night prayer meetings with the Liberian Christians, we have a short devotion and maybe three or four songs, but for the next hour or so, we share prayer requests and praises. It started out about six weeks ago with more prayer requests than anything else, but just recently the praises have been much more in abundance than the prayer requests! In the past month, we have gathered 71 names of unsaved loved ones and friends. We have already seen 20 of these come to accept Christ. After only two months of holding these Wednesday night prayer meetings, we are averaging seventy in attendance.*

In April of 1996 the Good News Baptist Church was birthed in Blolequin. On the day of its organization, a five-hour program was planned. We started the morning service in a thatched-roof, mud block building used for a refugee school. With over 300 in attendance, it was quite the talk of the town. After the morning church service, we went straight into the church organization program. Twenty-six Liberians signed the charter and then voted Teacha Jeff Abernethy in as the first pastor. From the beginning, Jeff made it clear he would only pastor long enough to help them establish a constitution, elect deacons, and train the members. Everyone seemed satisfied with the plan. Later in the afternoon, we celebrated with food. What church doesn't? The food committee had cooked 160 pounds of rice and five different Liberian soups - palm butter, potato greens, eggplant, okra, and potato soups. Not one grain of rice was left! When everyone's belly could hold no more, we took the Lord's supper with the new members. What a sweet time of fellowship that day was for us all.

One of the most memorable redemption stories in the early months of the church was the mother of a newly-appointed deacon, James. His mother, Nancy, was about 80 years old. In her younger days, she was appointed as a female zoe (an old Liberian term for *witchdoctor*), handling the circumcising of the young girls brought into the devil bush camp. The morning she was to be baptized in her obedience to Jesus Christ, she brought her circumcising tools to the church and laid them on the altar. She said in her testimony that *no longer would those wicked tools sleep in her house*. Flesh and blood did not reveal that to her, my friends. What *devil's tools* do we have sleeping in our houses that need to go?

The newness, the growing, the sharing, the learning: it all seemed right out of the pages of the book of Acts. My heart could hardly stand it. God was moving mightily in ours and the Africans' lives who lived in Blolequin and the surrounding areas. We chose to believe God for God-sized things - asking His Spirit to move through the region with grace and truth - going beyond our human expectations. Our prayer letter of September 1996, reads:

> *There have been several salvations and rededications. The most recent ones came when Jeff preached on the Judgment Seat of Christ. It made quite an impact on these people. Some of their African culture conflicts heavily with what the Word of God teaches. One example of this is their philosophy of borrowing things from other people. If a Liberian asks to borrow something from you, they may keep it for weeks, months, or even years. Jeff addressed this as **stealing** when they knew in their hearts that they were going to keep the item. The Liberian culture may call it **borrowing** but most of the time, they know the intention is to keep the items. The day after the message, one of the missionaries had a hand tool returned after eight*

months of it being "borrowed." We praise the Lord
for these unusual, but important victories in the
lives of these Christians as they chose to live in the
light of God's Word and not their culture.

Dancing Down to the Waters

The Sunday afternoon baptisms are still highlights of the Blolequin ministry days. Even now, I can hear the rushing of the creek, the harmonious and happy singing of the redeemed, the shuffling of feet in rhythm with God's joy. About a half mile out of town, a rather large creek ran parallel to the main road and was used as the baptismal spot for the Good News Baptist Church. Every three months, between eight and twenty people were baptized after the completion of a Baptism class taught by either Teacher Jeff or Teacher Mark. The convoy of Christ followers would start out following the morning service, literally dancing all the way to the muddy baptismal pool. There was singing, clapping, and laughter as we all celebrated. Be assured, I was right in the middle of it. As long as my hypoglycemia was in check (I would eat some protein food right before), I would sway and sing with the other African women. There's not an aerobic workout DVD anywhere that matches what it took to keep up with the celebratory moves of an African Christian. As my brother said many years ago, I had it in my blood. It was part of me. I really felt like a Liberian.

In rainy season, that same creek rose and the waters rushed forcefully through the baptismal spot. Fearing that someone might be swept away in the strong current, Jeff and Mark both held tightly to the person being immersed into the muddy waters. On the flip side, in dry season when the rains had ceased, the men had to walk quite a distance into the creek in order to find enough water. Each person being baptized had the opportunity to give a testimony before they were put under the water. Taking our portable megaphone, the person loudly testified of what Jesus had done for them to church members and curious bystanders. Sometimes it would be in dialect, so I could not understand everything they said, but it always gave me chills to hear the testimonies and then the resounding praise as the person was brought out of the water. What a celebration of new life and hope and obedience. As I read through my journals from our years in Blolequin, I was humbled to think that if I had lived out my fears of returning to West Africa, I would have missed one of **the** most incredible periods in our ministry. A seemingly insignificant place in the world became a hotspot of modern day revival. I'm not kidding. Revival broke out and God allowed us to watch the gloriousness of His moving!

Training Ground

Though I was dealing with a great deal of personal disaffection, I was falling more in love with the Africans around me. Deciding to use one of the things I loved best - the English language - I started two classes, dividing the students through the use of a simple placement test. Instead of using American grammar books, I wrote English curriculum especially for the Liberians. I did this when I was in the schoolroom with the girls, and they were working on worksheets and taking tests. On Tuesday nights and Saturday mornings, the school room would fill with eager-to-learn Liberian adults. For reading comprehension, we used the Bible. I loved challenging them on some of the familiar - and not so familiar stories. At the end of the six-month class, we celebrated with a feast and a graduation program. On my circa 1994 iMac, I created official looking certificates and diplomas. Delightfully, several students were able to get jobs in some of the refugee schools by showing those diplomas. One particular Liberian student scored so high on an achievement test given by a school where he was applying for a job, that he was asked to become the assistant field director for the refugee schools in that area. It felt so good to be able to boost vocational opportunities for our Liberian friends simply by teaching them something that God had given me a love for.

Jeff was also teaching twice a week. His leadership class, in which he handpicked eight men out of the church, went for six months. From those classes came future deacons and leaders to serve in the church both in Ivory Coast and eventually back in Liberia. Jeff and the men learned so much about each other, about

Liberian culture, and how the Bible was the final authority beyond Liberian or American culture. Our girls thought nothing of sharing the schoolroom and our home four times a week with Liberians as we gained momentum in our ministries.

Tom G. Barh, a young, single Liberian, worked occasionally for us at the Grande Maison, and was also part of the leadership class Jeff was teaching. One of his most memorable lessons was not learned in a class. It was one the Holy Spirit revealed to him after a Wednesday night prayer meeting. Tom, along with other Liberians, harbored the misguided belief that God listened directly to the "white" man's prayer more so than their own. Almost like a priesthood mediation, he had in his mind (certainly not from any teaching we ever did) that as long as the American missionary was among them, God would honor the prayers going up. Despite tireless teaching contrary to that assumption, Tom remained adamant that their prayers for this young church in the making was because the white missionary was there. One morning, he knocked loudly on our door and said, "*Teacha! Teacha! I know it's true now - what you have told us from the beginning. God does hear the prayers of the black skinned man just as He does yours!* This impassioned reaction came when he had seen the dozens of prayer requests being answered among his own people. When he realized that it was his own prayers and the prayers of his Liberian brothers and sisters being heard, he was ecstatic. Again, the Spirit of God had dealt with Tom on his fallacy of prayer. He became so free by the knowledge of that truth. Many tears of joy were shed in our house that morning as we saw that God was moving in the hearts of so many. We were simply overwhelmed by His faithfulness to those precious people.

Though we were occasionally having puppet programs in the yard of the Pink House - used still for storage and a woodworking facility for the guys - Michelle, Stefanie, and Melodie Sheppard desired to start a children's class for 2 - 5 year olds during the Sunday night service. It was great fun for the Liberian children, but even more a priceless learning experience for the girls. In their willingness to serve, they were also teaching the Liberians the benefit of children's ministry. Stefanie, who was eleven at the time, helped to establish a nursery on Sunday mornings for Liberian babies under the age of two. We bought toys and mats in the market and took full responsibility for running it at first. By example, we showed the women in the church how beneficial a nursery could be, eventually recruiting some of them to take a rotation. Our Sunday morning church services were much quieter because of those two children's classes.

An Amazing Movement of God

At the end of a six-month leadership class, a young man named Wilson spoke of his compelling burden to go to a town about ten miles away and start a church. After a survey trip to the town, the men were overwhelmed by the group of believers in the town of Diboke in their determination. Praying for a pastor to come and teach them God's Word, they, of their own accord, constructed a simple building and had thirty-five in attendance. God had truly been at work in that small town, preparing and softening hearts, persuading men to follow Him. It was a delight to hear Wilson's reports of what God was doing in those first few months he ministered there. God had heard the prayers of the Christians in Diboke and sent them a shepherd.

After Jeff preached a message entitled *Operation Andrew* taken from the story about Peter's brother, Andrew; many church members shared their desire in learning to lead people to Christ. In response to that, we began a soul-winning class for thirty-eight of our members, teaching them the academics of leading someone to Christ. It was happening. Liberian Christians were accepting their own responsibility for the spiritually dying world around them. It was no longer just the role of the American missionaries. We began a Saturday morning visitation program where the church members learned the practicalities of soul-winning. At first we went in groups, and if someone did not feel comfortable, we allowed them to learn by watching us. What a delight as we had the privilege to see some of the shyest people open their mouths and share Christ. God uses any one who makes himself available to His calling.

During the same time, a plan arose to schedule an evangelistic meeting in Diboke, to go and encourage Wilson in his church planting there. Though Jeff had preached in the town several times, I was really looking forward to visiting Diboke one particular evening. We had invited any of the Good News church members who wanted to go with us to the Diboke outreach. How amazed we were when more than sixty of our church members showed up to attend the outreach. Unfortunately, there were only four vehicles available to take about forty people. Though somewhat disappointed, I quickly felt the Holy Spirit prompt me to stay in Blolequin and have a prayer meeting with those who would stay behind. Nancy and I invited the twenty-three Liberian Christians who stayed behind for an extended prayer time in our house. Using our schoolroom whiteboard, we made a list of nine specific prayer requests to bring before the throne of God concerning the evangelistic meeting being held in Diboke. We divided into two groups. One group would stay on the living room side of our house, singing praises to God and sharing testimonies. The school room side of our home became the prayer room. After forty-five minutes, the two groups would switch. This kept us sharp-edged and clear headed for the long night ahead. Jeff's report of May 1997 reads:

> We traveled with four vehicles taking over 40 people. Everyone helped set up the meeting place, went around town distributing tracts, and inviting people to attend the meeting. Meanwhile, back in Blolequin, Kim and the other ladies were meeting with twenty-three Christians for a praise and prayer time. They wrote down nine specific prayer requests for the meeting in Diboke. One was that the invitation time would be orderly and quiet. I must admit that it was one of the easiest and most orderly services I have ever conducted in an African village. Every one of those prayer requests was answered - especially the one where many would be saved!

Meanwhile at the Grande Maison, we continued to pray and sang praises well past midnight, determining we would stay vigilant until the group returned to Blolequin. Nearing 1:00 a.m., we heard the vehicles, and rushed out of the house to hear details of the meeting. The weary entourage was surprised that we were still at our task. All in all, there were 122 professions of faith in Christ that night. Whether we were part of the team that stayed or went, God honored our prayers and faithfulness. It was an amazing night of ministry both in Blolequin and Diboke. God honored His Word in both places.

CHAPTER TWELVE

"It has repeatedly happened on foreign fields that when a heathen[sic] who has never heard of the true God, followed his innate convictions that there is a God and sought after Him, he found his way to some missionary that could tell him the way of salvation." —Thiessen, Systematic Theology

Here We Go Again

For a few months, it seemed the health of my family was stable. Granted, I still struggled with my condition of low blood sugar, but most of the time I was able to keep it under control. Stefanie, the daughter who had been so sick during our last term in Ivory Coast, was thriving, as was Lauren. One day during the apex of our evangelistic outreach, Michelle came to me holding her head and looking very pale. Obvious that she was coming down with something, it was not until after a long night of agonizing chills and a very high fever, that made it pretty clear she had malaria. We gave her the prescribed treatment and she responded to it very well, though within a couple of months, she came down with it again. That second time, it took four days before the malaria treatment began to work. Her sisters helped to bathe her feverish body and to coax her into drinking enough liquids to stay hydrated. Michelle had always been the child who never was sick, but those bouts with malaria had weakened her, causing her to lose quite a bit of weight. It hurt my heart to see her like that.

During our third summer in Blolequin, a doctor from Ohio brought his wife and two daughters out for an extended visit. While he mainly came to help Dr. Burrows in the medical clinic, we became fast friends with the Smith family. During their visit, Dr. Smith obtrusively noticed a slight nonuniformity in Michelle's spine. After further examining, he believed that she had scoliosis, an irregular curving of the spine. Since Michelle was just turning 14, he was concerned that waiting twelve more months (when we would return to the States for furlough) might be too late to correct it properly. With that important information, we sought out a doctor in Abidjan to have the condition further evaluated.

Upon recommendations from missionary friends, we chose to see a doctor at a French-owned hospital. After examining Michelle and performing an x-ray of the spine, the Ivorian surgeon came in and abruptly said, "*It is really bad! We must do surgery right away! Please sign these papers and we will operate tomorrow morning!*" Reeling from the intensity of his reaction, we, nevertheless, held off the impassioned surgeon. From my quick glance at Michelle, I noticed she had turned pale with the thought of imminent surgery. Showing us the x-ray, the doctor insisted that we see the curve was more prominent than expected. Still, none of us felt good about Michelle going under the surgeon's knife there in Ivory Coast. Michelle verbalized her fears about the findings. It was certainly hard enough to be a teenager and having to deal with the news of scoliosis. Add that to the fact we were in a country where French was the given language and where the medical system was a far cry from what was familiar to us. Jeff and I talked it through after leaving the hospital, both of us already knowing what needed to be done. While still in Abidjan, we bought tickets for Michelle and me to fly back to the States four weeks later.

Realizing that I was going stateside again, Stefanie and Lauren had a hard time understanding why they could not jump on the plane with us. Those international trips that split up families were never easy, but often necessary. My heart was torn between the daughter who needed me with her on the new medical journey and the two precious younger ones who needed me there in West Africa. Financially impossible to take the other two girls, we returned to Blolequin to make things ready for our rather quick trip. For me, there were meals to be prepared and frozen, lesson plans to formulate so that Jeff could continue with the girls' schooling, and loose ends to tie up with some ministry details. The weeks flew by, and before we knew it, the hard goodbyes were being said at the Abidjan airport.

Our family in Charlotte had already lined up an appointment with an orthopedic doctor known for his expertise on the spine. After seeing the surgeon in Charlotte, he told us that Michelle's irregular curve was at forty-one degrees. Technically speaking, any curve beyond 40 degrees was considered for surgery - yet another jolt to the seriousness of the situation. *Why had we not seen this before?* Thankfully, the surgeon opted to put her in a brace for a year to see if it could correct any of the curvature. He felt sure that the brace, worn correctly, would not allow the curvature to worsen during our remaining time in West Africa. Our brave fourteen year old had to wear a thick, heavy plastic brace twenty hours a day even in the extreme heat of West Africa. She was a trooper and did it, most of the time, with a good attitude. The less favorable option of surgical correction was not something any of us wanted to think about. At the time of this writing, though Michelle struggles with the pain in her back, she has never had surgery.

More Pet Peeves

Guinea pigs had been part of our daughters' lives since our years in Jamaica. When we moved into the Grand Maison, the Sheppard children and our own daughters really got into the serious business of raising guinea pigs. There were guineas pigs inside the houses and outside - all in cages, of course. The constant squeaking and squealing, shuffling and munching of fresh green grass, and the pungent smells of cages needing to be cleaned permeated our house. One day a pregnant guinea pig was in obvious labor, so the girls decided to help her out. She was having a hard time delivering and it was evident that the life was flowing out of her. In an incredulous effort to save the guinea babies, the girls bravely slit open the mama guinea pig's belly on a makeshift operating table outside. They noted that one of the babies was turned sideways at the birth canal, making it impossible for any of the babies to be delivered. Though the girls were able to extract all the babies from the dying mother's tummy, the babies only lived a few hours. It was an interesting lesson for the kids who were involved in this procedure. Dissecting dead frogs in Biology class had nothing on those missionary kids.

Not one to have ever wanted a zoo of exotic animals on or off the mission field, I discouraged the girls from pets they thought they wanted. I certainly did not want to be stuck with caring for discarded animals to which they had grown tired. But, since I could never stand to see any creature neglected or suffer, I knew I would care for them no matter how tough I sounded. Ten year old Stefanie was the main advocate for more pets. When she was nine, she had rescued a beautiful kitten from the house located behind us and paid some boys five hundred francs (at the time equal to one dollar). She named the kitten Bubba, and sixteen years and four international flights later, he is still very much a part of our family. I have joked about my next book most likely being a children's book on how God enabled us to get Bubba the cat into America two different times without having him quarantined or paying any fees.

Michelle received a couple of chameleons for her twelfth and fourteenth birthdays, for some reason naming them both Diesel. Chameleons are some of the most fascinating creatures to watch, especially when they eat. Their tongues are much longer than their bodies, and when that long, thick appendage propelled out of the chameleon's mouth for food, you better not blink or you will miss the whole thing. Not really a fan of holding the lizard, I was an admirer of Michelle's reptile friends from afar. Most chameleons can live up to ten years, but the ones captured from the wild and brought into captivity usually are not as hardy. Human interaction is not one of their favorite things and does put stress on them. Believe me, any lizard that came in our house as a pet was overwhelmed with interaction. Poor Diesels.

When Stefanie was eleven, she ran into the house with yet another pet she needed to have. African kids were always bringing animals to the white peoples' houses to see if we would buy them. If not, I imagine they would cook them in their soup pots later that evening. You certainly could not blame those young African entrepreneurs for trying to make a little extra money from the crazy Americans. Two boys had come to our gate one day selling a couple of small baby genets, though looking like cats where actually a part of the mongoose family. Stefanie and Nathan Sheppard saw the genets before their older siblings did and wanted them desperately. After the normal spiel about taking care of the animal or we, the parents, would personally put back the cat back into the wild, we agreed Stefanie could have it. She quickly named her genet *Darling.* I must admit, she really was very cute. Most likely, the mommy had been killed for food and the babies were orphans. Stefanie had to feed her with a dropper for a few days until Darling was able to acclimate to her environment and start eating other foods.

Three months after Stefanie brought Darling into our home, tragedy struck. Stefanie was in her bedroom with Michelle and two other missionary girls practicing a song they were planning to sing in church the following Sunday. There was one part of the song that was emphatic and the girls would stamp their feet. During one of those stamping times, Darling happened to be under one of the girls' feet. With the quick pounding of the young girl's foot, Darling's head was crushed, but not enough to kill her immediately. At the moment it happened, I was catching a quiet moment in the living room, reading and resting, when loud screams, high shrills of agony came from Stefanie's room. Before I could get out of the chair and rush breathlessly to the room, all four girls ran out in obvious torment. Stefanie was holding Darling, but the small genet's head was dangling at an awkward angle. It was obvious that the pounding to her head would eventually be fatal; it was just a matter of time. Over the next few days, Darling's head swelled greatly and she could only walk in circles. It was almost too much to watch. Poor Stefanie's heart could hardly take watching her suffer like that. Of course, I stepped up and did most of the caring for the slowly dying genet. *This was why I did not want the girls to have pets. Who was the one attached to this suffering creature?* We had to make a trip to Abidjan a few days after the accident, so the Sheppard kids volunteered to care for Darling. It was while we were gone that she mercifully died. Of course, I cried as hard as Stefanie when we heard the news.

Small Details

During the years of ministering in Blolequin, our missionary team hosted numerous individuals or groups. One summer, we had the opportunity of having a sixteen year old young man stay with us for six weeks. Josh Benfield was the oldest son of some of our dearest friends and had a great desire to experience African missions. Even better was the fact that our girls had known Josh since they were born, so it was like having a big brother visiting. He fit right into our family, except that he did not particularly care for our cat Bubba. Using that knowledge, if we ever had a difficult time getting Josh up in the mornings, we would send both our five year old Lauren and the skittish cat into his room. It never failed to work. Sounds of maligned displeasure would erupt from Josh as Lauren threw the poor cat into his bed. First the cat, then Lauren would dash out of the room, followed by a wild-haired, wild-eyed Josh - not wanting to be awake, but awake, nonetheless.

Josh was so helpful with our ministry and eager to learn everything he could. He worked on the church construction, which basically consisted of hanging panels of thick thatch and cutting bamboo and wooden pieces for framing. Learning to ride Jeff's moped, he drove into town to the local market and to do errands for us. He became quick friends with one of our church leaders and Awana director, Jackson. A week before Josh was to return to the states, Jackson was traveling to a remote village about an hour's away from Blolequin to direct an Awana event. He asked Josh to accompany him. While we knew the trip would be eye-opening and memorable for Josh, we wondered what his parents would think of us sending him so deeply into the bush without us. Those were always the dilemmas we faced when hosting high school aged students. Their parents had entrusted their child to us, to help make their mission experience a good one, but yet we also had to weigh the safety of certain opportunities.

It would have been ideal if we could have called Josh's parents and talked over the situation with them, and while we did have a phone installed in the Grande Maison, it only worked on the rarest occasions. After talking with Jackson and Josh, we decided to allow the American fellow to go on the Awana trip. Taking both guys to the bus station in town early the next morning, I almost regretted that I had done so. After buying two tickets, Jackson came back to tell us it was going to be an exciting trip. The money bus they were riding had no brakes, but *not to worry*, Jackson told me, the brake boy was strong and fast. *What?* Local money buses had very poor brake systems - if any. So, the driver would hire a teenage boy to stand by the door and when the driver needed the bus to stop, he geared down until it was hardly moving. The brake boy would then jump off the bus with a huge piece of wood - a wheel chock of sorts - hurling it in front of the right front tire. *Usually* the bus would stop.

Learning details that I did not need to know, I watched Jackson and young Josh board the bus for their adventure. I remember thinking, *Debbie and Glenn, please forgive us for leaving out the small details of how Josh traveled.* The next day, Josh returned with a plethora of stories. After the bus stopped - thankfully - at a town on the main road, the two men had to walk a couple of miles into the bush before reaching the area where the Awana event was to be held. Josh was indeed an anomaly there, but enjoyed learning and meeting some wonderful West Africans who live differently than he ever imagined. Josh thanked us over and again for allowing him an adventure of a lifetime. Some risks are just worth taking, I'm pretty sure.

The Outworking of Love

My little children, let us not love in word or in tongue, but in deed and in truth. (I John 3:18) That verse may be short but is loaded with great life principles, though never easy to apply. In my observation, we use the word **love** too freely. For some of us, love is easy to say, but is usually as far as we take it. If we acted out what love looked like each time we uttered it, our society would be a much different place.

A physically and mentally challenged African named Eugene was sent to teach us about learning how to *love* IN DEED. In his younger days, Eugene had been a school teacher in Liberia, and then as a Liberian refugee teacher in Ivory Coast, until disease crippled his body with weakness and mental incoherency. Thinking him too much of a burden, his family abandoned him as happens more often than you would think. He was forced on the streets to provide for himself though he was not really able to do so.

A few months after we had settled into our home in Ivory Coast, Eugene showed up at our gate, his clothes ragged and filthy, smelling of stale urine and garbage. His feet teeming with chiggers, his hair matted with dirt and parasites, he only asked to look through our *dumpa* - garbage pile. Instead, we invited him in our yard and offered him some food from our kitchens. Sitting on the front steps of the Grande Maison, he gratefully ate whatever was provided. After he left, chiggers crawled freely on the concrete stoop where he had sat, making it evident we may eventually find chiggers in our feet, too. As repulsive as that thought was, none of us wanted to tell him that he could not sit in that spot. Such a small gesture for a person with such great needs.

Walking past Eugene, as he sat on our front stoop, was provocative in many ways. It was not comfortable to see him in such a pitiful state nor smell the putridness of his sores, but feeling too ashamed to admit my discomfort, I instead asked God to help me love Eugene as He did. Saying we *loved* Eugene was to mean we would live out that love no matter how it made us feel. A smile. A dish of food. New sandals. A firm handshake without thinking of what might be on his hand. A drink of cool water. Taking time to listen to his bumbling speech and incoherent thoughts. Daily disinfecting the steps where he had been sitting without complaining. That's what love looked like to Eugene. I failed at doing those things (more often in my heart) so many times.

My love for Eugene was still a bit distant and cautious until RJ showed me how it should be done. A Liberian man, RJ, worked for us occasionally. Not academically astute, he was a hard worker with a big heart. On Easter Sunday, RJ preached a powerful sermon about loving in deed and in truth - without saying a word. He had asked for his pay early (he did most of our gardening) plus requested to borrow extra money that week. We did not think about it until the next morning when we saw him come through our gate with a bag of clothes, Eugene bumbling slowly behind him. RJ ran up the stairs and asked if he could borrow a bar of soap. After giving him the soap, we watched him walk with Eugene to the bathhouse located behind our house, but still easily seen from our upstairs bedroom window. After a few minutes in the bathhouse, he emerged with a clean, neatly clothed Eugene. RJ had even put a pair of new slippers on his rough, malformed feet. As Jeff and I stood at the window watching, the tears flowed freely. Jeff was scheduled to preach that morning at church, but he said something to the effect that he had already *seen* the best sermon.

RJ brought the *freshly scrubbed* Eugene in our yard and asked if he could ride to church with us that morning. Of course, he rode with us to church though we had never asked him before. Why had we never thought of how difficult it was for Eugene to walk to church? It was as touching an experience as I could ever remember. Plain, uncomplicated RJ ministering to physically debilitated Eugene in a palpable and beautiful way. The church members were very glad to see Eugene sitting in the pews that day, and even he seemed more lucid and in tune with his surroundings. A couple of days after that silent Sunday sermon, Eugene showed up at our house clothed again in rags, telling us that mean people had stolen the clothes off his back. Not able to fend for himself, he was at the mercy of those who cared nothing about him. Knew nothing about love themselves. Sin looked us in the eye and mocked at our pain.

Sadly, a few weeks later, we were told by the town police that Eugene had died in the middle of the night on a hard, wooden market table. While we were so thankful he no longer suffered physically, it was disturbing to think he had died alone. Nevertheless, I will be always grateful for how RJ taught me what it means to love IN DEED.

Another Attempt By the Great Deceiver

The outpouring of God's Spirit was being realized in Blolequin and the surrounding areas. Because of the burden for lost souls, the members of the Good News Baptist Church saw nearly two hundred people saved within a three month period. Evangelistic services were also being held in towns around us, and it seemed that God asked us to believe Him for thousands to receive Christ. Rest assured, Satan was cooking up yet another scheme to stop the results of this revival. During one particular week, every missionary woman in Blolequin became either heavily burdened, agitated, overwhelmed, extremely oppressed in our spirits. I was having a hard time focusing on the girls' school work and cried at the drop of a hat. The other women were having similar struggles.

Jeff and the other missionary men were working one day at the medical clinic located on the town's only main road when they noticed a large group of people marching back and forth in front of the clinic like demonstrators would do. The assembly of people was not particularly loud, and they carried no signs, so their purpose was not clear. Curiosity peaked, the missionary men finally asked some of the African Christians what was going on. Hesitating before answering, they eventually told our guys that the group pacing in front of the mission were members of the Devil Bush Society commissioned to get rid of the white missionaries, hoping to force us out of town. Too many powerful things were happening in the name of Jesus which in turn was hurting the Society's business. When the missionary men heard this, they shrugged it off as benign, but did take it as a good sign if Satan was upset at what was going on in the church.

Meanwhile, that week turned into a long one for the women as we struggled with an unknown axis, even noticing more obvious tension between us and our husbands. Near the end of the week, we all met for our regular missionary prayer meeting. Right off we noticed things were not right. Things felt different. Off kilter. Foggy. There was a palpable tension and fatigue which was unanswerable. One by one, we began to share prayer requests. Each woman shared her own personal struggles. One thing was for sure. It seemed to have only affected the women. Something was amiss. But what? Talking it out, one woman described it as feeling like Satanic oppression. A heaviness, much deeper than the physical, delving into her spirit. That was exactly it, the rest of the women concurred. At that description, the men recalled what they had seen in front of the medical compound, putting it inside the same realm as what we women were going through. The pieces locked together. We were under attack.

The reality of Satanic oppression that had filtered into our homes caused me to shiver, though it was certainly not the first time I had felt it. That night at our gathering, we prayed on our knees, not just sitting in our chairs. Husbands praying over wives, all of us beseeching our Heavenly Father to break the chains of darkness and set us free from the hellish pressure. We knew that we were working in one of Satan's strongholds because the Devil Bush Society had a camp not too far from the medical compound. It had been several years since missionaries had lived in Blolequin, so Satan had, no doubt, reigned supreme - so he thought. Still greater was God in us than he that was in the world. Another important lesson to remember.

An Intersection of Eternal Consequence

At the writing of this book, I still struggle with low blood sugar, though it is not as draining as it was those first few years in Blolequin. One particular Saturday morning in 1997, I had gone visiting with a Liberian woman named Rebecca. Usually I walked to our evangelistic jaunts, but that particularly day I drove our blue Mazda to the other side of town, hoping we could visit some people who had attended our church the Sunday before. I remember how I was finally feeling a connection with the townspeople as they allowed me to enter their homes and share their lives with me. Wearing African cloth swathed around my waist and simple slippers on my feet, Rebecca and I visited several homes, sitting on a wooden stump beside a fire or on a crudely made chair inside a mud brick room. After about three hours of visiting, I felt the telltale signs of low blood sugar: the tinge of a headache, cold sweats, and a shakiness which starts inside and moves outward.

The ladies with whom I generally visited were familiar with that look on my face when I needed to get back home, though I am not sure they ever really understood it. Eating food high in protein and complex carbs balanced out the blood sugar for a few hours. That particular day with Rebecca, I was enjoying myself more than ever. So, when the physical symptoms beckoned me to return home, I bucked and fought back. Hypoglycemia is relentless and before long, I knew that I **must** return home. Rebecca decided to stay for a while longer, so I left her. Walking back to my car, I kicked every rock my foot could find, feeling enormously sorry for myself. My conversation with God on that trek to my car was not uplifting, but merely a pity party where I attempted to get Him to join with me. He, however, is sovereign and knows the future. It is when we step into that precious place of trusting Him, no matter how we feel, no matter what is going on around us, that we are allowed to see a little more of what He is capable of doing in and through us. Trusting Him is our choice. Pity is the weaker option.

As I headed back to the car, sweating and shaky, the conversation with God went like this: *So, Father, I just don't understand.* **I know you can heal me**. *Here I am serving you in West Africa still having to deal with this low blood sugar stuff? Please, Father, why can't you take it from me? I wanted to keep visiting and telling these Africans about you. But no.....I have to go home to EAT.* Can't you just hear the whining in my voice, as I spewed out my discontentment? I would like to believe that God just looked at me with love, shook His head, and smiled. I am really not sure how He reacts to such blatant distrust. But He knew what was coming. He had ordained it. A divine appointment was really why I was where I was. In spite of me, He was going to use me.

Crossing the dusty junction to reach my car, I called out a quick greeting to the deacon's family who were sitting outside their house. In the same moment, an African man bumped into me, but I never even looked up at him until he spoke these words. *I say! Hello, Missy, I say! It is **you**! You will show me the way to God today!* Those enthusiastic words grabbed my attention and glancing at the man standing on the dirt path, I was surprised to see him grinning from ear to ear. Looking at me intently, he waited for my answer. *Had he been talking to me?* Already beyond the point of no return with my blood sugar condition, I could not get over the eager trust he seemed to have in me and became curious to know his story. James, a friend and deacon, asked the man to sit down on his porch. The man kept looking at me as if I would disappear in a puff of smoke, and then said, *I will do that, thank you, but it is this white woman that will show me to God first. I have waited such a long time.*

I was mesmerized by his fervency to find God. We all sat down and I opened my Bible. A few minutes later, after going through the creation story and ending with the story of redemption, Amos bowed his head and received Jesus Christ. His prayer was one of the most magnificent I have ever heard. He talked to God so personally and was beholden by the work of the Son, Jesus Christ in his life. He kept saying, *Now, I understand! How wonderful it is!* From there, he struck out into dialect because of his excitement, telling James the story of how he knew he would one day find God with a white woman's help. James' face showed that he was staggered by the story, and he prompted Amos to tell me the story in English.

Almost two years before, Amos, a Liberian refugee, had been diagnosed with tuberculosis and was being transported with some other TB patients to a clinic. He had become very sick. As he was riding in the back of a United Nations truck one night, he looked up at the stars and the vastness of the heavens, and was afraid. Afraid to die. His prayer went something like this: "Creator of all the stars, trees, and nature, I do not know you at all. I know that I am dying and I need to find you before I die. Show yourself to me." Amos told us he was lulled to sleep in the back of the truck, and somewhere in the remoteness of the West African jungle, God reached out to him just as He promises to do for anyone who truly seeks Him. Amos had a dream, describing a bright light that came to Him and told him that because he truly was seeking God, he would indeed find Him. The Light also told Amos that a white woman standing beside a blue car would be the one to show him the way to God.

Guess what color our car was? I was completely blown away by the story, and as you can imagine, extremely humbled to realize that God would include me in His kingdom's work in such a stunning way. If I had not been prompted to go home at that specific time because of my medical condition, I would have completely missed the divine appointment with Amos. While it thrilled me to know God would choose to use me in such a way, it also revealed to me how very small I was in the scheme of things. Living life for His glory often entails the unexpected, the unsought, the unwanted. Through those things, God glorifies Himself in a way that only He can do while our hearts learn to trust Him a little more with each display of providential splendor. **If we ask God to use our lives completely for His glory, we should then be prepared for our lives to seemingly spiral <u>out</u> of our control and ultimately <u>into</u> His will**.

To some reading this, you may have perked up and paid close attention to the *dream* part. I, personally, had always stayed away from people's stories of "dreams and visions" until my encounter with Amos. Through this experience, God has shown Jeff and me that He alone chooses how He reveals Himself to those who desire to find Him. Who are we to limit God to radio broadcasts, biblical books, or a televised church services? Amos had none of those things available to him. And, yet, God reached down to him in a dream simply because He could.

CHAPTER THIRTEEN

When your will is in God's will, you will have your will. —C.H. Spurgeon

Cultural Collision of a Seventh Encounter

Time was winding down and would soon be time for us to head back to the U.S. for our furlough year. However, God was truly using the Good News Baptist Church, and we felt strongly that because of the faithful work in Blolequin, the ministries in other towns, and ultimately into Liberia itself, that church would perform what God had ordained it for. In the previous story about Amos, I mentioned a deacon named James. He was married to Martha and had six daughters. Their story is heartwarming as well as particularly telling of some of the cultural struggles with which these African Christians had to deal. In the strictest Liberian culture, sons were what men desired most, not daughters. Basically, a Liberian man was not really considered a man unless he had been able to produce a son. Oh, I believe the men knew that daughters were important, but it was detrimental to the manhood of an African man not to have a son.

James and Martha had been married for sixteen years when they crossed the border into Ivory Coast with four daughters, fleeing one of the hottest fighting spots in Liberia. Martha was a Christian, but James was not. Not yet. A year after Martha and James arrived in Ivory Coast, they had their fifth daughter, and, as you might imagine, the birth of another daughter did nothing to induce a peaceful home environment. James' family began cursing and ridiculing Martha for her inability to have a son, which caused Martha to cry almost every night from the grief of it. She prayed to God to give her a son for her husband. Even her own family began to question Martha on having all girls.

After a few months of constant talking and strong persuading by his unsaved family, James finally brought another woman into the house to be his second wife. This was common when a the first wife could not produce an heir for the man. Martha was despondent, but there was nothing she could do. Her family would not have her back and where else could a woman with five girls go? After about six months of sharing her husband with this other woman, both Martha and the second "wife" became pregnant. Delivering first, the second woman had a son. It was a nightmarish situation for Martha, but for James' family, it was the proof they needed to pressure him into getting rid of Martha and her daughters. Martha was filled with anxiety and distress as her time to deliver came. Daughter number six arrived one very dark night.

Out of her deepest distress, she still loved this sixth daughter and proved it by naming her *I Love*. Martha knew that she might be the only one who really loved that little girl and asked God to give her a true heart of love for all of her daughters. Meanwhile, James' family refused to come see the new baby girl as is customary. After much undeniable tension between the two wives, James moved the second woman into another house. As time went on, James came to visit Martha and the six girls less and less, spending the majority of his time with wife number two and his first son. Even Martha's friends were telling her to go and sleep with another man, hoping she could have a boy child with someone else, helping her *shame to go down* - to use a Liberian phrase. Martha would not entertain such a plan. She stayed true to her Christian beliefs though it was a lonely road.

All of this coincided with the inception of the English church in Blolequin. To promote the upcoming Sunday services, an evangelistic outreach was planned at the refugee school, where James was a history teacher. It is also where we had acquired permission to begin having our Sunday morning services. Using a projector powered by a generator and hanging a large white sheet, we showed the *Jesus* film on the side of one of the school buildings one Saturday night. James and some of his friends were bored that night, so decided to attend the film. While watching the *Jesus* film, the Holy Spirit wrapped the truths portrayed in the film around James' heart, and he accepted Jesus Christ as his Savior that very night. James was truly never the same.

He began attending church and even moved back in with Martha and his daughters. However, he would still visit the other woman and his son. During the baptismal class he was attending, he asked to talk with Jeff privately about his predicament. Perhaps he was on edge because Jeff had, during that particular class, talked about polygamy and the struggles it causes in marriage. He told Jeff, *"Pastor, I think I have a problem. I have a second woman, but she is the one that has a son for me. My first wife has so-so (means "only") girls."* It was not an easy situation, but Jeff tried to give James some biblical truths to help him make a decision. Sin always brings its traps that seem to have no escape. ***But God...being rich in mercy, because of His great love with which He loved us*** always provides a way, always through His mercy and grace. (Ephesians 2:4)

Two weeks later, James came to Jeff with a smile on his face and said: *Pastor, I did it. My family thinks I am a crazy man. I took the woman and my son back to her parents and am living with my wife Martha again. I will not go to that other woman again* (meaning that he would not sleep with her, but was advised to provide for the child), *but Satan is on my back.* Do you understand that feeling? We try to do the right thing and Satan crawls all over us. That is what scripture means when it says we should be joyous when we enter all kinds of trials and struggles. Through them, we are able to cultivate spiritual strength and endurance. James was learning that lesson. God began working in his life. A year or so later, he was nominated as one of our church's first deacons. He had grown strong through obedience and much studying of God's Word. His testimony was beautiful and powerful to those around him. He learned to continue to care for his son from the other woman without having to sleep with her. These were all unchartered territories for most Liberians. We did not pretend to have the right answers for those situations, but continued teaching God's Word while the Holy Spirit taught us what His Word says.

When Martha first told me the story, I was amazed by her stamina and fortitude of enduring an overwhelmingly difficult situation. She was constantly demeaned in the eyes of James' family and hers. However, she and James both continued to grow in the Lord and chose to replace the cultural expectations with the solid promises of God. I felt so compelled to pray with Martha for a son, not as proof of anything, but simply as another avenue for God to receive glory. Finding herself pregnant for the seventh time, she told me of her enclosing fears. Both families taunted them, but they tried to hold fast in their growing faith. James had learned a valuable lesson, and even the night before Martha delivered their seventh child, he gave a powerful testimony at the ordination and installation program for the Good News Baptist Church deacons. He proclaimed that God would never leave him nor forsake him and that God was good all the time. He wanted to be found faithful to walk in God's promises and in His strength.

As was planned, Martha sent for me when she began her labor. After cutting the cord, the midwife first showed me the baby as Martha whispered, "*Look at my baby, Sister AK (*short for Aunt Kim*), and tell me what God has done for me.*" I heard the longing, the excitement, the fear, and the anxiety, as well as the fatigue of labor. Seeing immediately the obvious markings of **a baby boy**, while holding Martha's precious son, I kneeled on the dirt floor, thanking God from the depths of an ecstatic heart. I was so overwhelmed at what God had done, I could hardly speak. Martha did not want to believe what she was hearing as I was praying. I had to literally hold the little fellow up to her and show her the baby's boy parts. Wiping tears first from her eyes, she then reached for her son, smiled faintly, and whispered, *God, I thank you. God, I thank you so much. God, you are so good all the time.* She fell asleep holding her precious little baby boy.

I could not wait any longer. Hopping into my car, I drove to our church building where James was working with some other men on a construction project. Smiling at him slyly, I asked him the same question Jeff had asked the night before during the deacon installation service, "*James, are you sure that God has blessed you? How do you know?*" He answered me in the same way. "*Yes, God has been so good to me. He has promised to never leave me nor forsake me. He is good all the time.*" With those beautiful words spoken from a heart of faith, I had the profound pleasure of telling James that he had a son. I'll never forget the look of awe that came on his face when he comprehended what I said. He just knelt down and thanked God right there.

James and Martha named their new son after my husband, Jeffrey. They were already praying that Jeffrey James would follow and serve God just as Pastor Jeff does. At the time of this writing, I do not know of the whereabouts of Jeffrey nor his sisters. For you see, less than five years after Jeffrey's birth, James and Martha were taken to heaven just a year apart in two separate incidents. That news was hard to hear, and even now, I cannot comprehend why such faithful servants of God would be taken as they were raising their children and being used in the Good News Baptist Church. Still, God's ways are higher and I will praise Him. And, as James said, *God is good all the time.*

Transplant of a Spiritual Kind

Because the civil war seemed to be cooling off, at least in the remote areas of Liberia, we wanted to see the Good News Baptist Church officially transplanted into Zwedru, Liberia. Though there would remain a remnant of believers in Blolequin, they would be called a *fellowship* of the Good News Baptist Church. Several members had already traveled back to Zwedru, working hard to put up a temporary building. In the following weeks, the church leadership sent a couple of deacons, their families, Bibles, a wooden pulpit, choir robes which had been donated, pews, Sunday School materials, and other items the church had purchased in its time in Ivory Coast. Thankfully, there was a smooth transition, and to this day, the Good News Baptist Church is active and alive in Grand Gedeh County, Liberia. I kept waiting for Apostle Paul to send a letter from Zwedru expounding the goodness of the Christians there - it was that exciting.

For much of the revival period in Blolequin, I was personally struggling with some serious pride issues, discontentment, and jealousy. Hard to share, but I really desire that you understand how real missionaries are and how we struggle with many of the same things as you. It was one of the spiritually ugly times of my life. After my few weeks in America for medical treatment, I came back to Blolequin resolved to enjoy our thriving ministry to the fullest. Honestly, I did. But when Satan could no longer discourage me from living in Ivory Coast by focusing on my physical ailments, he waylaid me with discontentment. Not just that, I chose to underscore certain living conditions surrounding me as a personal affront to my spiritual growth. *Some of the greatest spiritual lessons have been written in the darkest prisons.* Whether a prison of physical confinements or a prison of one's spirit, locked away in its misery, the days are long and life becomes skewed. Hope is a fleeting light. Bright then dull. I fell soundly for the lies which said "others" were the reason I was not happy. I became so obsessed with my plight, I started counting the times per day I was wronged, reiterating all the ways God had not provided for me as He had for someone else. I bottled a selfish desire to be recognized in our ministry into a destructive brew. I wanted the throne. The recognition. How deplorable was my soul!

Gradually, God got my attention in a Spirit-to-spirit collision about my nasty pride and unresolved issues with a co-worker. He desired to break me, mold me over again, in order to recreate me into a fitting vessel. Still, I whined. I complained, though, in my spirit, I knew my circumstances did not matter. It made no difference that He had not given me what I thought I wanted, things I coveted which someone else had; it made no difference that I felt taken advantage of and my miserable plight misunderstood; it made no difference that I felt my situation was more difficult than others.....no matter, no matter, no matter. All those were excuses to allow my flesh to run rampant. I had seen His marvelous workings in the Blolequin ministry, and I desperately wanted to submit to His calling, but that would involve asking forgiveness and confronting issues I had buried for more than two years. Issues that I had allowed to consume me, control me. I had no desire to look them in the eye and see how deformed my soul had become as my wretched flesh had reigned.

Before writing this, I prayed much about my extremely sensitive struggle and how much to share. Feeling it best to leave the most of the specifics in the deepest sea where God placed them when I confessed, I will only share part of it. Too many of the details affect others for whom I love and hold great respect. I also feared that if I started telling the story, *my flesh would rise up and want to tell it in its own way.* I desire to give no place to Satan in this matter. The bottom line is this: We all have choices. We decide whether we will live with godly joy and contentment. These choices should have nothing to do with the wrong or unfair things that come into our lives. If they do, we have been owned by sin itself.

In a loving, but penetrating way, God revealed my spirit's ugliness to me. He does know how to get our attention, believe me. During that time, I was having a problem with one of my upper molars. An infection near the root of the tooth caused my gum above the tooth to swell, becoming tender, ultimately festering. When I would press on the gum with my finger - to try and find some relief from the throbbing - pus would slowly ooze from the swelling. Please forgive my bluntness, but I am making a point. Promise. The book of Isaiah is my favorite Old Testament book. Deciding to study it in detail for a few weeks, the first four days I was confounded by chapter one. Especially three particular verses that kept repeating themselves deep within my spirit.

> *"Ah sinful nation, a people laden with iniquity, a seed of evildoers, children that are corrupters; they have forsaken the Lord, they have provoked the Holy One of Israel unto anger, they are gone backward. Why should ye be stricken any more? Ye will revolt more and more; the whole head is sick, and the whole heart faint. From the sole of the foot even unto the head there is no soundness in it; but wounds and bruises and putrefying sores: they have not been closed, neither bound up neither mollified with ointment."*
> (Isaiah 1:4-6)

Those putrefying sores reminded me of the one in my mouth, and using that visual image, God commanded that I look closely at verse six: *But wounds and bruises and putrefying sores: they have not been closed.* It was exactly what my soul looked like. Rottening. Full of pus. Disgusting. I buckled under the weight of the conviction. Extremely weary of indulging my consuming flesh, I could do nothing but look inward. What I saw was not pleasant, but I would not allow myself to look away until I saw myself as God saw me. Later, after pouring my heart out to my merciful Heavenly Father, I was ready to start making things right on the outside, too. As I went to find the person whom I had wronged, that person was on the way to find me. God's grace was working in both of us - it was so beautiful and freeing. Just as the Good News Baptist Church was being transplanted into another physical location so that it could be used to further Christ's kingdom work, I felt my spirit in the process of being transplanted with new life. No more rotten sores or bruises. I felt whole, completely in fellowship with my Heavenly Father.

That revealing story has this to say; **in spite** of my personal struggles and sin, God used me and allowed me to be a part of His kingdom work even during the two years that I was living directly again His will. I do not know why. I doubt I would have done the same, but then again, that's why I am not God. He is amazingly loving, infinitely wise, and overwhelmingly merciful. Recently I heard a preacher use these words: "God does not love a future version of us. He loves us in real time. We will never do enough, be enough to deserve His love. To measure up to His glory. But Jesus points to the cross and reminds us, *I know that, my child and have made provision for that. I paid it all. I am enough.*"

A Little Different This Time

The Grand Maison had been a great place to live and minister, so it was sad to leave it behind. I had grown more in my spiritual life and ministry than in a very long time. We had truly seen God move in ways I had only read in missionary biographies. Experiencing God *close up* does not leave room to wallow in sin just because we are too overwhelmed to deal with it. Living close to His holiness is always a purging experience. Be careful when you say you desire to be closer to God. The reality of that is not a benign thing. It will forcibly change you from the inside out.

In June of 1998, we readied ourselves to leave Ivory Coast. Packing up things to keep, selling things we do not need, and emptying a house full of memories, was not easy or fast. Finally, all that behind us, we said our goodbyes as the multi-faceted trip back to the States commenced. Tired but excited about our year in the States, we boarded the plane; each with his own memories of the years past. The long plane trip was always a time to slow down, ponder, remember, and pray. At one point, Jeff and I were exhilarated to realize that those past three years in Blolequin was only the second *normal* time in our African missionary career where we had been able to stay in one place. As we had done in Tappita, Liberia, in our first term, we had been able to work, teach, and see a particular ministry come to fruition. It was indeed a venture we wished to repeat. I also pondered how the present departure from Ivory Coast was much different than the one in 1992, when I declared to Jeff my hatred for the African people and my vow to never return. Not even knowing who that person was, I never wanted to invite her back on a plane or in my life.

Bubba our cat was with us on the flight, which was both miraculous and humorous. Jeff had tried to hold up under the torrential pleading to bring Bubba to the States, but he could not. He was sorely outnumbered. The four females whom he loved dearly, dragooned the resolve right out of him. With the decision made that we would lug a simple one-dollar African house cat to the states, we then had to get the proper immunizations and paperwork for said cat. That chore was placed soundly on me by my dear husband and for good reason. I could not imagine leaving that beautiful cat whom we had all learned to love, so I had been right in the middle of the pleading. I admit it.

Hailing a taxi a couple of days before our departure, I thrust a howling Bubba in the back seat with me and whisked off to a vet. The decision to campaign for Bubba to travel to the states took on a cruel form as the poor creature endured injections and extensive prodding before we were given the official *declaration of good health* papers required by American customs. The vet also gave me a couple of tranquilizers to give Bubba during the trip if needed. Both the cat and I were exhausted by the time we returned to the guest house. I was tempted to take one of those tranquilizers myself by the end of that day.

Departure day arrived and we headed to the airport, checking in early enough so we would hopefully be able to take the cat into the cabin with us. Most airlines only allow a limited number of small animals to travel in the cabin during a flight. The rest must travel in an oxygenated area in the belly of the plane. I popped *half* a tranquilizer into the agitated cat's mouth to save all of our sanity. He was clearly disturbed about being kidnapped from his motherland, chortling loudly, letting everyone know that none of this was his idea. After we were in the air for a couple of hours, and when everyone was sleeping, I bent down to check on the cat in his cage. Lying on his side in a rather odd position, I noticed his tongue was hanging out, his eyes rolled back, and his chest barely moving. I quickly punched Jeff, waking him out of his sleep, and said with a loud whisper, "*The cat! Look at the cat! I think he's dying! What are we going to do? Look at him!*" Jeff reluctantly - yes, very slowly and reluctantly, not telling me what he was thinking - bent down and looked into the cat's cage. His eyes were huge as he sat up in his seat and said, "*What are we going to do with a dead cat on an airplane?? How will we dispose of his body?*" This reaction told me exactly what he was thinking and hoping. I knew he would be NO help with this brewing crises, so I spent the next couple of hours shaking the cat, talking to him, and forcing him to open his eyes much like you would do with someone who had suffered a concussion.

Thankfully, he did survive the trip, and we were able to get him into the country without having to put him through the costly quarantine process. Jeff put his foot down on that issue, saying that we would not be spending money on paying quarantine fees for a cat from Africa. So, we all prayed for God to get Bubba through customs, and He did. It was again an amazing time of growing our faith in seeing what God could do even for the smallest child. So, Bubba became nationalized into the American way of life and learned to eat Fancy Feast instead of a homemade fish and rice concoction. When I took him to the American vet a few weeks later, I asked the vet to test the strength of the tranquilizers I was given in Ivory Coast. He called a couple of weeks later to tell me the drug was strong enough for a 50 - 60 pound dog. No wonder he had that reaction on the plane. And to think, the vet in Ivory Coast had recommended given him the entire pill.

Looking ahead to the year of furlough, we wondered how it would turn out. As far as our girls, our oldest daughter Michelle would have the biggest transitional year since she would be entering high school that fall. Stefanie and Lauren were still both young enough to see life as an adventure. I say it again, *bless missionary kids and the resilience they most often portray living where they are taken, experiencing things they may not ever have chosen.* And for the parents and children in American churches that open their arms and hearts to those MKs when they return stateside. Thankfully, all three girls had those kind of friends when they arrived in Charlotte.

Before leaving Blolequin, our field administrator, Evan Gough, visited the different Baptist Mid-Mission ministries in Ivory Coast. Because those of us who were originally assigned to Liberia as missionaries had been given permission to minister temporarily in Ivory Coast, Mr. Gough wanted to determine the feasibility of continuing that since Liberia was not an option yet. It was suggested that Liberian missionaries, who desired to continue working in Ivory Coast, consider French language training before returning. For years, Jeff and I discussed our desire of working with John and Merri Holmes in a BMM ministry in Bouake, Ivory Coast. For various reasons, citizens from English speaking West African countries such as Liberia, Ghana, and Nigeria, had settled in the Bouake region, located more on the northeastern side of Ivory Coast. While John and Merri were busy with a French-speaking church ministry, they felt it would be beneficial to also add an English fellowship. That sounded just right for us.

CHAPTER FOURTEEN

If we obey God, He will look after those who have been pressed into the consequences of our obedience. —Oswald Chambers

Parlez-Vous Francais?

As we settled back into America for our one year furlough, we visited supporting churches and enjoyed time with family. We also needed to look more seriously into French language training if we wanted to officially move our missionary citizenship to Ivory Coast. When trying to decide where to attend language school, we felt Word of Life in Lennoxville, Quebec, would be the best for our family. Feeling it would be easier for Jeff and me to immerse ourselves into learning French if we were not worrying about our daughter's stumbling their way through a school that only spoke French, we looked into English schools up there. After talking in detail with our girls and weighing what we felt was best for our family, putting them in English schools there in Lennoxville was what we decided.

In the summer of 1999, we bought a used conversion van, installed a TV and VCR, piled in blankets and pillows and a litter box for the cat, and headed north; a long, twenty hour trip north. Michelle had recently acquired her learner's permit and saw no reason why she should not be able to drive the big van on the interstate for a bit. After a grueling twenty minutes or so, weaving in and out of her lane, her daddy could take it no longer. She was relinquished to the backseat with her sisters. Another transition. More uncertainty. Going into unfamiliar territory again. But our family was made for adventure, so no matter how sad we might have been at leaving family and friends, there was also anticipation and excitement, at least for the first six or seven hours. The next thirteen hours were...well, long.

It was an exemplary year in some ways, though I initially struggled with the uncertainties of the move. It wouldn't be normal if I didn't contend with God's calling in some way, right? Taking our three girls to another country so soon and enrolling them in unfamiliar schools - was that asking too much of them? As a mother, it seemed I always worried over my children, wondering how our following God's calling would truly affect them. Michelle was a sophomore in high school, Stefanie in seventh grade, and Lauren going into fourth grade. God proved again that He is faithful to provide and enable those He has called. Our daughters were given to us in the full wisdom of God's sovereign purpose for our lives. Our children, whom are given by God, are equipped to thrive where He leads us as parents.

Then there was the language school schedule. How would it all work? I, always a night person had four hours of morning classes and Jeff, always a morning person had four hours of afternoon classes. That was our first challenge. We both had required hours of labs and studying plus the primary responsibility of being parents to three girls who were swimming in their own uncharted seas. Life went on, meals were cooked, homework was completed (for all five of us), rooms stayed relatively cleaned, clothes were washed, and we worked at find time for much needed sleep. Off we went on this new adventure. All five of us in school. The girls thought that was crazy. We knew it was.

Having always lived in the southern United States or the tropics of West Africa and Jamaica, the cooler days of Canada, even in August, were refreshing. Living on the second and third floor of an old farm house located in the middle of the Word of Life campus, we had a panoramic view of the rest of the campus and beyond. Besides very tired blue carpet and furniture from the 70's, our living area was fairly comfortable. The master bedroom was on the same floor as the living and kitchen area. On the third floor, the girls shared a bathroom. In the larger bedroom, which Lauren would need because she had the bigger toys or so the older sisters reasoned, were also the washer and dryer. Poor third girl of the family. Seemed she always was delegated to the less favorable rooms. If one of her sisters insisted on washing clothes while she was trying to sleep, we would often find her coming down the stairs and crawling in our bed. As the weather got cooler, the house remained cozy and warm because it was heated by a simple but yet impressive system of radiators filled with hot water. So much for my concern that we would all die in our sleep while the temperature dropped below freezing outside.

Northern White

On the morning of October 4, 1999, I looked out the classroom window and saw white stuff falling from the sky. Perplexed, I leaned closer to the window pane to comprehend what I was seeing. *Snow*. But that had to be impossible, I reasoned in my head. The professor chuckled at the amazement of the southern students to see snow falling in October. He said it was quite common for snow to fall at that time of year and would continue through at least the middle of April. I had never heard of such. Walking the short distance home at lunchtime, I had the ominous feeling we were all going to die, be buried alive in the snow in the Canadian winter. Why was I the only one who seemed concerned with snow in October?

I remember when the first heavy snow fell early one morning as the girls got ready for school. My heart pounded at the dread of putting them on a school bus and sending them off. *Surely* classes would be cancelled because of deteriorating weather conditions. In the South, school was often canceled just because of a forecast of snow. If that would have been the case, there would have been no school for four months. The bus arrived on schedule, but the very southern momma went to have a talk with Mr. Bus Driver. Certainly he must have been amused by my concerns for his driving in the *blizzard. Blizzard?* he said, as he look at the snow falling. He assured me in the kindest way that he had been driving a school bus for a very long time and had never lost a student or a bus in the *blizzards.* Was that a chuckle I heard under his breath as he smoothly closed the bus door, leaving me blinking snowflakes out of my eyes? I shuffled my way back into the warm house, praying for God to keep them safe. I was so trying to be brave, but my imagination was, again, on overdrive. Out of the entire winter, only one day did the high school cancel classes. Not because of snow, but because of frozen pipes in the bathrooms. Baffling how the people of the North live. I was impressed.

In the heart of the Canadian winter, we experienced subzero temperatures for the very first time. I must admit I became obsessed at watching the slightly rising and mostly falling of our thermometer right outside our living room window. For most of January and February, the temperatures remained steady at -10 during the day and plunged to below -40 at night. One night we were at a school event in another building on campus when we were told to be very careful as we returned to our homes. The thermometer had dipped to minus 50 degrees. We were instructed on how to cover even our faces because of the possibility of any exposed body part becoming frostbit. Returning home that night was the quickest I had ever moved in the snow. I was petrified of turning into a literal snowman. Surprisingly, after a few weeks, it seemed our bodies grew accustomed to the cold. The snow really was beautiful, but there was just so much of it.

The girls had mixed experiences that year as they attended public schools for the very first time. Lauren's fourth grade class took a field trip to a ski resort one day during school. It was her first time skiing. She loved her teacher and was even picking up some French during a class that she took in the afternoons. Riding the bus was a hard experience because she was bullied by some of the older kids, and unfortunately, picked up some unsavory words during that year - needing to be reprogrammed in what was acceptable to say and what was not. Stefanie did her seventh grade there and had a great experience in the junior-senior high school, making many new friends and learning even to enjoy a Quebecois delicacy, Poutain - French fries smothered in a brown gravy. Michelle braved her sophomore year despite mean students who made fun of her and was not friendly. We only found out of her struggles years later, because she never complained. One of her greatest accomplishments during that time was taking karate classes. Only the African cat, Bubba, did not enjoy the arctic environment. Menacingly, the girls would sometimes throw the poor feline on the second floor porch which was covered with two or more feet of snow. Like a bunny rabbit,

Bubba would hop his way through the snow, back into the house, licking his fur for hours. I imagined him pining away for the warm sun of his homeland.

We enjoyed meeting several families at the local French-speaking church we attended that year. Our girls felt comfortable to try out their French vocabulary with the families at the church, though we realized that none of us were really hearing good Bible teaching that year. All of us struggled to understand the pastor's French, and while he was a great preacher, no doubt; it sounded like Greek to us. Our family devotions became paramount to all our spiritual growth and were great family times of learning more about each other. There was one family who spoke well both French and English. Becoming fast friends, they invited us often to their farm. Those trips to the Rouilliard's house remain a highlight of our entire year in Quebec. Seeing how cows were milked with machines and exploring the vast acres of land, our girls thrived there. For the first time in any of our lives, we drank milk given to us by that family - straight from the cow. Yellow and thick, it was not at first extremely appealing, but it did grow on us.

Another highlight of our Canada adventure was working on the Rouilliard's maple farm in March. As the temperature rose to slightly above freezing, buckets were ready to catch the sticky syrup soon to run from the inners of the maple trees. The kids ran from tree to tree, hauling buckets into a large wooden shed complete with syrup-making equipment. The process was fascinating. In celebration of the running of the syrup, we were allowed to take some outside, drop syrup on fresh, clean snow, and eating it. Simply marvelous.

In the deepest part of the Canadian winter, we attended the famous Ice Festival in Quebec City. I really wanted to experience the festival, but was not keen on the idea of spending hours exposed to the brutal cold. Michelle, our sixteen year old, thought herself way too cool to dress properly. Insulted that the bulky winter clothes would make her look *fat*, she chose to wear blue jeans. Regular blue jeans that when wet, made her legs feel they were almost falling off from the coldness. Nothing needed to be said about her vanity. She learned her lesson in the most brutal way. The rest of us bundled up with every piece of winter paraphernalia we had, and hopped into our van for our adventure. The ice sculptures were fascinating and the ice tents, where all the food was served, was kept warm by heaters. We were delighted to enjoy the 32 degree heat inside those tents. What a different world it all was. So thankful to get inside a warm van after a day at the festival, there was no one more thankful than our Michelle. Warm. Finally.

Overall, the year was amazing and interesting. We learned so much, made many new friends and stayed pretty tight as a family in spite of the hectic schedules. By the end of July, 2000, having finished a full year of language training, we packed up the conversion van along with the moving truck we were sharing with a couple of other families, and headed South. Equipped with more French than when we first arrived, though nowhere near proficient, we looked forward to a brand new ministry in the second largest city in Ivory Coast, Bouake. Before that could happen, Jeff would be taking a survey trip to Bouake with John Holmes, looking for a house suitable for our family. There was much buying, packing, and planning ahead of us. Also looming ahead as shadowy phantoms were two of the biggest tests I would ever endure. But I did not know. God is so merciful not to allow us to see the future. The following twelve months would try my soul like nothing in the past ever had.

The Growing Pains of Parenthood

If the year spent in Canada had been challenging but yet satisfying, the next year was quite the opposite. Michelle started her junior year in high school, flapping her wings, as most teenagers will do. Stefanie was an eighth grader, also believing that she was old enough to take charge of her own life. Why we as parents get so freaked out about those inklings of independence that surface, I don't know. It is quite the natural reaction as children get older. Soon they will leave the nest, so why not get some practice in? Emphatic, vigorous, and often time extremely messy, these emotional confrontations between parents and teenage children can be exhausting.

Don't get me wrong. I am not condoning the disregard of parental authority. I do believe, however, that we as parents could do a better job at preparing our children for the real world where *flapping* those wings will be crucial. If we snip the wings or quell every flap, they never grow the confidence and knowledge on how to do life when they finally are on their own. Instead, out of our own fears or need for control, we tie their wings until they are eighteen. At the portal of young adulthood, we untie their wings, expecting them to know how to "fly" well. Finding a balance takes work on both sides, but it also takes concentration and a purposeful living in the moment with our teenagers - even when that is not pleasant. From Christmas 2000 until the end of July 2001, it pains me to say I did not do a very good job with either of our two teenage daughters. I had no margins. No guides to alert me to the dangers. Life started closing in, definitely skewing my **Godview** - again. I will take responsibility for those few months because I chose - again - to live in fear and not in obedience.

My brother Eddie was perceptively very ill and was needing to have another surgery. Watching my brother's health decline rapidly, I felt sure he would not live very much longer, and the ramifications seemed intolerable. At the same time, seeing the rebellion rising up in our two oldest daughters, I did not feel I had the energy to deal with them, so I didn't. Without realizing it, I ceased to function except on a minimal level. I had been in that debilitating place before, so I should have remembered to put safeguards in place. I did not.

For the first time in our years of ministry, Jeff was forced to write a prayer letter because I felt that I could not. Now, Jeff has many talents, many strengths, but writing is not one of them. Out of necessity, he wrote to the best of his ability. He asked me to proofread it before sending it, but for some reason, that did not get done. A couple of weeks later, we received an anonymous letter in the mail from someone stating that our prayer letter was a *shame and disgrace*. The person had mailed back a copy of the prayer letter, marked and bleeding with derogatory commentaries. Having no idea what we were going through personally, a *well-meaning* but thoughtless Christian brother or sister crushed our spirits…cutting deeply. Why this person felt they needed to do something of that sort, we'll never know. I've sent prayer letters before with minor mistakes, but never had anyone demeaned us quite like that. Please take care not to judge missionaries any harder than you judge yourselves. You just never know the boggy path they are walking down.

A Well-Laid Plan

In January of 2001, it was discovered my brother desperately needed quadruple heart bypass surgery. Because of many years of dialysis and strong medicines, his arteries were as fragile as procelain. When the surgery was finally attempted, only one bypass could be completed. Any more was simply too risky. Beyond that complication, he had been living with a fourteen centimeter aortic aneurysm. Needless to say, Eddie's health experiences have been recorded in the annals of medical phenomenas. Not too many people walk around with an aneurysm of that size, positioned so closely to the heart. He was indeed a *walking time bomb*.

Sometime in February, after Eddie had the bypass surgery and was recovering, Michelle came to us with her well-laid plan for her senior year. She did not want to go back to Africa to do her senior year at a school she had never attended. The International Christian Academy (ICA) run by a mixture of mission agencies was located in the city of Bouake which was where we planned to minister. Jeff and I personally had never felt we should send our children away for their high school education while we did ministry in a different place. ICA seemed to be an answer to our prayers. Our high school daughters could attend classes there while I home schooled Lauren for another year or so. The best of both worlds.

Michelle, evidently, had been thinking about the uncertainties of changing schools again. She was also becoming well immersed back into American culture, along with having a boyfriend which, no doubt, weighed heavily into her plan. I understood her struggles of not wanting to attend another school. When we had returned from Blolequin, she started ninth grade in Charlotte, did tenth grade in Canada, and eleventh grade back in Charlotte. Now we were asking her to transfer to a third school in a matter of four years. Little did she know that I had already been bargaining with God about all that upheaval in her life. While listening to her very grown up plans, I lamented the loss of my oldest daughter, who in the past years, had lived valiantly in some very difficult places in West Africa. Where had she gone? Who was this independent creature who wanted to push away from us? My heart struggled to beat. It hurt so much to realize the pain she was feeling, the fears she was measuring in her young heart.

Those all-consuming trepidations for my children rose back up in me. When they were younger, the fear of going back to Africa manifested itself as deep concerns for their health and safety. Now, the fear of returning again to Africa portrayed itself as caring for emotional adjustment. I realize what I am saying here and how I am saying it will most likely not be embraced by all who read this book. When it comes to our children, some parents like me, lose their heads. Honestly, where in Scripture does it say we should completely obey God - *oh, except concerning our children*? **Our children are not ours**. They are His. If we trust Him, we must trust Him with everything. God gives us discernment to choose what is best for our family at different phases of life. Every year will not hold the same challenges. That changes with time. If God has placed a child in our home and God wants to move us to another place and then another and then another, rest assured the emotional adjustment of that child is of utmost importance to God. *He is on it.* Living out our trust and faith in God through these situation are paramount to our children being able to see God work in the lives of their parents.

Having it all planned in her mind, Michelle told us she wanted to live with her grandparents in Charlotte and finish her senior year. We could go back to Africa to do what we felt God had called us to do. Everyone would be happy, right? Her plan was simple and fulfilling...for her. If you ask Michelle today, she would tell you that she was as spiritually far from God as she has ever been. That decision was not as pious and caring as it sounded. It was her way of getting what she wanted. Her flesh was definitely in charge. I had seen the same thing in myself many times.

Again, Jeff's reaction to this and my own were completely different. Seeing this as an opportunity to divert, to postpone, to not have to go back to a new ministry, a new town, a new home and not to have to face leaving my dying brother and my hurting parents, I sided with Michelle. My stance floored Jeff. *Where had all that come from?* He realized at that point he was standing alone on what he believed God wanted for our future ministry. I was too locked inside my own fears and fatigue to acknowledge his position. Again, for the umpteenth time, I bucked against his leading, his desire to follow God's purpose for us as a couple, as a family. Why? Why? Why? Would I never learn? It is difficult to even share this story with you because of my shame, my pride. My intent to fulfill Kim's will. No wonder I had a daughter bent on doing her own bidding. The example she had in front of her was doing no less.

The year before, I had been bent on heading back to Ivory Coast and starting a new ministry in Bouake with the Holmes family. Now, in light of my brother's precarious health and the rebellion of our daughters, I buckled. Forgetting many of the things that God had taught me about myself in that past years, I simply closed my mind to His calling. When I cried to my friends about my dilemma, they sympathized with me. Though it was nice to have the compassion of people around me, it was also the worse thing for my spiritual growth. Often when friends and family see missionaries' prevailing conditions and hardships, it may seem natural to encourage us to look somewhere else. *Stay home. Go somewhere else. You've done enough.* We hear, "*Do something different. For the sake of your health. For the sake of your family.*" Any of that advice may be the right thing depending on the missionary family. But, sometimes the hardest thing to do may be exactly right.

Want to truly make a difference in the life of a faltering missionary? Help us pray for God's will, and without giving us a way out, direct us to seek God. Walk with us. Listen to us. Encourage us. Without appeasing. Without commentary, and often, without understanding. Through the years, we have had a handful of dear friends who have coveted to pray with us about some very hard things. Missionaries desperately need churches and people to come alongside and *bear* our burdens with us instead of assuming we should just lay down the heavy burden and pick up a lighter ones. Each calling is individual. We should never assume to know how the calling of another should look.

CHAPTER FIFTEEN

You gain strength, courage, and confidence by every experience
in which you really stop to look fear in the face. You are able to say,
'I have lived through this horror. I can take the next thing that comes along.'
—Eleanor Roosevelt

Even For One of These

I did not know until much later that Jeff had actually written a letter of resignation to Baptist Mid-Missions, and that it was tucked away in his desk drawer. He was not willing that our family should be split up in order to do ministry. As he waited for God to speak, he knew nothing else to do. Things seemed to be falling apart on all sides. Little Lauren was the only one who carried the excitement of returning to Africa with her dad. Stefanie was in her own little world with a boyfriend, sports, and her all-consuming social life. If you have gone through the junior high years with your children already, you know what I am talking about. Michelle continued in her plans to remain in the States. My brother was deteriorating rapidly and was considering having a risky surgery to take care of the aneurysm. All this was weighing on me physically, mentally, emotionally, and most definitely, spiritually. I knew deep down we were supposed to return to Africa, but I could not seem to put myself into the planning.

Back in 1992 when I told Jeff that I could absolutely not return to Africa, I had meant it. God had a different plan for us at that point in our life. This time, however, was a choice of my will. I did not want to go back because there were too many mountains in the way, and I simply could not see how I could move them. I was choosing not to go back simply because it looked too hard. Jeff, having learned from the last time, sought advice and counsel from our pastor. Not sharing too deeply about my own issues, we concentrated more on Michelle's reaction to our future plans. The advice he gave us was rather unconventional, but we felt completely at peace with following it. Michelle was seventeen and wanted desperately to make decisions for herself. What she did not understand was that our decisions never, ever affect only us. There are always others involved. It was suggested we ask Michelle to pray for one week before making the ultimate decision of whether she could return to Africa. It seemed the right thing to do. Somehow she needed to know her decision would affect the entire family. Was she that intent on having her way?

We went home and called a meeting with her. Jeff asked her to listen one more time as he expounded the reasons why he felt God calling our family back to Africa. He shared his heart beautifully. Though he might have thought it was entirely for Michelle, it touched me deeply just listening to him. He cried, he talked, he dreamed, he called names of African Christians he would like another chance to teach, he painted the most exquisite picture of ministry I had ever heard. Then he paused and looked at Michelle. *"Sweetie, after saying all that, I want you to know that I love you. You are more important to me than anything. So I want to ask you to do something. For one week, please pray harder than you have ever prayed. Turn your heart completely to God. Seek confidence in your heart that this decision you are wanting to make to stay in the States is from Him. That it is right. And, after a week, if you can come back and tell us that you believe it is the right thing for you, then we will all stay."*

Shocked by this, Michelle started crying and so did I. Jeff continued, *"If you really believe you cannot go back to Africa, then we will stay here and see what God has for us. God gave you to us seventeen years ago and then gave us your sisters. We are not going to break up this family. Not yet. Not like this. There will be a time when you will go out on your own and make your choices. But this is not that time. But, Michelle, if you heard my heart and if you can trust that I am trying to follow God, and return with us with a willing spirit, then we will all go back to Africa."*

We've all heard of Custard's last stand. This was Jeff's and it was powerful. It spoke to me in a way that I did not expect. It convicted me of my unwillingness, my disobedience, and my lack of submission to my husband, though it was several days before I could voice what I was feeling to him. Things in my life still seemed uncertain and crazed, but my heart began to open little by little. I looked my fears straight in the face and cringed from the bigness of them. There is absolutely no strength in giving in to fears. They are impotent in the reality of our God's greatness. This became my mantra. *God is bigger...*

Michelle was unusually quiet and docile for the entire week, so there was no guessing what she was thinking about this heavy thing laid on her. After the week passed, we sat back down to listen to her decision. She had been crying, I could tell, and she had a hard time looking at us, but this is what she said with her sweet, trembling voice, "*I don't want to go back to Africa. I have made a life here and I enjoy my friends so much. I know what you are doing is important though, and that I am part of this family. I really am thankful for you both and I am thankful to be chosen to be in this family. So, I choose to go back with you if it means that even one African will not burn in hell. I could not live with that.*" Our beautiful, strong-willed firstborn daughter had let God have His way. It took my breath away! Could I do any less? I don't know if she even knows what part she played in this discouraged, tired mother's heart and in my own decision to follow God with complete abandonment. For the sake of one African being eternally saved by God's redemptive power - that was the best reason for setting aside self and leaning into God through the raging storms.

Ministry Bits and Pieces

By the end of February 2001, the plans for our family to return to Ivory Coast had accelerated. Jeff took a survey trip to Bouake with our new co-worker, John Holmes, finding two choices of housing for our family. Upon Jeff's return to the States, we started packing the things we needed to take with us. As summer approached, we scheduled physicals for the whole family and bought quite a bit of packing tape. To even more encourage our hearts, Michelle decided to take a trip during that summer with Word of Life to the Philippines and Japan. God used that trip to refocus her heart and energies into others instead of herself.

Though she had made her choice to return to West Africa with us, we knew she was still struggling with the reality of it. The trip to Japan and Asia was exactly what she needed that summer to get her mind off herself.

Our supporting churches rallied and provided funds or supplies that we needed for the ministry in Bouake. There is nothing more encouraging than a church that stands with their missionaries. We were so blessed with more than a dozen like that. Through the numerous field changes since the inception of our missionary career in 1985, almost all of our churches stuck with us, prayed for us, and encouraged us as God called us to yet another place of service. It is heartening to see churches who have become more pliable and understanding about the fast changing face of global missions instead of staying rooted in 1980's ways of doing missions. Those days are long gone. *The world is truly at our doorsteps.*

The Steps Ordered By God

Thankful that God is not bound by time, He does understand that we are. Precise, exact, perfect - that is His timing in our lives. During the first week of a very busy July, my brother called, telling me he had decided to have surgery to repair the aneurysm that was growing beyond a whopping fourteen centimeters. His doctors, when asked by Eddie how death would most likely come if the aneurysm ruptured, described a horrible thing. That is not the way Eddie wanted to go nor did he want his family to watch him go that way. So he chose to take the risk and have the surgery. In his place, I would have certainly done the same thing. That he cared enough to do it **before** we left for Africa, however, spoke volumes. I was both glad he had considered me, but yet also concerned.

"*Any particular reason why you are choosing to have this surgery before I go back to Africa*?" I candidly asked him on the phone. "*Yea, well, you would worry too much if you were over there, and besides, I think you need to be here for mama and daddy,*" he said in a quiet voice. Pricked to my very core, I did not elaborate on his answers, but I knew exactly what he was saying. He thought he was going to die. The weekend before his Monday morning surgery, our family of five went down to stay with my parents. Jeff was already lined up to preach at my home church that weekend, but he and the girls would need to return back to Charlotte on Sunday night. Monday morning they all had to be at the doctor's office for mandatory physicals. I had rescheduled my physical when I realized it was on the same day as Eddie's surgery. I was going to be in that hospital waiting room ...no matter what was to come.

The Saturday morning before Eddie's surgery, I woke up with an urgency to plan a special day for Eddie's family, my family, and our parents. I called and told him what I was thinking. He affirmed he had been thinking the same thing. In the early afternoon, we all climbed in two cars and headed to Southport for an excursion. Eddie and Judy rode in the car with us. It was a magical time that I would never trade. We ate at his favorite seafood restaurant on the water and fed the sea gulls. The positioning of the aneurysm hampered his breathing and his blood flow, so he could not move as fast as he had in the past. We walked slowly, taking our time. Praying the moment could be frozen in time. Michelle had brought her camera and the pictures from that day are some of my most prized. We topped off the afternoon by getting ice cream at a small dairy bar in Oak Island. Later that night, when I laid my head on the pillow, I could not stop thanking God for giving me the desire to plan that day with Eddie and the family. *Carpe Diem* is not just a phrase to say in a passionate moment. There are those moments, those times, which are meant to be grabbed fiercely by the horns and lived out. Just do it.

Eddie had to check into the hospital by Sunday night in preparation for his surgery the next morning. I went with with my mom to see him later that evening. While we visited, his legs were itchy as they often did, he looked pale and older than his years, and his eyes were just tired. When mom went out of the room to get some lotion for his legs, I leaned forward, looking deep into his eyes. With arched eyebrows and moist eyes, I asked, "*Where are you going tomorrow, huh?*" He smiled weakly, looked at the wall past me and said, "*Well, there is a big part of me that wants to come back here and be with my family, but I'm pretty sure I'm going to see Jesus. That will be good, too. It will be all right, my sister.*" He awkwardly patted my hands and tried to smile at me. To break the waves of fear heading towards me, I jokingly told him he **could not** leave me to raise our mommy and daddy alone! We both laughed and then I kissed his cheek lingeringly. It would be the last time I would ever do that.

As on the morning of any surgery, I never went back to the prepping room to see him since I felt there was nothing that could supersede the time we had shared the night before. Eddie's family lined the walls near the surgical suites as an aide pushed the gurney towards the surgery door. Asking the aide to stop for a moment, he lifted his head and looked pointedly at all of us standing there, lingering on his wife, Judy. Then he smiled peacefully and lay his head back down. *He's really going to heaven today. He knows it. I know it. Who else here knows it but would dare not say it?* My heart was pounding with the reality of it. I willed away the thoughts as just a result of my ever active imagination. But this time...

Sitting in a hospital waiting room was not at all unfamiliar to our family, but we never learned to like it. Eddie had his first surgery in that same hospital when he was thirteen, more than twenty-seven years before. We had spent a lifetime sitting in waiting rooms over the years. That day, like most of the times, at least a dozen friends sat with us. Never underestimate the simple act of sitting quietly with someone and waiting. Unless you have experienced it, you cannot imagine how loudly it speaks. Don't be afraid to go because you don't know what to say. If that is your concerned, you have missed the point. *Being* is most always better than *saying*. Read the book of Job, if you do not believe it.

The first time the nurse came to give us an update on the progress of the aneurysm surgery, there was the slightest hint that things were not going well. With the second report, she told us, though the doctor had repaired the aortic aneurysm successfully, Eddie's heart seemed unable to beat on its own. She assured us, as she is trained to do, that the medical staff was doing everything they could. Still, Eddie's wife, Judy, wanted us all to go with her into the chapel to pray. As part of His marvelous grace, the very morning of my brother's surgery, God sent me two dear missionary friends whom we had known during our Jamaican ministry. They had heard about Eddie's surgery and happened to be in town visiting a grandmother, feeling led to come to the hospital to be with me. David and Anita Fenley ministered to me in ways I could never tell them. When I first saw them earlier that morning, it was another affirmation to my soul of what was going to take place that day. My brother was going to heaven. He was really going to leave us. God's grace kept me calm. Held me still in the moment. Focused. His grace never failed me.

After we all had settled in the small hospital chapel, different friends praying for the doctors, for Eddie, for his heart to beat on its own. I felt an oasis of calm, fleeting but memorable. As I prayed quietly in my own heart, I sensed my focus changing. I began to pray for us, the family, for strength for the following days as my mind's eye willed me to see Eddie's spirit heading towards heaven. Healed. Completely whole. It is not that I saw his spirit ascending, but the portrayal in my mind was helpful for what my heart knew we would soon need to accept.

Click. I heard the click of the chapel door opening and without looking up, I knew. It was time. My breathing accelerated and my eyes became moist. The same nurse entered quietly, but this time, there was no update - only a summons to Eddie's immediate family to meet with the doctor in the *consultation room*. I sat still as the cold, overwhelming wave of death toppled me. All those years of worrying about losing my brother while I was on the mission field had not come to fruition. God had seen to that. During my heart-wrenching thoughts, a dear friend of our family kneeled in front of me, took my hands, and tenderly prompted me to stand up and go to that dreaded room. "*Your mom and dad need you. Go to them and be strong,*" she lovingly said as she hugged me. With eyes filled with pain and disbelief, I shrugged out of the cloak of God's grace and exclaimed, "*How can I? How can I ever get on that plane in three weeks and leave them? How can I? I cannot!*" Again, I had gone before God and His promised grace.

Strength Made Perfect

The next few days were a blur as we dealt with the loss of a son, brother, father, grandfather, husband, uncle, and friend. In the good moments, when we could remember how riddled his body had been with disease and fatigue, we rejoiced in where we knew he had gone. The song, *If You Could See Me Now,* played a soothing and integral part of the funeral service, reminding us of heaven, wholeness, and the hope of seeing him again. Still it was those raw moments when waves of grief threatened to sling me to the bottom of the cold ocean and pin me under, telling me that things would never be the same. They never are after the loss of a loved one.

In spite of the reality that death brings, one thing always remains the same: ***Jesus Christ, the same yesterday, today, and forever.*** I held on to that as the only buoyant truth in my life. I spoke during his funeral, talking of his life, helping us all to process what had happened. It all became clear: *Eddie and God had planned this whole thing.* It was beautiful how God had honored Eddie's prayers to die peacefully for the sake of the family he loved so much, and while I was still in America and could be with my parents.

A few days after the funeral, I had to return to Charlotte, to the reality that in two very short weeks, I would have to do what I had always dreaded. What I always said would be the one thing God should not require of me: to leave my parents alone in the States with no child to nurture them, love them, or be with them. *And now this.* With not even a month in between burying one child and saying goodbye to their other child for at least three years, I began to fear what this would do to them. *Didn't I know better by then?* We usually know better, but living out our faith sometimes seems to require more energy than just giving in to the fears. That, I know, is a lie from the Deceiver, but it is one which seems very convincing at times. I reeled under the pain and grief.

Michelle, though resolved to return with us to Africa, started to cling more tightly to her boyfriend and so had Stefanie to hers. Our home was tense, quiet, dreary as we moved toward the departure day. I could not imagine how God or Jeff could dare ask me to get on that plane. Some nights, I trembled at the hold those fears had on me. Jeff prayed over me night after night, and when I asked him *how* could I do this hard thing, he told me, through his own grief and tears, to just hold on and follow him. He knew that he was following God, so I could confidently follow him - no matter how

I might feel. I wanted to run and fight, but I kept trying to conjure up the burden God had given us to return to West Africa. Though I was numb and could not really revel in the reality that God had a plan for us in Ivory Coast, I chose to just accept it in my head. I would try to follow and be obedient. I would try to allow Truth to reign. That was all God or Jeff required of me at this point. It was all I had to give.

My journal of August 14, 2001, reads: *The day I thought I could never get through has passed and God was gracious. I think I found out something: the dreading, the worrying about something is most of the time harder than the actual event. God promises His grace will be sufficient, but it comes at the point of need. The timing of all of this seems surreal, but I am learning that God loves me as well as my parents. He knows the exact needs of their hearts and how He will meet them. Maybe I need to get out of the way so that God can work something beautiful in and through them.*

Saying goodbye at the airport was poignant and laborious, but my parents were classically strong. I remember trying to apologize for leaving them, but they held me tightly and said I should never apologize for following God in my life. They affirmed to me that it was one of their greatest joys watching me follow God and my husband in the ministry. They vowed that they would be fine. Thankful for my dear friends, Glenn and Debbie Benfield, whom I had asked to be there for my parents if they need anything. Not having any other blood sibling, I was grateful for the Christian siblings God has put in my life. One last hug for my dad and then my mom, I let go and walked away. Tears filled my eyes so that I could hardly see in front of me.

Michelle and Stefanie, feeling that their worlds were totally disintegrating around them, took loving, but firm prodding to get them on the plane. I did as Jeff had told me to do: I held on to him for dear life as we walked through the boarding gate. I took one last glance at my parents. *Please, God, don't ask me to do this! How can I leave them?* Then I turned and walked stoically onto the plane. Numb. I just felt numb.

Picture it: eleven year old Lauren leading the pack, the only one excited about this part of the trip. With her beautiful brown eyes and her red hair gleaming in the afternoon sun, she had said her goodbyes and was ready to find her seat on the plane. Stefanie and Michelle were holding on to each other, sobbing intermittently, so much that Jeff walked back to our sweet girls and put his arms around them, reassuring them, encouraging them. Except for Lauren, it looked like we were heading toward a death chamber. Reflecting back, I can only imagine what the other passengers on the airplane thought about our family as we bumbled down the aisle, looking for our seats, faces contorted and wet with tears. I sat heavily down in my seat and looked out the window for a very long time. I felt nothing, but still I prayed, *God, I'm here. It's all I can give you. It's all there is. Thank you for loving me. Help me.*

CHAPTER SIXTEEN

*The steadfast of mind You will keep in perfect peace, because
he trusts in You. Trust in the Lord forever, for in God the Lord,
we have an everlasting Rock. Isaiah 26:3,4*

Turning Outward and Upward

In counseling students who are depressed or discouraged,
I often say: the longer you choose to think only of yourself, to
remain *inward*, the harder it will be to see God in each hard
situation. Even in my deep grief, I knew that I would need to be an
example to my daughters. I had no strength of my own to do that
nor any clue how to live out my faith when my heart was so broken.
My prayers for those first few weeks back in Africa were short and
sweet. *Help me, God. Teach me. Use me somehow. Strengthen me.*

The house we had chosen to rent in Bouake was located right
across from our new co-workers, John and Merri Holmes. Because
there was quite a bit of unfinished work and painting to do, for
the first ten days we stayed in the Holmes' house (as they were
not coming out for three more weeks). Upon arriving in Bouake,
we registered Michelle and Stefanie at the International Christian
Academy and also contracted the painting job for our house.
The yard was cozy, shady, and very accommodating, except for
the dog. There in that tropical lush oasis lived a big, black dog.
The missionaries who lived in the house before us had returned
permanently to the States, so they asked us if we would like to
keep Beau, the dog, since he was already extremely protective over
the yard and a great guard dog. I, for one, was scared of him. He
weighed almost a hundred pounds, was mainly black, and had
small penetrating eyes.

The first time our family of five went over to take a look at our
house, Jeff coached the girls to enter the yard with the intention
of being friends with the dog right away. Still I was concerned
about this dog turning on one of my girls and really hurting them.

It would have been wiser if I had been more concerned about my own relationship with the dog. Jeff and the girls walked in first, confidently, patting Beau on the head, receiving a slight wag of his tail for their effort. *Oh, he looks pretty friendly. It should be fine,* I kept telling myself as I entered the yard with fear and trembling. Of course, he sensed my fear, so when I forced myself to gingerly pet him, he snarled at me, just enough to intimidate me. I did not run because I was frozen with fear, standing very still, crying quietly, waiting to be devoured by the black beast of a canine. The girls laughed at me, but I was not amused. I had been bitten by a dog when I was about nine years old and had never really gotten over that fear. Because I knew that Beau and I would need to coexist in that yard, I kept trying. When we finally moved into the house a couple of weeks later, Jeff suggested that I feed the dog for a week or so. That did the trick. It only took a couple of weeks of lavishing care on him before Beau and I fell in love with each other. He would stand in front of me and block me from going into the house until I would sufficiently rub his head.

Before classes started at ICA, the girls suffered tremendously with homesickness, boredom and anger, spontaneously lashing out in their pain. I did not have the inclination nor strength to coddle them. I was dealing with my own pain. Jeff had to return to Abidjan to buy a car and pick up needed supplies for the work on our house. He took Lauren with him because there were a couple of missionary families with children her age whom she could play with while he got things done. That left me with our two older precarious daughters and the unpredictable African painters, answering the gate and fielding all kind of requests mostly in French, and trying to learn the taxi system in order to get around town when we needed groceries. There was no television, no internet, no electronic diversions at first, except our video camera. Imagine that. Even so, those quieter days did give important times of reflection for all three of us, and the silence encouraged some great discussion about spiritual things as well as some renewed mother-daughter bonding. When classes finally started for the girls, it did not take them long to fit in with the other missionary kids and make new friends. As we did not have money to enroll

Lauren in ICA, I brought out a homeschooling curriculum for her to do on the computer. Before we were able to move into our own house and while the two older girls were in classes at ICA, Lauren and I would do some of her school work on our front porch. Our huge black dog, Beau, would sit near us and seemed to listen to the stories she was reading out loud.

Week by week, we were finding our momentum, learning to love our new home, though it lacked many of the things to make it comfortable. My journal of September 6, 2001, reads:

> We had wanted to go to Blolequin to get our things
> that we left there in storage (for more than three years
> now). It would certainly give us more things in the
> house to use. As of right now, we have a borrowed
> stove, a borrowed freezer, which we are trying to use
> as a refrigerator, an old wooden table and chairs
> that came with the house, four cooking pots, no
> cabinets, no hot water, two air mattresses, two foam
> mattresses, eight plastic plates, eight plastic cups, no
> fans, no curtains, and one cat! I sure need to pray for
> a good sense of humor these next few weeks.

Daniel, the son of good friends arrived from the states for a nine-month short-term stint. He was valuable in helping Jeff with maintenance and setting up things in our house, but one of the biggest blessings to me was his ability to entertain and distract the girls from their problems. Our family of five quickly made room for one more. Daniel was full of life and compassion. It was great to have a big brother for the girls.

Housekeeping Items

I quickly learned to anticipate the "produce lady" coming to my gate three times a week with her wheelbarrow ladened with the fresh fruits and vegetable from the Bouake Farmer's Market. Since the time we lived in Tappeta, Liberia, I had never really enjoyed shopping in the local markets. The looks and jokes about us, the jacking up of prices because of our white faces, and the beggars who would follow us around, it just was not worth it for me. So, when Marie - a fabulous Ivorian woman entrepreneur - introduced herself to me the first few days after our arrival in Bouake, I fell in love with the concept of produce delivery. Her prices were fair, her quality was indisputable, her integrity was solid, and her business manner was easy. She never pushed me to buy more than I wanted.

She did learn my family's love of pineapples, so always brought an abundant supply of the golden fruit. Never had we tasted such exquisite pineapples as what Marie sold us. She inspired my desire to cook healthy, from-scratch meals for my family as often as possible. Other than adding meat or beans and a just-baked baguette from the local bakery, Marie's wheelbarrow held all the delectable freshness my culinary imagination could muster. Less than a half mile and located on the same street as our house was a Belgian woman named Brigette. Whatever my menu called for as far as herbs and spices, her delightful garden held it. She grew dozens of herbs, dried spices sold in small sachets, and beyond that, there were scores of beautiful flowers spread throughout her botanical wonderland. Anytime I planned to cook something Italian, I would run down and have her hand pick a feisty, aromatic bundle of herbs which turned any pasta into a delicacy. To this day, I pine for those delightful and simplistic days of cooking. It was a far cry from the food situation in other West African places where our family had lived. Bouake was growing on me.

Our house was laid out appealingly. Built by a French company several years before, it had a flavor of Europe combined with the easy flow of West African style. It was, as far as aesthetics and comfort, the best house I had ever lived in outside of America. With a front terrace cooled by many mature shade trees, the house also had a large suite of buildings located in the backyard. We had storage galore and also a guest suite which Daniel made his own by painting the walls orange and insisting that the rogue plants be able to grow through cracks in the shower. How we laughed about that. As far as our living setup went, we were all very thankful and enjoyed what God had provided for us. But, outside those gates was where Jesus prompted us to go. Not always easy, not always safe. But yet that was why we were there.

Everywhere We Go

Our coworkers, John and Merri Holmes, knew better than us how the dynamics, the *feel* of the city had changed since they returned from furlough. We spoke about it in some of our gatherings, wondering what it would mean for future ministry in the city. Robberies around town had escalated and tensions were high especially in the evenings. In spite of the palpable jumpiness around us, no one could really put their finger on it. Some disturbing incidences had happened since the last year's election which concerned any expatriate living in Ivory Coast. Though we did not want to become paranoid about Ivory Coast's growing political issues, we knew serious conflict could escalate overnight. Hadn't we watched Liberia practically disintegrate into civil war within a matter of five years? Almost without any distinct warnings?

On September 11, 2001, most every American knows exactly where they were when the twin towers fell. We were thousands of miles away from New York City, but that searing incident still greatly affected us. On the morning of the attacks, I was trying to call my mother in North Carolina to reminiscence about my grandmother who had died on that day one year ago. All circuits were busy, and after trying for almost an hour, I still could not put a call through. Before long, the Holmes called and told us what had happened in NYC. Driving to ICA, located three miles from our house, we were able to watch the unbelievable news on satellite television. For us being so far away from America, it felt right to share the news and emotions with an American community. The campus was quiet, pensive, rocked with the news that America had been deliberately attacked. Our vulnerabilities of living in a foreign country as Americans never felt as strong as when the attack happened in our own country. What would stop it from happening to American communities anywhere in the world?

Bouake was located slightly in the northern part of the country where a majority Muslim population lived. When the news of

9/11 came to our part of the world, tensions shifted toward the Americans in town. Our western dress, stance, and actions seemed to stand out even more than before. In little less than a month after 911, riots played out in our city, but the reasons behind them were not clear. It hardly seemed that the terrorist attack in New York City had anything to do with the tension building in the small city of Bouake, but the timing seemed surreal. So thankful that Daniel was with us for those few months; he became protective over me and the girls when we traveled in the city and Jeff could not be with us. He went to the grocery store with me as well as other places. We joked that I had my own personal bodyguard. God knew what we would need and His timing was again...perfect. More and more, we (especially the girls) stayed at home after dark and were alert to our surroundings.

It was at this fragile time when English church services began. We shared the same building as the French church, located in a storefront building on the other side of town on a dirt street. Right in the middle of scores of needy people. Spiritually and physically. On Sunday mornings, our English services were held when the French church finished. Bible school classes in English and French began for several African men who desired to become pastors and Christian leaders. Those classes were held on our terraces for four hours every weekday morning.

Growing Through the Pain

Meanwhile, I continued to struggle with the reality of the death of my brother and being separated from my parents during our time of grief. It did help to have a working phone, so we were able to talk on a weekly basis. As it became evident my dad would need knee replacement surgery, I wrestled with God about not being there to help my mom with his recuperation. During family devotions one night there in Bouake, I shared my fears with the rest of the family. I remember being prompted to pray, *God, I will trust you with my parents at this time. I ask for my dad's surgery to go well and that you will guide the doctor's hand. I am asking this to be the very best surgery that this doctor has ever performed*. Several days later when my dad was in rehab, I was able to talk with him for a couple of minutes. He told me how well he was doing and that the doctors were very surprised at his progress. Then he said, *"Kim, the morning after the surgery, the doctor came in and told me that he felt this was probably the best replacement surgery he had ever performed."* Totally amazed, I then told dad how I had prayed and we both wept on the phone out of the magnitude of God's amazing grace. Again God reminded me that He loves my parents much more than I. He was able to care for them far better than I ever could.

Christmas was very hard. Just knowing my parents were spending their first Christmas after the death of their son, and that I could not be there, gnawed at me in the worst way. I had to give it over to God so many times during those few weeks. His grace had no limits, He kept reminding me. On the positive side, we began to see more spiritual depth both in Stefanie and Michelle. After Christmas, Michelle asked me to disciple her. She really did not know what God wanted her to do with her life and she desired to know Him more. What an honor and a privilege for a teenage daughter to ask such a thing. Six months earlier, I could never imagine that request coming from our strong-willed daughter. While I still was not doing any ministry outside the home, I was thrilled to be able to have those special times with Michelle in the afternoons. My spiritual and emotional healing continued as did explosive spiritual growth in her heart.

In the fullness of time, when He knew I was ready, God whispered my next ministry assignment to me through the sincere requests of the Bible school men. They asked if I would be willing to teach the Bible to their wives. Surprisingly by then, I felt more emotionally ready to step out and take on added responsibility in the ministry. Before we had left America, I asked Jeff not to expect very much out of me ministry-wise for a few months. Teaching those African women the Bible was a blessing for me as well as for them. We were able to get to know each other, share our struggles and fears, and give testimony to God's strength even when relating as women from different cultures. God always transcends cultural barriers. He is the same magnificent Heavenly Father in every language. **In every place.**

Each of the five Bible school wives were on different reading and academic levels, so it was hard to design a specific lesson with homework and extra reading. Gleaning from my experience back in Blolequin when I had written curriculum for the Liberians, I did the same. Giving the women assignments to complete at home, Jeff and I both encouraged the men to take the time to help their wives with the questions and reading. Not exactly what the men had in mind when they asked for my help, but it was also a teaching experience for them to learn that they should be proactive in the spiritual growth of their wives. During the time we were studying the book of Ruth, an unexpected and painful loss happened to one of the Bible school families.

Baby Ruthie, the daughter of Jackson and Lucy, was four months old when she contracted cholera. Cholera is no respecter of persons and anyone within its confines can become deathly sick. Though there were some healthy adults who had survived the ravaging of cholera, the odds were overwhelmingly against the small body of a four month old. Baby Ruthie lived mere hours after it was first realized that she had cholera. One night she was eating, cooing, and sleeping soundly by her mother; the next night she lay lifeless, wrapped tightly in the bedcovers on which she died. One of the other Bible school men came late one night to tell us the news, so we got dressed and went quickly to the grieving family. What do you say? Where are the words to comfort a mother whose arms no longer can feel the sweet, warmth of her baby?

We had ministered in West Africa long enough to know how the acceptance of death and the manifestation of grief is much different than in America. This time we would experience it, not just know it. For we had been invited to join them in the center of this families' grief. I had only heard the crying, the lamenting of the death of a child, but this time we would feel it closer to us. This couple needed us to be their friends, their counselors, their reminders of the Light in the worse kind of way. I was not sure if we were prepared for such responsibility. But when are we ever? Still, we must go if we love the person, entering into their suffering, bringing nothing but ourselves. No words are needed at this stage of grief and that is where many falter. We feel uncomfortable in the silence, in the painful groans and inner lamentations that fester to the mouth of one in such agony. So we talk. To quieten them. To make ourselves feel better. To feel like we are helping. There is time for all of that, but those first few hours of grief is not it.

Kerosene lanterns threw shadows like golden nymphs dancing across the mud brick wall of Lucy and Jackson's house. I heard the agony of a mother who had lost a child before I even saw her, reminding me too painfully of my mother's similar cry at the casket of my brother the year before. It is not a place one wants to go willingly. The rhythmic prayers in dialect and the interjected wails all told the story. As my eyes became accustomed to the light that the amber hue of the lanterns offered, I could see maybe a dozen Africans sitting with the grieving parents. None of them were talking. As the American missionaries walked into the room, all eyes turned toward us. I felt as if we were expected to bring some kind of magical release, a potion of mindlessness that could ease the hearts of these two. The pressure to do something seemed palpable, but I forced myself not to give in. My Americanness trumped my knowledge of how Liberians greet each other when there has been a death: I went to Lucy, knelt down beside her and held her. Unfamiliar to physical affection, she grew quiet for a moment as if stunned. Then reality snatched her sanity and carried her back into a dark, unforgiving place. We sat down on the dirt floor with the others, leaning our backs against the rough wall, quietly joining into the suffering. After about thirty minutes, Jeff raised his voice and prayed with words heartfelt and hopeful. I followed suit with an appeal for God's mercy, a hedge of protection around this dear family. Then we resorted again into silence and sat with them longer. After a couple of hours, we slipped into the night, back to our home where our three daughters still lived and breathed. I felt unworthy of my blessings, but blessed nonetheless.

Family Roguery

Every family has its vices and virtues. Ours were no different. As the three girls topped the hill of the long, bumpy teenage road, things got interesting, loud, and intense. Sometimes even a little violent. One Sunday morning, Stefanie, who was a freshman in high school, and Michelle, a senior, were getting dressed for church. Jeff, Lauren, and I had gone ahead earlier for a special program. The two older girls were getting rides with someone else. Ready to put her makeup on, Stefanie realized one of her favorite eye shadows, which she had brought from America, was missing. She was sure that Michelle had it, so she went into Michelle's room "jack diesel" (as Stef describes it) and started knocking things over, pulling things out of her sister's dresser.

That was considered an act of war by big sister Michelle. You can imagine what happened next. Or perhaps you think missionary girls are different. That they never fight. Always share. Forever considerate of each other. Yea, okay. Prepare to have your bubble popped. Michelle ran into her room like a mad woman. They both danced around each other like two tomcats preparing to fight. Vicious hitting, scratching, hair pulling ensued. Screams and shouts projected all around. Michelle, in a rage, pulled back her arm to hit Stefanie with more force than ever. Stefanie flinched to miss the blow that...what? She heard the scream of agony before looking down and seeing Michelle writhing on the floor. *What had happened? I didn't hurt her that bad, did I?*

Michelle was yelling that her shoulder hurt. By that time, Stefanie was crying, too, and could barely see that Michelle's right shoulder had popped out of its socket. The wailing proceeded to become more desperate. The dogs barked anxiously outside. It so happened that our security guard, Seydou was in the yard that morning. Never coming in the house without being invited, he must have known that something was really wrong. *Wonder how?* So, he quickly entered the house. What he found were two silly American girls sitting on the floor crying their hearts out. One from tremendous pain from her awkwardly dangling arm and the other from compassion...and guilt? Assessing the situation without understanding the words, the father in Seydou came out as he looked at Stefanie firmly saying, *Telephone, telephone!* In other words, *Stop crying, little girl, and call your daddy!*

Though we were concerned for Michelle's pain and what had happened to her shoulder, when we found out the cause for the injury, we felt irritated. Teenage girls fighting like that. A doctor at a nearby clinic was able to put the shoulder back in its socket, but the pain and humiliation from that day stayed with those two girls for a long time. Twice more Michelle's shoulder popped out of socket in the next few years, but never again from the violent retaliation of a missing tube of makeup. Oh, the continuing joys of girls!

CHAPTER SEVENTEEN

I care not where I go, or how I live, or what I endure so that I may see souls saved. When I sleep, I dream of them; when I awake they are first in my thoughts. —David Brainerd

A Dreamy Experience

We had come a long way from having to fly or drive long distances to buy groceries such as we did the first few years we ministered in Liberia and Ivory Coast. Bouake was home to one medium-sized grocery store and a couple of smaller ones where one could find the culinary staples needed. While I was extremely grateful for the easier access to general food items, as the first year wore on, there were days when I was less inclined to drive to the stores. Not because of the shopping itself, but because of all that was located outside the store.

Hovering expectedly outside the main grocery store were a dozen or so teenage boys, too poor to afford school uniforms, forced to become young entrepreneurs. Their profession? Watching over parked cars, supposedly protecting the cars from bandits. Mixed in with the crowd of boys were scores of beggars. When I parked at the grocery store, the sight in front of my eyes was an unavoidable look at the fragility of mankind. Some of the beggars were mangled, often with one or more limbs missing; some had no feet and had learned to walk using their hands. Blind, crippled, deformed in the worst kind of ways, they would come or be brought to a designated place, waiting for the *rich* to arrive and perhaps have mercy on them. The cold hard fact was if a person was to have mercy and placed money in their grimy dish, it would most likely be taken by some greedy, heartless healthy person passing by. *Was that a reason not to give them something?* I struggled constantly with the dilemma, but chose to give them food which they could eat right then. Still there were so many beggars outside of a store ladened with food and sustenance...so close, but yet so far from them. It was a heady issue, and I never felt like I could do enough. Sometimes I did not even try. It was reminiscent of our days in the towns that bordered Ivory Coast and Liberia while we were doing intense relief work with Liberian refugees. No matter how much we did, there was always more needing help. I had to set aside my proneness to try and fix the system, asking God to show me what my good and acceptable part was.

Those young entrepreneurs vied for any shopper's attention, insisting on her commitment to use only one of them as their exclusive car security guy. Not liking the setup at all, it soon became clear that I would need to "choose" a security guy, if for no other reason, than so the twenty others would leave me alone. I chose Miguel. He seemed friendly, intelligent, and kind-hearted with bright eyes and a pinch of a an awkward smile. In past visits to the grocery store, I recall seeing some of the other young businessmen pushing him around. Always one to favor an underdog, I passed the so-called scepter over his head and my choice was made. Choosing Miguel was cue to the others to no longer pressure me. Miraculously, the plan worked. I was amazed how uncanny Miguel's perception was. Anytime he saw my gold Honda in town, he would find me, whether at the grocery store or four streets away at a bakery or hardware store. Out of nowhere, he would arrive and gesticulate his intention to watch my car, pointing first to his eye and then to my car with a serious, CEO kind of look. What a guy.

The little business deal between Miguel and I went on for several months until I found myself beginning to dread the trip to the grocery store. Though Miguel's help blunted some of the frustrations of parking and shopping downtown, the area around the grocery store was so busy, so loud, that it began to stifle me. As we neared the first year anniversary of our arrival in Bouake, little irritations were becoming big. Unfortunately, this spilled over in my feelings about Miguel. He began to irritate me in small ways that I soon allowed to become big deals. One day I arrived at the grocery store, deciding I would ignore them all: the beggars, Miguel, the other young businessmen, the smells, the noise...everything. Just check off my list and get home. I felt my heart hardening to my environment because it was simply too uncomfortable. My human shield of protection went up without one single petition to the one true Shield and Protector of my heart. It was a sad place for a missionary to be.

After all the years of dealing with the unique elements of West Africa: the constant begging and the unquenchable needs of those around us, I knew myself. I was retreating. God knew that, too, but He had different plans. The night after I ignored Miguel, I had a dream about him. He was older, taller, and walked toward me with a smile on his face and a Bible tucked under his arm. In the dream, I asked him (in French) how he was and what he had been doing. He then told me that he had attended Bible college and was now pastoring a small church in his village not too far from Bouake. *Incredibly, he thanked me for taking him to church and introducing him to Jesus.*

I woke up from the dream, my face wet with tears, my breathing struggling to return to normal. My subconscious reached out and slugged my reality with the fact that I had **never** even once invited Miguel to church nor told him about Jesus. God profoundly convicted me in the dark of the night, leaving no doubt of what He was saying to me. He forbade me to retreat from this young man. His plan was to redeem Miguel. Did I want to be a part of it?

The next morning, I went to the store parking lot and found Miguel. When he saw me, he looked a little timid, probably because of how I had treated him the day before. He was, obviously, a little unsure of the white woman's moods. Remembering the intense message of the dream, I smiled at him, placed some money into his hands, apologized for yesterday, and then invited him to church the following Sunday. He seemed excited that I would ask him to go, and after working out the details about the time for the French service, I promised to pick him up. For two weeks, I picked him up and went with him to the French service. After that, he was able to find a ride with someone else. He seemed to really enjoy what he was hearing, and within the first month, Miguel accepted Christ. Though I do not know where he is today, I would like to think that he is well, growing in his faith, and will one day be a pastor to his people in a village near Bouake. Winning others to Jesus. And to think that I was going to put my walls up and turn away from him. *Oh God, never allow me to do that again. You alone, be the Shield and Protector of my heart and mind. You alone know how much you have purposed me to handle. I want to trust you.*

A Revelation of Reaping

Late one afternoon, our night guard, Seydou, arrived to work as usual. Most missionaries and ex-pats (those who were not Ivorian nationals) who lived on our street hired night guards. Bouake was not a safe city, and so, most of the houses in our neighborhood were behind high walls and locked gates. A far cry from our first African home in Tappeta, Liberia, where our house was open and vulnerable, located beside a main path used by the townspeople. Later, just as it was getting dark, there was a knock at our gate, so Seydou went to check it out. We watched as he stood talking to someone for quite some time. He soon came to the house and spoke to me in French (he knew no English) about our visitor. Not quite understanding what he was saying, I asked the name of the visitor. It did sound like he was saying, "Say Koo, Say Koo." Still not sure, Jeff walked to the gate with Seydou, and an instant sound of pleasant recognition come from Jeff. Up the driveway with Jeff walked a skinny, haggard, but albeit, familiar man. It was Sekou! We had not seen him since March of 1990, when we evacuated from Liberia because of the impending civil war. He was one of the Bible school men I taught to read when Michelle and Stefanie were very small. Riddled with the mental debilitation of severe malaria, he was a very slow learner and it seemed he would never be able to read but the simplest of words. With God's help, I endured the teaching, but honestly I never thought Sekou's reading ability would come to anything. True to God's character, He sent Sekou to find us, giving us a glance of His inner workings.

How he found us, I do not remember, but we were so thrilled to have him spend the next five days with us in our home. Still simple and somewhat slow, there was also a bearing of spiritual understanding which went farther than even my own. One of the first things he wanted to do was to read a chapter of the Bible to us. As he read, I felt like I needed to keep pushing my chin up to close my gaping mouth. He read with power and fervency and a clarity I would never have thought possible. By the time he finished reading, tears overcame me as I beheld one of the greatest gifts God could have given me in reference to our early ministry. If we are faithful to do what He has called us to do, God's plan shines beautifully.

Over the next five days, he told us how he found his way back to his birth county of Guinea spending ten years trying to reach his Muslim people for Christ. He had been beaten - *we saw the scars* - he had been poisoned - *it was evident by the horrible issues he still experienced with his stomach* - and he had been imprisoned, tortured both mentally and physically. Each time he told us another story of the persecution and his relentless resolve to see some of his people come to Christ, my eyes streamed with tears. It literally took my breath away to realize I had a personal investment in the ministry of that modern-day Apostle Paul. All those years ago, all those moments of frustration and discouragement, all those feelings that he would never be more than he was, all those thoughts dissipated into the reality of what God had done through him and for him those past ten years. He had seen several Muslims come to Christ, but still carried a profound burden for his country that would eventually take him back there. Who knows what he would face next time? Would he live? That was Christ. Would he die? That was gain. Sekou's heart was set on the prize of the high calling of Christ Jesus.

While he stayed with us, we noticed Sekou spending long hours with our night guard after he arrived for his night shift. Seydou was from the neighboring country of Mali, but that did not change Sekou's burden for the man's obvious need for Christ. The two men discovered almost immediately that they spoke the same dialect, and because Sekou had been a Muslim before he became a Christian, he had a much better witnessing platform than we ever did with Seydou. Within three days of intense conversation and discussions that went well into the nights, we were thrilled to see Seydou come to us with a Bible in his hand, using it as a banner of praise, pointing up, and smiling. He told us, in his simple French and with the help of Sekou's translation, that he had put his trust and faith in God's only Son, Jesus Christ. He saw Jehovah God's love by the way we had lived for the six months since he had known us, but now he understood more who Jesus was because Sekou had explained it to him in his own dialect. It was indeed an afternoon of rejoicing.

The next morning, when it was time for Seydou the guard to return home after his night of work, he asked Sekou to come with him to preach to his family. How beautiful the love that Seydou displayed for his family! And how Sekou blessed us in many ways during his visit. Just hearing his stories about what God had taught him during his ministry in Guinea, and then seeing his desire to do things for us while he was with us, absolutely moved our hearts and encouraged us in our ministry. Over and over he thanked me for taking the time and having the patience to teach him to read when no one else believed in him. I was humbled to think of the times I had been impatient and almost gave up on such a pure treasure of God.

Who are we as mere humans to decide who God can and cannot use? Who are we to assume that God cannot use someone like Sekou? Seeing the "rest of the story" with Sekou has challenged me to never give up on anyone or any situation simply because my finite mind cannot wrap itself infinitely around the ending. *God can and will do incredible things, reach whom He knows is seeking Him, through anyone He chooses to use.*

CHAPTER EIGHTEEN

Faith never knows where it is being led, but it loves and knows the One who is leading. —*Oswald Chambers*

Family Changes

When a child graduates from high school, it is a marker of exceptional importance for both parent and child. But, what do we do with the polarizing emotions that come by living with a child with one foot out the familial door? *I will be so glad when she can be out on her own! She is driving me crazy. What will we ever do without her here? I can't stand to think of her growing up and leaving us?* At least a year before Michelle's graduation, I started counting the days and dreading the time she would return to America and attend college. No respecter of persons, time passed way too quickly, and Michelle's high school graduation was upon us. To have been so anxious about attending a new school for her senior year, she had been blessed with making many new friends. Probably the most memorable event of her senior year was her role in the school play. *Don't Rock the Boat* was a comedy which called for an actress with a Southern drawl but lots of Hollywood style. Michelle nailed the part. It was so much fun watching her blossom along with the other students at ICA. Her senior year was just what it should have been. Fun, challenging, and enjoyable. Our discipleship times together continued through the end of June - sweet and distinctive were those days when we sat in her room or outside on the terrace with our Bibles, looking for nuggets of truth. I prayed those truths would strengthen and empower her as a young adult in the world she would soon be entering.

She decided to attend Liberty University and perhaps study to be a nurse. I remember well the day she received her acceptance letter. The glow on her face was priceless. I ached to realize that I would not be able to gaze on that beautiful face day after day after she left. After a festive graduation weekend with her new friends, we spent a few days helping Michelle pack up her room before traveling to Abidjan. Always our child who had the hardest time with transition, she meandered around the house and lingered in the yard with the dogs, before climbing quietly into the packed car. The next day we arrived at the airport to put Michelle on a plane *all alone*. My mother's heart was screaming for one more week, one more year! But the time had come for her to flap her wings and fly on her own. What **were** we thinking to send her on a plane by herself? She was just a little girl, wasn't she? Had could she traverse the ocean alone? The goodbyes were painful for all of us, though I personally held on to the fact that I would see her in a few weeks. When she arrived in Charlotte, she would be staying with her grandparents. The plan was that I would fly back to the states a couple of weeks before her classes started at Liberty, so I could help her settle into her dorm room. Jeff and I both felt it would be good for me to remain in the States for her first month in college, just so she knew I was close by.

Saying goodbye to Michelle was hard for all of us, and so was waiting for her call telling us that she was safely in Charlotte. We returned to our home in Bouake as a family of four. It was one of the quietest trip we had ever taken as a family. Even the two younger sisters were quiet, struggling with what their new normal was supposed to look like. I had just about had it with *change* and my heart ached as I tried to embrace the reshaping of our family. The first week or so, I would lie on Michelle's bed and let my mother's heart have its cry. Sometimes I would find Stefanie in there or maybe Lauren. It soon became evident that we needed to redo the room before we made it into a shrine. So we repainted it and changed it into an office. For me, it helped to redirect towards the future. We had to choose to make the best of how life had changed. Things would never be the same and that needed to be all right.

We could tell that our two other girls were struggling without their sister, so we decided to take a short vacation. Surely a change of scenery as we still transitioned from a family to five was a great idea. Some missionary friends who worked in San Pedro were in the states for a brief trip and welcomed us to stay in their home during our visit. Our friends owned a chimpanzee, which proved to be quite entertaining for Stefanie and Lauren. Sad to say, they taunted the chimp, stealing her blanket and food, playing hide-go-seek with her toys. Loving to hear the chimp cry with frustration, the two girls found all kind of ways to get a rise from her. One afternoon the chimp was taking a nap in its small wooden house. The girls gently tugged the blanket away from the sleeping animal and climbed on a high platform built for the chimp to use for exercise. As the girls sat on top of the platform looking around and talking sister stuff, one of them looked down to where the chimp *had been* sleeping. She was gone. Stefanie, immediately sensing danger, asked Lauren, *Where is the chimp?* In answer to that question, they heard her chained leash bumping cumbersomely along the rungs of the ladder to the platform. The girls looked toward the top of the ladder just in time to see two hostile, beady eyes glaring at them. Too high up to escape by jumping off the platform, they knew they were in a precarious spot, so they did the only thing they knew - as girls - to do. They screamed.

When I say they screamed, please use your imagination. It was not the high shrill, playful scream which little girls often conjure up. Those screams were blood-curdling, desperate, screams of alarm, of death, of last word and testament. It was the sound of one preparing to receive the fatal sting of a bullet, the sharp claws of a lion or the deadly impact of a car. Jeff and I were inside the house relaxing, no stress, no inclination that we would need our adrenal glands to jump into action until we heard **the** screams. We bolted from our chairs, willing it to be a dream, not daring to imagine the horror of what we would find. Blood coursed through our veins and pumped into our legs for that classic *flight or fight* phenomenon. We were ready to do battle. Flinging open the side door, we wailed, *What? What? Tell us what's wrong?* I half sobbed, half blubbered the words as we scanned the situation.

If you are parents and have dramatic kids like ours were, you are laughing your head off right now - simply because you know exactly what we were feeling. We saw the chimp jumping up and down on the platform, daring the girls to jump or die, and we saw the sheer terror in the eyes of our daughters. A life or death situation? Absolutely not. The screams did not match the scenario in front of us. Unable to stop the rush of adrenaline, we used it to woo the chimp down from the platform and stood like angry statues as the two sheepish, but still shaken girls climbed down. Needless to say, it took quite a while before any of us were back to normal. You can be assured that the chimp and his area of the yard was strictly off limits to the two affronted chimp bullies. They may have learned their lesson, but we continued to occasionally glare at them for a couple more hours as our bodies expelled the last bit of adrenaline.

Soon it was time for me to hop on an airplane, reducing our family left in Bouake to three. I felt so badly for them. But on the other side of the ocean was my oldest daughter, edging her way into a whole new world. I wanted to be there to move her into her college dorm room and enjoy more late night talks. Six weeks had passed since I had seen Michelle, and when I came down the escalator at the airport, the sight of her was stunning. No less stunning was the fact that there was a tall, handsome young man standing beside her. She introduced him as Frank Clark. *You know, mom, I emailed you about him a couple of times. Meme and Pawpaw have met him and really like him.* It did not take long to see that they were falling in love, though it did take quite a bit more convincing to get that across to Jeff when I talked to him a couple of days later on the phone.

In the Dead of the Night

Five weeks passed quickly. After visiting with my parents and seeing that they were doing rather well, and having helped Michelle to settle in at Liberty, I boarded yet another plane and flew back to Ivory Coast to reunite with the rest of my precious family. The three of them had come down to Abidjan to meet me, even though Stefanie had to miss a day of school to make the trip. I showed them pictures and talked of the experience about putting Michelle in college, describing her room, her roommates, and her reactions to being on her own. During my absence, Stefanie had quickly and efficiently picked up the mantle as older sister and was caring for

216

Lauren in a way which made me proud. Content to be with my three loves, jet lag soon got the best of me. I went to bed early as the three of them started a new movie I had brought back in my luggage. The plans were to head back to Bouake the next day after doing some grocery shopping. That was **our** plan. *A man's heart plans his ways, but the Lord directs his steps (Prov. 16:9).*

Slightly irritated by a sound making its way into my slumber, somewhat disturbed by the feeling of someone staring at me, I inched open my eyes to see Jeff's beautiful brown eyes peering into mine - willing me to wake up. Before I could comprehend even where I was and what time it was, he barreled out the latest news. The girls had awakened him while it was still dark outside, telling him that something strange was happening in the city. At first, sleepy Lauren thought it was a volcano, her feeble attempt to properly identify the red tracers being scattered across the city sky. Heavy gun and artillery fire relentlessly sparked the black sky like fireworks. Jeff remembers thinking: *I hope this is just army maneuvers,* but deep inside he knew better. When light edged its way into the early morning, he went to the top floor patio of the guesthouse where a man was holding a radio close to his ear and looked worriedly towards downtown. Jeff asked him what was going on. It was as Jeff suspected, but much worse. Rebels had attempted to take over three cities in the country, but had not been entirely successful in Abidjan. However, Bouake and another city had been completely taken under rebel control. *Bouake? Are you sure?*

In the twinkling of an eye, everything changed...again. The four of us sat together in the living room of our apartment and talked about what we had heard. Trying to process the fact that we would not be traveling back to Bouake that day, Lauren and Stefanie started crying. They asked us hard questions. Unanswerable questions. We were extremely concerned about the Holmes family and others in the city of Bouake. To echo our fears, rockets and artillery fire continued to vibrate the building. Having hardly any food in the apartment, we ate from the snack items I had brought back from America for the first day. Stefanie, Lauren and Jeff had no extra clothes - packing only for a brief overnight stay. Thankfully, I had brought a few items for each of them from clearance racks while shopping in the States. We tried to take our mind off what was going on by going through all the Action Packers packed full of stuff from the states.

The following day, we needed to find some food, though the American Embassy issued a mandate that no American citizen should travel in the cities of Abidjan or Bouake - except for emergencies. Finding food seemed to fit that exception, so we prayed for God to show us how to best get food for the day. It may sound bizarre and totally irresponsible, but Jeff took Stefanie and Lauren with him on a couple of food hunts. They wanted to go and would have been extremely worried about their dad out there alone, so we let them go. That way, I could stay behind and be the worried one while they were all three away from me. Why I didn't go with them is a mystery. While most of the little food shanties located near the guest house were shut down tightly, the three hungry and brave souls were able to find a lady selling a limited selection of food items. Jeff bought an onion, a couple of cans of corned beef, a large cabbage, and a small bag of rice. I made corned beef and cabbage soup that fed us for two days.

By the fifth day after the attempted coup, more people seemed to be moving around the city. The government troops were slowly getting a handle on the rebel activity - at least in Abidjan. In Bouake, our coworkers, John and Merri Holmes, were in a completely different situation. Mortar, rockets, and gunfire were constant. The Holmes family camped out most of the time on their hallway floor away from windows for fear of stray bullets and rockets being launched just northeast of our homes. After talking with them on the cell phone one day, we were extremely concerned for their safety. The International Christian Academy community was also put right in the middle of the fighting several times that first week. It was a horrid time for the staff, their families, and many of the students who were experiencing the attacks without the support of their parents. We were thankful, so thankful, that Stefanie did come with Jeff to pick me up from the airport. Otherwise, she would have been staying out at the school when all the fighting started.

From Out of Nowhere

One afternoon Jeff and the girls went out to find more food. As they were walking back with flour and more canned meat, they first heard and then saw a large group of young men carrying machetes and chanting an unknown, but obviously war-inducing song. Our white skin could have easily been misconstrued as French, who were being targeted because of their government's stance about the Ivorian civil unrest. The angry mob was heading straight toward where Jeff and the girls were about to cross a side street. Not knowing who was friend or foe, Jeff was immediately concerned about coming in close contact with the group of men, so he grabbed the girls' arms and darted behind a large white column.

Standing still, hearts beating rapidly, they vaguely heard whispering coming from one of the doors of an abandoned building behind them. "*Come, I say, you white people, come inside!*" were the distinctive English words Jeff heard. Realizing almost immediately those were Liberians who were afraid and hiding, Jeff maneuvered the girls through the open door of the building, taking shelter with a dozen terrified Liberians not willing to be involved in another country's war. The mob marched in time with their impassioned singing, bent on being involved somehow in the latest fighting. When Jeff felt the group of men were far enough away, he and the girls hightailed it back to the apartment where I was anxiously waiting. Stefanie and Lauren's eyes were huge when telling me the story, but not out of fear. More out of excitement and awe that they had come so close to danger and that God provided a way of escape. Spiritual lessons for our young daughters were in the making, no doubt.

As the long, turbulent week passed and the political condition of the country deteriorated, we looked toward the inevitable possibility of evacuating to the States. If the situation continued, most likely the Abidjan airport would temporarily shut down. Our window of escape could be a narrow one. Prudence was the name of the game, so we sought God in prayer and kept our ears open to what other missionary groups were deciding to do. It took almost a week before the Americans and French were allowed to evacuate

219

the city of Bouake. John Holmes had done his best to retrieve a few things that we would need from our house across the street. Beyond that, we realized we would not be able to go back and recover anything else in our house.

Stefanie began to pray that her cat, Bubba, could be evacuated. It was heartbreaking to think he was stuck in our house in Bouake, not understanding why he was alone. We really did not see a way to have the cat transported down to Abidjan. John Holmes was extremely allergic to cats, so we would not even consider asking that of our friends, especially after all they had experienced that week. Then we thought of our friends from England who attended our church. Trying to call Guy and Sheila, there was no answer. Hope seemed slim that the cat could be rescued. Stefanie was beside herself, going into her room to pray and think. She came out a little later and asked Jeff to call our English friends one more time. She stood by him, biting her nails, beautiful eyes wet with tears. Guy promptly answered the phone that time and after explaining the situation, he said that they would be more than happy to bring Bubba to us.

My journal of September 25, 2002, reads: *You can only imagine all the thoughts going through our heads right now. We love our ministries here so much, but it seems they have all been taken away from us for some reason. At least for the time being. Please pray for us to have God's wisdom, God's peace, and God's strength during this time. We want to do what is exactly right for us.* Within a week, the entire country was feeling the squeeze of impending war. Gas was scarce, grocery stores were not restocking, and banks were running out of available funds. The country was collapsing before our eyes, and surprisingly, momentum was building in favor of the rebels.

On the eighth day after the coup d'état, our missionary friends were evacuated out of Bouake, staying overnight in Yamossoukro, a nearby town, eventually arriving in Abidjan. The guesthouse where we had been holed up for almost ten days was filling up quickly, but we procured another small apartment for some of our evacuee friends while several others would stay with us in our apartment. We opened our hearts and door wide for several families needing a place to stay. Knowing the approximate time of their arrival, we ordered pizza and had chilled Cokes when our war-weary and travel-ladened colleagues arrived. As the cars parked, Stefanie stood with bated breath - trying to be happy to see everyone, but more than anything, wanting to see her cat. Soon, our dear friends held up a cage which harbored a not-too-happy cat. Bubba had made it! It was wonderful to see how God answered the prayers of our children once again.

Listening to the stories that the missionaries from Bouake told gave cognizance that things would most likely get worse before they got better. Bouake had already turned into a seething cauldron of unrest, a slaughterhouse. The rebel forces had taken full and complete control of that entire region. Concerned about our African Bible school students left behind there - particularly those from Liberia, we were told that any person speaking English was arrested or shot on the spot. Evidently, Liberia was one of the many countries the president of Ivory Coast was accusing of aiding the conflict. Paranoia was running wild. So many things started making sense to us. The deteriorating conditions in Bouake during that past year. The succession of carjackings. The house robberies. Bank robberies. A West African mafia at work - acquiring the finances needed to make sure the uprising would seal the deal. It worked...right underneath our noses. I swallowed hard at the reality of how close we had lived to such evil intentions. But God had known all the time. We were always safe in His arms - no matter where in the world we might be. No matter how close to evil. Greater is He...Greater is He.

So, What Next?

The missionary men went the next day to purchase our tickets to fly our families back to the states. With the realization that we were indeed flying back to the states, we knew that we needed to get the cat to a vet for a another *clean bill of health* certificate. But travel around most of the city was still unsafe, so we decided against it. It did not seem prudent to risk our lives making sure a cat had traveling papers from a vet. Another test of faith. The girls prayed earnestly, but if Jeff is honest, he will tell you that he prayed a different prayer. *I remind you that he is a big talker when it comes to the cat. Bubba still lives with us to this day, sixteen years old, thriving, and well loved by all, **even Jeff**!*

The day came for us to travel to the airport with the exact four action packers which I had brought back with me from the States just ten days earlier. Because the airport was located on the opposite side of town from our guesthouse, and we would need to travel through some dubious areas, we put the children in the middle part of the car, telling them to keep their heads down. The thirty minute taxi ride, in my memory, induced a vulnerability like I had only experienced while traveling into Liberia during the middle of civil war. Perhaps it was because our daughters were with us and a taxi driver had control of the steering wheel instead of Jeff. Praying earnestly for God's protection, we felt the palpable difference in tension as we crossed over to the other side of the city. There were checkpoints everywhere, but because they were manned by government soldiers, we were not given too hard of a time. The gleaming steel of AK-47s held tightly and the rigidity of the soldiers on guard underscored the degenerate conditions the city was under.

Riding through the city, I felt a strange detachment, which I assumed was acting as a protective coating over my raw nerves. There was a calmness even in the projection of calamity. It was like I knew this was an ending. A shift of some kind. I felt no longer connected to that place. Keeping those thoughts to myself, we hauled luggage, kids, and a cat into the airport. As Jeff checked the baggage in, I scoured one of the airport pharmacies to find something to use as a tranquilizer for Bubba during the long trip home. In my simple French, I asked a pharmacist what would be good to give a cat on a flight, but he just laughed at me. I really don't blame him, but I was in no mood to laugh at myself. So, I asked God to give me wisdom for the rather unorthodox task. This was for our sanity too. If that cat stayed awake the entire trip, every passenger in the plane would either jump out the window or throw us out.

Valium: I picked up the white and blue box. A muscle relaxer, it could also make one sleep. I bought a box (yes, you could buy anything over the counter in Ivory Coast) and went to meet up with the family. Briefly taking time to read the instructions for taking Valium *in French*, I took a deep breath, broke a tablet into fourths and gave Bubba one of the small pieces. I had no idea if I gave him enough to actually make him sleep or if it would be too much and kill him. At least he would die peacefully. We took his cage to the custom's officer to be cleared for check in. The official, of course, asked for Bubba's certificate of health. We tried explaining how the cat had been brought out of Bouake only two days before, giving us no time to get him to a vet. The official remained adamant that the cat could not travel without proper papers. We begged, we pleaded, we begged some more. Finally, my nerves frayed to shreds, and I began to bawl like a baby right in front of the uniformed man. I could not help myself. The tears just kept coming and my sobbing was noticeable to everyone around us. Everything in the past year came crashing down and I could barely stand the weight on my chest. Only by sheer will did I not howl just like the cat was doing inside his cage. The custom official's face became concerned and then softened as he patted me on the back. "*Of course, you can take your cat. We are sorry for all of the hard times you people are catching in our country. Take your cat. Don't cry anymore.*" I had honestly forgotten about the reaction that tears had on African men - even those who are wearing uniforms. My girls and Jeff praised me for a great performance. I did not tell them until later - it was **not** a performance at all. I had snapped and it felt rather good releasing all those pent up nerves.

Walking out on the tarmac, I looked up at the gray skies and felt the thickness of the humidity hugging us. I also felt the reality of what it all meant. My journal of September 26, 2002, reads:

> *We know that you will all be relieved when we are out of Ivory Coast, but you must understand that ONCE AGAIN - for the second time in twelve years - we are faced with walking away from our ministry, our precious African Christians, and a whole house full of memories. The "things" are insignificant. But walking away from our ministry and people whom we*

223

*love so dearly and have poured our lives into is nearly
breaking our hearts. Pray for us as we seek to hear
from God. For what He has for us next.*

Having stowed away our carry ons, we sat down heavily in our
seats and were silent for a few minutes. Jeff was deep in thought.
So was I. There was a sadness which went beyond what was
immediately happening. That shift again nudged at me. Something
was different, but I could not tell what it was until Jeff slowly
looked at me with those beautiful, but soulful brown eyes. As I
heard the clicking of his seatbelt, I heard him say, *We're not coming
back. Not here. I am sure of that, but I don't know what that means.*
Looking up, he prayed, *God help us know what you are doing.*
Nodding, I took his hand for a moment and we both smiled...sadly.
Bravely. Neither of us knew what else to say. But this I did know:

Wherever it was, God was already there. As He had
always been. ***In Every Place.***

EPILOGUE

When one door closes, another door opens; but we so often look long and regretfully upon the closed door, that we do not see the ones which open for us. —Alexander Graham Bell

A Fictional Reality

Tom Clancy once wrote, *The difference between fiction and reality? Fiction has to make sense.* How true that is. For more times than I could count, we found ourselves somewhere precariously between fact and fiction. Surely, missionaries were only allotted one dramatic evacuation in their lives? Had God not gotten that memo? The long twenty-something hours flight home was full of ponderings and questions. What could this mean?

Within a couple of weeks of being in the states, we were summoned to Cleveland for a meeting with our field administrator. The room was packed with nearly two dozen missionaries with aspirations, passion for ministry, but no safe place to act on those things. Being the person solely in charge of drawing out the feelings and frustrations of those who have experienced sudden trauma and displacement could not be easy. But someone has to do it. Vernon Rosenau did it well. A seasoned missionary in Central African Republic before being led to BMM's home office, he had an inside channel to the thought process of missionaries displaced. The meeting was long, hard, but so very good for all of us. As everyone was going their separate ways, Jeff and I asked to talk with Vernon privately. It was then that Jeff voiced aloud what we had only been barely whispering since we had been home. *We do not sense God telling us to wait this one out. He is moving us. Where? We don't know. We can't see that far yet, but we know that we are to move away from West African ministries though that breaks our hearts to say it.*

As purposeful as we had been in the ministries God had given us in the past, we had no doubt that He would give us that zeal

225

again. Four long, torturous months passed and the heavens seemed silent. Have you experienced that painful and perplexing silence? We heard nothing, felt nothing, saw nothing that stirred us or made sense for us. Missionaries cannot live like that for long for a couple of reasons. First, we are wired to plunge into the thick of things. We are called to touch lives, make a difference. Secondly, it is expected by those who have invested in us, who are watching us, that we be busy in the work. But if the work was not defined yet? What then?

Let me say that most of our supporting churches had been simply wonderful and supportive in our seasons of unsettledness.

When we had been home a mere six weeks, I came down with an unexplained fever that reoccured for more than a week. Never did the thought of malaria enter our minds, but when my fever topped at 104.3 and I became delusional, Jeff carried me to the ER for evaluation. We had already seen a couple of doctors, but they all assumed it was a kind of flu. Meanwhile, my body was becoming weaker; I had hardly any strength to lift my head off the pillow. One positive side was that I no longer had the energy to worry. Worry does take energy. The hospital emergency doctor finally pinpointed that I indeed had malaria and the correct medication was prescribed. Still, it took several weeks for me to regain my strength. I knew that God had used the case of malaria to weaken my flesh so that He could deal with my spirit. We had things to work on...again. Would it never end?

Even Jeff was becoming discouraged with the waiting. Visiting our churches became his priority during the interval. But at night, when we shared a little pillow talk, going to our Father in prayer, we poured out our hearts to Him and to each other. *Did we hear God really say to leave West Africa? Maybe we made a mistake. Reentering some sort of African ministry seemed the easiest. Should we?* **When we are discouraged, frustrated, and impatient, our tendency is to bargain with God. To be tempted to take shortcuts. To find relief by going down a comfortable and familiar road.**

One *ordinary* day we received a call from our Field Administrator, Vernon Rosenau, telling us that he and his wife were passing through Charlotte later that week. Could we have dinner with them one evening? Thankful for the chance to sit down in person with Vernon and Jan, we heartily agreed. Over an *ordinary* dinner with *ordinary* (yet wonderful) people, God revealed His **extraordinary** plan. Vernon began to tell us of an *ordinary* conversation he had recently had with the North American field administrator, Steve Butler, while passing in the hall. They talked about the Abernethys. Steve then asked if Vernon thought we had what it would take to do college ministry. This is the question that changed our lives forever. Our response to it was crucial. *Jeff and Kim, we know that you have a gift of teaching and hospitality. Two very important tools needed in doing college ministry. Have you ever thought of getting involved in a campus ministry somewhere?* An *ordinary* question asked, yet teeming with eternal connotations.

As the question sunk in, we simply froze in our seats, trying to comprehend what this meant. Long had we waited for the instrument God would use to nudge our hearts and realign our ministry zeal. My husband turned and looked long at me, seeing the same spark in my eyes that he felt in his heart. Finally. We were again at home in our calling though - in all honesty - the waiting is also that. The conversation turned to logistics, places, possibilities, and a suggestion that we call Steve Butler for further guidance. Later that night in bed, neither of us could sleep as we mulled over dozens of questions that we knew had no immediate answer, but still...it felt good to dream, to wonder, to gaze at something that now had a shape. But with the shaping of a future calling comes the insecurities, the doubts, the fears of not being able to live up to someone else's expectations. Jeff particularly struggled with this.

In Africa he had felt at ease with the people. He felt in their presence no expectations to go beyond what he felt capable of teaching. But a college campus? Teaching young American and international students who were immersed in Academia in a way he had never felt comfortable? Could he really do that? Jeff affectionately says that God called us away from the African jungle to the spiritually hardened concrete jungle of campus ministry.

By the middle of March 2003, we had visited a Campus Bible Fellowship ministry in Miami, Florida, and fell in love with the magnitude of that ministry. The next step was to speak with BMM administration about our desire to transfer to the North American field and move under the auspices of Campus Bible Fellowship. A few more small details were worked out, and our path was cleared to walk forward. By another spectacular move of God, He reminded us of His implicit care for our daughters. CBF leadership approved us to remain in Charlotte and begin a ministry at UNC-Charlotte. We had been extremely concerned about another major transition into our girls' lives so soon after the Ivory Coast evacuation. God had already designed the plan - reminding me for the upteenth time that He loves our children far more than we do. How beautiful, so very beautiful is His love and care for us.

An Angel With a Gun

Before we could move forward completely, Jeff wanted to return to Ivory Coast and our home in Bouake. Making plans with three other missionaries, who desired the same, they waited for a window of opportunity, which arose in April of 2003 - almost seven months after our evacuation. Through a connection with some of the International Christian Academy staff, after arriving in Abidjan, the four missionary men were able to drive their car in the midst of a French military convoy heading directly to Bouake. Though the fighting between Ivorian rebels and the government army had diminished some, tensions were high and no one trusted anyone else. Because of a previous agreement with the French government, its military was commissioned to bring in medical and food supplies to suffering Ivorians behind rebel lines. Bouake had fast become a central point for rebel activity.

Even the French military was susceptible to military checkpoints, especially when it was discovered that there were Americans in the midst of the convoy. What could have turned out to be a half dozen long and harrying stops was actually quite delightful (if that word can be injected into a war situation). Jeff and the other men were given soccer balls by churches in

America to use for that very thing. Just as in Liberia, many of the rebel soldiers were still teenagers, and the sight of a shiny, new soccer ball pumped up in front of their eyes was too good to be true. Minds turned from wielding metal instruments of death to maneuvering one of the soccer balls on a makeshift field. John Holmes, one of the missionaries traveling with Jeff, jumped into the spontaneous game, and soon the Americans became allies instead of suspicious spies. After a bit, the convoy continued towards Bouake.

All four of the missionary men's houses were in the same neighborhood, so they each felt relatively safe to sleep in their own homes for the three nights they planned to be in Bouake. Unbelievably, when Jeff arrived at our home, he met Seydou - our night guard. Tenacious, faithful to the end, Jeff was able to give him a good amount of money so that he could travel with his family away from the mayhem in the city. After packing the few things he wanted to ship back to America, he carried many of the larger pieces of furniture to the International Christian Academy to be stored. Before he left, I begged him to bring back my precious mahogany table which he had crafted for me back in 1995 while we lived in Blolequin. Built from one large piece of beautiful, rich mahogany wood, it was one of my price possessions from our West African years - mainly because Jeff had built it with his own hands. I also had asked him to bring back a red cushioned chair of my grandmother's that we had brought out with us when we moved to Bouake.

He called me one night from a cell phone that he had bought for the trip, telling me that it was not going to be possible for him to bring the table or the chair. None of the other men had enough items that they wanted to transport back to America, so a twenty-foot container was out of the question. I tried hard not to cry while he was on the phone. It was not my intention to make him feed bad. He was already going through so much just by making the trip. But my heart had not yet come to grips with yet more losses - tangible items, true - but heartfelt losses just the same. That table was built during the time Michelle had become a teenager and it was also the table we sat around while having family devotions when Lauren accepted Jesus as her Savior. So many family memories were embedded in the essence of that table. My heart burrowed under the pain of it. And my grandmother's chair. Why had I insisted taking it out there? Why did I always choose to live life on a risky level? I knew better. Didn't I?

It was decided that the table and the chair would be stored at the International Christian Academy. A year or so later, we heard that our items had traveled to another Christian academy in another African country. My table was still being used by other missionary families which does give me great joy. Even my grandmother must be smiling from heaven, never having imagined that an old red chair of hers would have traveled so far around the world.

The day before Jeff and the others were to depart Bouake, they invited some of the soldiers in town to buy the items left in the houses. If the truth be told, Jeff was somewhat nervous about a group of rebel soldiers entering our home. Who would protect him if they became unruly? How would he understand their clipped market French? But yet, the missionary men had decided it was a nice gesture to offer some of our things to these soldiers.

God has told us in Scriptures that He never leaves us, though we often doubt it when we *feel* alone and when things are tough. Then there are those times when He *shows up*, a term I have always had problems with, because it incites that God sometimes is not with us. That is never true. God is always with us. He never just *shows up*, though the manifestation of His loving care can sometimes blow us away when it is presented to us in full color.

The large metal door that gave access to our house screeched on its hinges and opened widely as several army vehicles entered the yard. At least two dozen soldiers dressed in their fatigues and waving their guns edge noisily toward the front door of our house. Jeff breathed deeply and went to the door to let them in. In the ruckus, one lone soldier stood out among the others. Quietly and confidently, he came straight to Jeff and said **in perfect English**: *I am in charge of this battalion of soldiers. Thank you for allowing us to purchase items from you. Don't be afraid. I will be here with you the whole time.* He seemed to look deeply into Jeff's eyes, a calming stance, an almost familiar demeanor. Jeff felt better.

Throughout the next hour, this captain stayed by Jeff's side. If Jeff went into one of the side rooms, the soldier went with him. When Jeff sat down to take money for the items bought, the soldier wrote out the receipts in French. When Jeff stood up, the soldier stood beside him. When the other soldiers became loud and raucous, the captain spoke firmly and quietness ensued. It was a baffling thing, but it was also a blessing beyond description. As the soldiers took their wares outside to the vehicles, Jeff and the captain followed behind. Thanking the soldier again for all his help, Jeff turned to shake his hand and the captain inclined his head. He waited until every soldier left the yard. He then walked to the gate, looked back at Jeff one more time, and closed the metal door behind him. **An angel with a gun** indeed.

Already There

Returning home with that amazing story of God's protection, we felt nothing but enthusiastic anticipation for the ministry ahead. In the years since we became campus missionaries, God has reaffirmed His commitment to His glorious plan to use us as shining lights on a spiritually-dark university campus. We've had the privilege of meeting and teaching students from all over the world, and a few of those have become followers of Jesus, carrying the Gospel back to their own people, in their own language. We have many stories of God's grace and power displayed through the ministry of Campus Bible Fellowship International in Charlotte and all over the world. God is alive and well on the college campuses. So thankful are we that we can carry the Light to those who live in such relative darkness and confusion.

It has taken God many years to teach my self-determining heart to rest complete and sure in His ways. To finally settle into the not-so-settled life He has called me to live. It is not in the predictable and safe where we usually pause to see God, but when life turns us upside down and shakes us out onto an unfamiliar shoreline; that is when we must let Him lead us.

My prayer is that you, too, will not be afraid of the changes God may bring to you and the challenges God may place in your life to ultimately grow you into a stronger and more effective servant for His kingdom. To change you from the inside out. **Be assured. Wherever He is taking you, He is already there.**

In Every Place.